Model Security Policies, Plans, and Procedures

Model Security Policies, Plans, and Procedures

John J. Fay, CPP

BUTTERWORTH
HEINEMANN

Boston Oxford Auckland Johannesburg Melbourne New Delhi

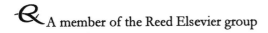

Butterworth–Heinemann supports the efforts of American Forests and the Global ReLeaf program in its campaign for the betterment of trees, forests, and our environment.

Library of Congress Cataloging-in-Publication Data

Fay, John, 1934-
    Model security policies, plans, and procedures / John J. Fay.
      p. cm.
    ISBN 0-7506-7183-1 (alk. paper)
    Personnel management—United States. 2. Industries—United States—Security measures. 3. Industrial safety—United States.
4. Employee rules—United States. I. Title.
HF5549.2.U5F39 1999
658.3—DC21   99-22511
                                CIP

British Library Cataloguing-in-Publication Data
A catalogue record for this book is available from the British Library.

The publisher offers special discounts on bulk orders of this book.
For information, please contact:
Manager of Special Sales
Butterworth-Heinemann
225 Wildwood Avenue
Woburn, MA 01801-2041
Tel: 781-904-2500
Fax: 781-904-2620

For information on all Butterworth-Heinemann publications available, contact our World Wide Web home page at: http://www.bh.com

10 9 8 7 6 5 4 3 2 1

Printed in the United States of America

Table of Contents

Policies

Plans

Procedures

POLICIES

pol·i·cy \n, a high-level overall statement of the general goals of an organization.

AFFIRMATIVE ACTION

The Company affords equal opportunity for employment to all individuals without regard to race, color, religion, sex, age, national origin, citizenship status, veteran status, or disability, and also observes the fair employment laws in each respective jurisdiction in which we operate. As government contractors and/or subcontractors, we are responsible for making good faith efforts to bring the percentages of females and minorities in our Company up to the levels of availability in the relevant labor markets. We are committed to these goals.

The Mandate

The mandate for affirmative action can be found in:

- Title VII of the Civil Rights Act of 1964 which prohibits employment discrimination on the basis of race, color, religion, sex, or national origin. Additional federal laws prohibit discrimination based on citizenship, disability, or age, and require equal pay for equal work regardless of sex.

- Fair employment obligations specified in government contracts. A series of Executive Orders require government contractors to maintain written plans providing for affirmative action in the employment and advancement of minorities and females. Contractors are also obligated to have plans and make special provisions for Vietnam-era veterans, special disabled veterans and the disabled.

- The 1978 Uniform Guidelines on Employee Selection Procedures regard as illegal any selection policies or practices that have an adverse impact on employment opportunities of a sex or minority group unless justified by business necessity.

- State laws on fair employment, many of which are more far-reaching than federal legislation.

Responsibilities

Managers and supervisors are expected to maintain an employee-relations atmosphere in which any employee can work in an environment free from verbal abuse, racial and ethnic jokes, religious and age-related slurs, and racial and sexual harassment. Managers and supervisors must make every reasonable effort to settle employee complaints internally and without delay. If an employee complains of discrimination in the work area, the manager and/or supervisor must work with that employee. If a complaint cannot be resolved at the working level, the matter will be referred to Human Resources.

Managers and supervisors are expected to help all individuals achieve their work goals by emphasizing each person's abilities and by accommodating individuals with disabilities wherever reasonably possible. Reasonable accommodations may include:

- Acquiring or modifying equipment or devices.

- Job restructuring.

- Permitting a part-time or modified work schedule.

- Reassignment to a vacant position.

- Adjusting or modifying examinations, training materials or policies.

- Providing readers or interpreters.

- Making the workplace more readily accessible to and usable by people with disabilities.

Both prudent financial risk management and the effective, productive use of all our human resources require that each supervisor and manager be committed to assuring equal opportunity for the employment and advancement of all individuals and to conducting the business of the Company with due regard to the human dignity and innate worth of each individual.

Implementation

Managers and supervisors have ultimate responsibility for the overall implementation of this Plan on a timely basis. Responsibilities include but are not limited to:

- Assisting in the development of actions to increase the utilization of minorities and females in underutilized areas.

- Identifying problem areas and establishing goals and objectives.

- Actively supporting local minority organizations, women's organizations, community action groups, and community service programs.

- Reviewing the qualifications of all employees to ensure that minorities and females are given full opportunities for transfers and promotions.

- Keeping informed of new developments in Equal Employment Opportunity.

- Periodically auditing to ensure that all facilities are in compliance in areas such as:

  - Posters being properly displayed

  - Company facilities being desegregated

- Minority and female employees having full opportunity and encouragement to participate in all Company-sponsored activities.

- Evaluating and compensating all supervisors on the basis of their Equal Employment Opportunity efforts and results, as well as other criteria.

BUSINESS ETHICS

The Company is committed to conducting its business with the highest ethical standards. Honesty and integrity are essential standards never to be compromised in our business dealings. We are subject to a wide variety of laws, customs, and regulations, and if we are to be successful, we must find innovative ways to achieve our business objectives while maintaining the highest level of ethical and legal behavior in all aspects of our business. It is important that each employee clearly understands his or her responsibility for conducting business activities in accordance with the Company's ethical standards. In addition, we must comply with all applicable laws wherever we operate. By consistently applying high ethical standards to all of our business dealings, we will continue to promote a work environment that is conducive to individual and company success.

Compliance

Every employee has a responsibility to comply with the Company's standards of business conduct. Compliance with the law and company business standards is a condition of employment. Should questions arise, the employee also is responsible for seeking clarification of the Company's standards from his or her supervisor.

Every employee also has the responsibility to report any suspected misconduct, illegal activity, fraud, abuse of company assets, or other violation of ethical standards. Such activities can seriously impact the Company's operations, damage the Company's reputation, or subject the Company or the individual to significant liability.

Management must fully support the employee's exercise of these responsibilities. This includes promoting throughout the workforce an awareness of compliance issues and providing a simple method for reporting any unethical or illegal conduct. The Company has established several ways for employees to report violations of its ethics standards. These include a toll-free hotline that is available 24 hours a day and will be answered at all times by trained personnel. There will be no retribution against anyone making such a report, and every effort will be made to protect the employee's identity.

Antitrust

The activities of the Company are subject to antitrust and competition laws. In general, these laws prohibit agreements or actions that may restrain trade or reduce competition. Violations include agreements among competitors to fix or control prices; to boycott specified suppliers or customers; to allocate products, territories, or markets; or to limit the production or sale of products. Special care must be exercised to ensure that any activities with representatives of other companies are not viewed as a violation of any antitrust law.

Government Contracting

In pursuing business with governments of various countries, the standards of conduct and prohibited practices may be different from those adhered to in commercial business. For example, in the United States, the giving of or offering to accept business courtesies from the government is severely limited. Courtesies could even include simple items such as meals and entertainment. These laws are often complex and impose serious civil and criminal penalties for violations on both the Company and employees participating in improper practices.

International Trade Laws

Employees must be mindful at all times that situations exist in which acts carried out in one part of the world can result in prosecution under the laws of another country. The most important of these situations are described as follows.

Anti-Boycott

A boycott is the refusal of a person or group of people to do business with certain other people or countries. The reasons for a boycott can vary widely. One example is the Arab boycott of Israel. The U.S. anti-boycott laws generally prohibit U.S. companies and their subsidiaries from cooperating with international boycotts that the U.S. government does not sanction. U.S. companies and their world-wide subsidiaries must report to the U.S. government any demands or requests they receive to engage in boycotting activity.

Export Control Laws

The Company must comply with all applicable national and multinational export control laws. For example, U.S. export control laws apply to the export and re-export of U.S. goods and technology. Under certain circumstances, these laws prohibit subsidiaries of U.S. companies, including those located outside the United States, from dealing directly or indirectly with particular countries.

Foreign Corrupt Practices Act (FCPA)

The FCPA was enacted to prohibit payments outside the United States by or on behalf of U.S. companies (and their subsidiaries) to bribe foreign government officials to secure business. In addition, the FCPA requires the Company to use proper accounting controls and maintain accurate and reasonably detailed books and records.

Securities

Laws in some countries, particularly the United States, prohibit the use of nonpublic information obtained as a consequence of Company employment (including information about customers, suppliers, or competitors and proposed acquisitions or divestitures) for the personal profit of the employee or of anyone as a result of association with the employee. Use for personal profit includes taking advantage of such information by trading or providing information for others to trade in securities. At least once annually the Company requires employees a through a business ethics questionnaire employees to report any situation that could involve a securities violation.

Futures and Commodities Trading

The Company's trading activities are governed by the Commodities Exchange Act, the rules of the Commodity Futures Trading Commission, antitrust laws, money laundering laws, and trade sanctions statutes. Each employee involved in such transactions must adhere to procedures dictated by both the applicable laws and Company procedures.

CONFLICTS OF INTEREST

Employees should avoid any situation that may involve a conflict between their personal interests and the interests of the Company. In dealing with current or potential customers, suppliers, contractors, and competitors, employees should act in the best interests of the Company to the exclusion of personal advantage. Each employee shall make a prompt and full disclosure in writing to his or her supervisor of any situation that may involve a conflict of interest. This includes:

- Ownership by an employee, or a family member, of a significant financial interest in any outside enterprise that does or seeks to do business with, or is a competitor of, the Company.

- Serving as a director, officer, partner, or consultant or in any other key role in any outside enterprise that does or seeks to do business with, or is a competitor of, the Company.

- Acting as a broker, finder, or other intermediary for the benefit of a third party in transactions involving the Company or its interests.

- Any other arrangement or circumstance, including family or other personal relationships, that might dissuade the employee from acting in the best interests of the Company.

Customer and Supplier Relationships

The Company does not seek to gain any advantage through the improper use of business courtesies or other inducements. Good judgment and moderation must be exercised to avoid an adverse effect on the reputation of the Company or its employees. Offering, giving, soliciting, or receiving any form of bribe is prohibited.

The Company's business is always to be conducted in a way that clearly and consistently communicates respect and value for our four stakeholder groups: employees, customers, stockholders, and society. Therefore, any business conduct or participation in any business entertainment that might be demeaning, devaluing, humiliating, or intimidating to any one of these groups, including contractors and vendors, will not be tolerated.

Business Courtesies

Gifts, favors, and entertainment may be given if they:

- Are consistent with customary business practices.

- Are not excessive in value.

- Cannot be construed as a bribe or payoff.

- Do not violate applicable law or ethical standards.

- Will not embarrass the Company or the employee if publicly disclosed.

Gifts, favors, entertainment or other inducements may not be accepted by employees from any person or organization that does or seeks business with, or is a competitor, except as common courtesies usually associated with customary business practices. An especially strict standard applies when suppliers are involved. Favors or entertainment that are appropriate in sales programs may not be appropriate or acceptable from suppliers. Employees should not accept gifts in cash or a cash equivalent.

Business Inducements

Sales-related commissions, rebates, discounts, credits, and allowances are customary business inducements, but careful attention is needed to avoid illegal or unethical payments, and to ensure compliance with various currency exchange controls and tax regulations. Such business-inducement payments must be reasonable in value, competitively justified, properly documented and made to the business entity to whom the original sales agreement or invoice was made or issued. They should not be made to individual officers, employees, or agents of that entity or to a related business entity. They should be made only in the country of that entity's place of business.

Similarly, commission payments related to Company purchases of goods and services should be made only to the seller or provider in the country of its place of business or in the country in which the product was delivered or service rendered. Although discouraged, "facilitating" payments are permitted if they are legal, are necessary, follow an established, well-recognized practice in the area, and are for administrative actions to which the Company is clearly entitled. These payments should be properly approved and recorded.

Inside Information

Confidential Company information (including business strategies, pending contracts, unannounced products, exploration or research results, financial projections, or customer lists) may not be given or released, without proper authority, to anyone not employed by the Company, or to an employee who has no need for such information. Nonpublic information obtained as a consequence of Company employment (including information about customers, suppliers or competitors, real estate acquisitions, exploration or research activities, and proposed acquisitions or divestitures) may not be used for the personal profit of the employee or of anyone as a result of association with the employee. Use for personal profit includes taking advantage of such information by trading or providing information for others to trade in securities or by acquiring a property interest of any kind, including real estate and oil and gas interests.

Competitive Intelligence

The business world is highly competitive, and success in it demands an understanding of competitors' strategies. While collecting data on our competitors, we should utilize all legitimate resources but avoid actions that are illegal or unethical or that could cause embarrassment to the Company.

DEADLY FORCE

The policy of the Company is to maintain a safe working environment for all. Security is therefore focused on the protection of human life. For example, firearms are prohibited on Company premises except in very unusual circumstances and only after approval has been given by a member of the Executive Committee. Unfortunately, some rare situations require the application of deadly force as a means for protecting innocent life. In these situations, the Company will follow all applicable laws, and in addition will observe international standards pertaining to human rights.

Guidelines

These guidelines are based on United Nations Principles for the Use of Force and Firearms and the Code of Conduct for Law Enforcement Officials.

- Protection of human life will be entrusted to law enforcement or the military wherever possible. The Company's general practice will be to prohibit the carrying of firearms by employees and contractors, including security contractors. The use of firearms or other deadly force will be exercised only in extreme situations where nonviolent means have been exhausted. And in these extreme situations, protective measures and non-lethal, incapacitating weapons will be considered as a first option.

- Any persons authorized to apply deadly force must have no prior history of human rights violations and must be thoroughly trained in the restrictions imposed by this Policy.

- Deadly force will be limited to the absolute minimum necessary. Every effort will be made to minimize damage and injury and preserve human life.

- Medical aid will be given to any injured persons.

- Next of kin of killed or injured persons will be notified.

- A full report of the incident will be made public.

Where firearms have been authorized for use, the Company's responsible management will:

- Ensure that those who are authorized to carry weapons have been trained, carefully selected, and properly licensed.

- Carefully specify the circumstances in which firearms may be used, i.e., only in self-defense or in defense of others in imminent threat of death or serious injury, and only after a clear warning has been given. The warning restriction may be lifted, however, when such warning would create an unacceptable risk.

DRUG AND ALCOHOL ABUSE

A major purpose of this Policy is to reduce accidents, fatalities, injuries, and property damage that result from use of illegal drugs and alcohol by persons working for or on the premises of the Company.

This Policy is also intended to promote overall a safe, healthful, and efficient working environment. Being under the influence of an illegal drug or alcohol in the workplace poses serious safety and health risks to the user and to all those who work with the user. The use, sale, purchase, transfer, or possession in the workplace of alcohol or an illegal drug poses unacceptable risks for safe, healthful, and efficient operations.

The Company recognizes its contractual obligations to its clients for the provision of services that are free of the influence of illegal drugs and alcohol, and will endeavor through this Policy to provide such drug-free services.

Definitions

As used in this Policy:

"Alcohol" means any beverage that contains ethyl alcohol (ethanol), including but not limited to beer, wine, and distilled spirits.

"Biological testing" or "chemical testing" or "drug testing" or "testing" means the scientific analysis of urine, blood, breath, saliva, hair, tissue, and other specimens of the human body for the purpose of detecting a drug or alcohol.

"Collection site" means a place where individuals present themselves for the purpose of providing body fluid or tissue specimens. A collection site will have all necessary personnel, materials, equipment, facilities, and supervision to provide for the collection, security, temporary storage, and transportation or shipment of the samples to a laboratory.

"Company premises or Company facilities" means all property of the Company, including but not limited to buildings and surrounding areas on Company-owned or leased property, parking lots, and storage areas. The term also includes Company-owned or leased vehicles and equipment wherever located. It also includes premises where the Company performs contract services.

"Contraband" means any article, the possession of which on Company premises or while on Company business causes an employee to be in violation of a Company work rule. Contraband includes illegal drugs, alcoholic beverages, and drug paraphernalia.

"Controlled substances" has the meaning assigned by 21 U.S.C. 802 and includes all substances listed on Schedules I through V as they may be revised from time to time.

"Drug" means any substance (other than alcohol) that is a controlled substance as defined in this Policy.

"Illegal drug" means any drug which is (1) not legally obtainable, (2) any drug which is legally obtainable but has not been legally obtained, (3) any prescribed drug not legally obtained, (4) any prescribed drug not being used for the prescribed purpose, (5) any over-the-counter drug being used at a dosage level different than that recommended by the manufacturer or being used for a purpose other than that intended by the manufacturer, and (6) any drug being used for a purpose not in accordance with bona fide medical therapy. Examples of illegal drugs are cannabis substances, such as marijuana and hashish, cocaine, heroin, phencyclidine (PCP), and so-called designer drugs and look-alike drugs.

"Legal drug" means any prescribed drug or over-the-counter drug that has been legally obtained and is being used for the purpose for which it was prescribed or manufactured.

"Medical practitioner" means a licensed doctor of medicine (MD) or osteopathy (DO) or a doctor of dental surgery (DDS) authorized to practice by the State in which the person practices.

"Medical review officer" means a licensed doctor of medicine or osteopathy with knowledge of drug abuse disorders. The MRO has the knowledge and medical training to interpret and evaluate an individual's positive test result together with his/her medical history, and any other relevant biomedical information.

"Possession" is meant to also include the presence in the body system of any detectable amount of drug.

"Random testing" means a testing process in which selection for testing is made by a method employing objective, neutral criteria which ensures that every person subject to testing has a substantially equal statistical chance of being selected.

"Rehabilitation committee" means the individuals who develop and determine an employee's rehabilitation plan and a schedule for the employee's return to work.

"Reasonable cause" means a belief that the actions or appearance or conduct of a person are indicative of the use of an illegal drug or alcohol. Such a belief is based on objective facts. A reasonable cause or "for cause" situation is any situation in which an employee's job performance is in conflict with established job standards relating to safety and efficiency. The term includes accidents, near accidents, erratic conduct suggestive of drug or alcohol use, any unsafe performance behaviors, and unexplained deviations from productivity.

"Under the influence" means a condition in which a person is affected by a drug or alcohol in any detectable manner. The symptoms of influence are not confined to those consistent with misbehavior, nor to obvious impairment of physical or mental ability, such as slurred speech or difficulty in maintaining balance. A determination of being under the influence can be established by a professional opinion, a scientifically valid test, such as urinalysis or blood analysis, and in some cases by the opinion of a layperson.

Affected Persons

This Policy applies to all employees and to contractors and persons employed by contractors. The Company will require by contract that contractors provide to their employees drug testing, education, and training that conform to this Policy, and allow the Company reasonable access to inspection of property and records for the purpose of monitoring compliance.

Job Applicants

All applicants for employment will be subject to testing. If evidence of the use of illegal drugs by an applicant is discovered, either through testing or other means, the employment process will be suspended.

If the applicant refuses to take a test, the employment process will be suspended.

If an applicant attempts to substitute or contaminate his or her specimen to be tested, the employment process will be suspended.

Current Employees

The Company may test employees for any reason at the discretion of the Company.

An employee's consent to submit to testing is required as a condition of employment, and the employee's refusal to consent may result in disciplinary action, including discharge, for a first refusal or any subsequent refusal.

An employee who is tested for any reason other than for random testing may be suspended without pay pending completion of whatever inquiries may be required.

Drug Testing Situations

Pre-Employment Testing

The Company will not hire or contract for the use of any person as an employee unless that person passes a drug test or is covered by an anti-drug program that conforms to the requirements of this Policy.

The Company will require, as a pre-qualification condition, drug testing of any applicant who the Company intends to hire or use, and any applicant will submit to testing as a pre-qualification condition.

Prior to collection of a urine sample, an applicant will be notified that the sample will be tested for the presence of certain controlled substances.

Post-Accident Testing

Each employee involved in an accident will, when directed, provide a urine specimen as soon as possible after an accident but in no case later than 32 hours after the accident. An employee involved in an accident is, at the discretion of the Company, any employee whose performance either contributed to the accident or who cannot be completely discounted as a contributing factor.

An employee who is seriously injured and cannot provide a specimen at the time of the accident will provide the necessary authorization for obtaining hospital reports and other documents that would indicate whether there were any controlled substances in his/her system.

The specimens to be collected will be urine specimens.

The Company will ensure through its trained supervisors that the collected specimens are forwarded to and processed by an approved laboratory.

Random Testing

Random drug testing will be conducted on a monthly basis. The number of employees tested each month will assure attainment of an annualized rate of 50 percent.

The Company will use a random selection process which utilizes a random number table or a computer-based random number generator matched with a selected employee's social security number, payroll identification number, or other appropriate identification number.

An employee will submit to testing when selected by a random selection process.

Reasonable Cause Testing

The Company will require an employee to be tested, upon reasonable cause. The decision to test will be based on a reasonable and articulable belief that the employee is using a prohibited drug on the basis of specific, contemporaneous physical, behavioral, or performance indicators of probable drug use.

An employee will submit to testing, upon reasonable cause, when requested to do so by the Company.

The conduct which forms the basis for reasonable cause should be witnessed by at least two supervisors, if at all practicable. If only one supervisor is available, only one supervisor need witness the conduct. The witnesses must have received training in the detection of probable drug use.

The documentation of the employee's conduct will be prepared and signed by the witnesses within 24 hours of the observed behavior or before the results of the tests are released, whichever is earlier.

The Company will ensure that the employee is transported immediately to a collection site for the collection of a urine sample.

Testing after Rehabilitation

A person who returns to duty as an employee following rehabilitation will be subject to a reasonable program of follow-up drug testing without prior notice for not more than 60 months after return to duty.

Record Keeping

The Company will keep the following records for the periods specified, and permit access to the records as provided by paragraph 2 of this section:

- Records that demonstrate the collection process will be kept for 3 years.

- Records of employee drug test results that show employees failed a drug test, and the type of test failed, and records that demonstrate rehabilitation, if any, will be kept for 5 years, and will include the following information:

  - The functions performed by employees who failed a drug test.

  - The drugs which were used by employees who failed a drug test.

- The disposition of employees who failed a drug test.

- The age of each employee who failed a drug test.

- Records of employee drug test results that show employees passed a drug test will be kept for 1 year.

- A record of the number of employees tested, by type of test, will be kept for 5 years.

- Records confirming that supervisors and employees have been trained as required by this Policy will be kept for 3 years.

Information regarding an individual's drug testing results or rehabilitation may be released only upon the written consent of the individual, except that such information must be released regardless of consent upon request as part of an accident investigation.

Matters Affecting All Persons

Prohibited Activities

The undisclosed use of any legal drug by any employee while performing Company business or while on Company premises is prohibited. However, an employee may continue to work, even though using a legal drug, if Company management has determined, after consulting with appropriate health and/or human resources representatives, that such use does not pose a threat to safety and that the using employee's job performance will not be significantly affected. Otherwise, the employee may be required to take leave of absence or comply with other appropriate action as determined by Company management.

An employee whose medical therapy requires the use of a legal drug must report such use to his or her supervisor prior to the performance of Company business. The supervisor who is so informed will contact the appropriate health and/or human resources representative for guidance.

The Company at all times reserves the right to judge the effect that a legal drug may have upon work performance, and to restrict the using employee's work activity or presence at the workplace accordingly.

The use, sale, offer to sell, purchase, offer to purchase, transfer, distribution, or possession in any detectable manner of an illegal drug or alcohol by any employee while on Company premises or while performing Company business is prohibited.

No employee shall be on duty if the employee uses any illegal drugs or alcohol or tests positive for the use of such substances, except as provided in the section titled Prescribed Drugs.

A person who tests positive for the use of an illegal drug or alcohol will be considered medically unqualified to work.

A person who refuses to be tested will not be permitted to work. Such refusal will be treated as a positive test, and cause the employee to be considered medically unqualified to work.

Prescribed Drugs

Any employee who is alleged to have violated the section of this Policy titled Drug Use Prohibitions will have available as an affirmative defense, to be proven by the employee through clear and convincing evidence, that his or her use of a controlled substance (except for methadone) was prescribed by a licensed medical practitioner who is familiar with the employee's medical history and assigned duties. The MRO may provide an opportunity for an employee to discuss a positive test result, and clarify if a prescribed medication was involved.

This section does not release an employee from the requirement to notify the Company of therapeutic drug use.

Responsibilities

Each individual required to submit to drug testing shall, as soon as practicable, provide the required biological specimens for testing. Failure to meet this responsibility is an offense punishable by termination.

Individuals in supervisory positions shall, as soon as practicable following an incident which requires drug testing, collect the required biological specimens for testing, and arrange for their prompt delivery or transfer to the drug testing laboratory. Failure to meet this responsibility is an offense punishable by termination.

Failure to Pass or Refusal to Take a Drug Test

The Company will not employ any person whose drug test upon medical review has been determined to be positive, or who refuses to take a drug test.

Discipline

Disciplinary action consisting of discharge without benefit of rehabilitation may be applied to any employee who:

- Uses, possesses, distributes, transfers, conceals, sells, offers to sell, purchases, or offers to purchase illegal drugs on Company premises or on Company business.

- Substitutes or contaminates or makes attempts to substitute or contaminate a specimen to be presented for testing.

Disciplinary action up to and including discharge may be applied to any employee who:

- Shows positive for an illegal drug or alcohol in a test conducted under the provisions of this Policy. For this violation, the Company may allow the offending employee to return to work following a 30-day suspension, contingent upon passing a drug or alcohol test.

- Refuses to take a test when asked to do so.

- Is found to be in possession of contraband.

- Fails to cooperate with the MRO during the investigation of a positive test result.

Suspension without pay for the duration of investigation may be applied to an employee who is the subject of a drug-related inquiry by the Company or a law enforcement agency.

Disbarment from the Company's work or workplace may be applied to any contractor or contractor employee who violates this Policy.

Notification of Test Results

The Company will notify each applicant of the results of a pre-employment test provided the applicant requests such results within 60 days of being notified of the disposition of the employment application.

The Company will notify each employee of the results of tests when the test results are positive. The employee will also be advised what drug was discovered.

Appeals

An employee whose test is reported positive for drug or alcohol will be asked in a confidential meeting or telephone conference to offer an explanation. The purpose of the meeting or telephone conference will be to determine if there is any reason that a positive test could have resulted from some cause other than drug or alcohol use that is in violation of this Policy. If the employee is desirous of a second opinion, he or she may request a retest by an alternate laboratory, approved by the Company, of the same specimen at the employee's expense.

An appeal that merits further inquiry may require that the employee be suspended until the inquiry and the appeals processes are completed. The suspension will be without pay but will not suspend provision of fringe benefits.

An employee whose appeal is successful will be made whole, i.e., compensated for lost pay and reimbursed for expenses related to specimen re-testing.

Confidentiality

All employee information relating to testing will be protected by the Company as confidential unless otherwise required by law, overriding public health and safety concerns, or authorized in writing by the employee.

The Company will ensure that no person will obtain the individual test results retained by the MRO, and the MRO will not release the individual test results of any employee to any person, without first obtaining written authorization from the tested employee. Nothing in this paragraph will prohibit the MRO from releasing to the Company the information delineated in the sections dealing with Notification of Test Results and Record Keeping.

The Company will maintain confidentiality of drug testing information that is entered into an employee's qualification file, and will not release such information without first obtaining written authorization from the tested employee.

Employee Assistance Program (EAP)

The Company will maintain an EAP program. The EAP program will, at a minimum, include:

- An education and training component of not less than 60 minutes for employees that addresses the effects and consequences of drug and alcohol use on personal health, safety, and the work environment.

- Not less than 120 minutes of instruction for supervisory personnel. The instruction must address the specific, contemporaneous, physical, behavioral, and performance indicators of probable drug use; intervention tactics; reasonable cause, including the two-supervisor rule; post-accident testing procedures; and supervisory responsibilities for the execution of this Policy.

- A written statement that outlines the EAP. The statement will be kept on file and available for inspection at the Company's principal place of business.

Rehabilitation

Rehabilitation in lieu of termination may be offered to an employee who has been found to be in violation of this Policy when:

- The violation does not involve selling or distributing illegal drugs or serious misconduct.

- The employee agrees to undergo rehabilitation in a rehabilitation program approved by the Company.

- The costs of rehabilitation will be paid for by the Company only within the limits of the medical benefits provided in the employee's medical benefits plan. Time spent away from the job for rehabilitative reasons will be counted as leave without pay, and will in no event exceed 90 days.

The Company will establish a rehabilitation committee that will develop and determine an employee's rehabilitation plan and a schedule for the employee's return to work. The committee will consist of a Company representative, the medical review officer, and the individual in charge of the employee's personal rehabilitation program.

After returning to work, the employee must continue in an after-care program and be subject to follow-up testing for not longer than 60 months following return to work.

Inspections and Searches at the Workplace

The Company may conduct unannounced general inspections and searches for drugs or alcohol on Company premises or in Company vehicles or equipment wherever located. Employees are expected to cooperate.

Search of an employee and his or her personal property may be made when there is reasonable cause to believe that the employee is in violation of this Policy.

An employee's consent to a search is required as a condition of employment, and the employee's refusal to consent may result in disciplinary action, including discharge, even for a first refusal.

Illegal drugs, drugs believed to be illegal, and drug paraphernalia found on Company property may be turned over to the appropriate law enforcement agency and full cooperation given to any subsequent investigation. Substances that cannot be identified as illegal by a layperson's examination will be turned over to a drug testing vendor for scientific analysis.

Other forms of contraband, such as firearms, explosives, and other lethal weapons, will be subject to seizure during an inspection or search. An employee who is found to possess contraband on Company property or while on Company business will be subject to discipline up to and including discharge.

Laboratory Analysis and Medical Review

Testing Laboratory

The Company will engage a laboratory certified by the U.S. Department of Health and Human Services. The testing laboratory will be required to permit:

- Inspections by the Company before the laboratory is selected to perform testing.

- Unannounced inspections, including examination of records at any time.

Medical Review of Testing Results

The Company will designate or appoint an MRO who will:

- Review the results of drug testing before they are reported to the Company.

- Review and interpret each confirmed positive test result as follows to determine if there is an alternative medical explanation for the confirmed positive test result:

  - Conduct a medical interview with the individual tested.

  - Review the individual's medical history and any relevant biomedical factors.

  - Review all medical records made available by the individual tested to determine if a confirmed positive test resulted from legal prescribed medication.

  - If necessary, require that the original specimen be re-analyzed to determine the accuracy of the reported test result.

  - Verify that the laboratory report and assessment are correct.

- Determine whether and when an employee involved in a rehabilitation program may be returned to duty.

- Determine a schedule of unannounced testing, in consultation with the rehabilitation committee, for an employee who has returned to duty after rehabilitation.

- Ensure that an employee has been drug tested before the employee returns to duty after rehabilitation.

The following rules will govern MRO determinations:

- If the MRO determines, after appropriate review, that there is a legitimate medical explanation for the confirmed positive test result, the MRO is not required to take further action.

- If the MRO determines, after appropriate review, that there is no legitimate explanation for the confirmed positive test result, the MRO will refer the individual to the employee assistance program.

- Based on a review of laboratory inspection reports, quality assurance and quality control data, and other drug test results, the MRO may conclude that a particular drug test result is scientifically insufficient for further action. Under these circumstances, the MRO will conclude that the test is negative.

Retention of Samples and Re-testing

Specimens that yield positive results on confirmation will be retained by the laboratory in frozen storage for at least 365 days, during which the Company may request retention for an additional period.

If the MRO determines there is no legitimate medical explanation for a confirmed positive test result, the original specimen will be re-tested if the employee makes a written request for re-testing within 60 days of receipt of the final test result from the MRO. The Company will require the employee to pay in advance the cost of shipment, if any, and reanalysis, but the Company will reimburse the employee for such expense if the retest is negative.

If the employee specifies re-testing by a second laboratory, the original laboratory must follow approved chain-of-custody procedures in transferring a portion of the specimen.

Since some analytes may deteriorate during storage, detected levels of the drug below the detection limits, but equal to or greater than the established sensitivity of the assay, must, as technically appropriate, be reported and considered corroborative of the original positive results.

Amnesty

The Company will provide an amnesty period that will start on the effective date of this Policy and conclude not sooner than 30 days or later than 60 days.

The amnesty period is intended to allow employees who may be abusing drugs and alcohol to abstain from such abuse and therefore be capable of passing any drug or alcohol testing that may be administered as set out in this Policy.

EQUAL EMPLOYMENT OPPORTUNITY

The Company will ensure equal employment opportunity (EEO) by prohibiting adverse treatment of persons on the basis of race, color, religion, sex, age, national origin, citizenship status, veteran status, or disability. This policy covers all terms and conditions of employment and personnel actions, including but not limited to recruiting, hiring, training, education, promotion, demotion, transfer, compensation, benefits, layoff, separation, and the administration of various employee plans and programs, and the maintenance of a positive work environment.

Responsibilities

In addition to ensuring EEO to protected classes such as minorities and females, this Policy places a duty on the Company, its managers and supervisors, to take positive steps to improve job opportunities for women, minorities, individuals with disabilities, disabled veterans, veterans of the Vietnam era, and protected-age-group employees.

Each manager and supervisor is responsible for applying the principles and spirit of EEO in the hiring and promotion of employees, and ensuring that all employees are encouraged to develop and grow in the Company regardless of irrelevant employee characteristics.

Furthermore, it is the Company's policy that employees and applicants are protected from coercion, intimidation, interference, or discrimination for filing a complaint or assisting in an investigation under applicable laws or regulations.

Implementation

The Human Resources Department will assist management in carrying out its EEO responsibilities. The HR Department will monitor EEO efforts and provide management with periodic reports concerning progress toward goals.

Any employee or applicant who feels he or she has been discriminated against due to his or her race, color, religion, sex, age, national origin, citizenship status, veteran status, or disability, should report such incident to his or her supervisor, manager, the Human Resources Manager, or any member of management.

The adherence by all employees to this Policy will be constantly monitored. Every employee is expected to be aware of and comply with the Company's commitment to EEO.

Details

- All employees will adhere to the letter and spirit of Title VII of the Civil Rights Act of 1964, the Age Discrimination in Employment Act of 1967 as amended, and the Americans with Disabilities Act.

- All positions will be open to any individual based on that individual's qualifications and ability.

- Private and public employment agencies performing recruiting services will be regularly advised that applicants are to be referred without regard to race, color, religion, sex, age, national origin, citizenship status, veteran status, or disability.

- All solicitations or advertisements made by or on behalf of the Company will include the phrase "AN EQUAL OPPORTUNITY EMPLOYER."

- The selection of employees for any training will be based upon skills required and the best qualified applicants to be trained for those skills.

- In placing procurements with subcontractors and vendors for materials or services required in connection with the Company's performance under a government contract or subcontract with a prime contractor, we will comply with all the applicable provisions of applicable Executive Orders and the Rules and Regulations of the Office of Federal Contract Compliance Programs of the Department of Labor.

- We will not segregate any work unit, facility or function based upon race, color, religion, sex, age, national origin, citizenship status, veteran status, or disability.

- We will provide equal pay for equal work to ensure that individual compensation is based upon the job held and the merit of the individual within the job. Employees will have the latitude to move from job to job, progressing within the approved wage and salary ranges, without regard to criteria other than merit, ability, and length of service with the company.

- Language that could have the effect of offending the dignity of any employee is prohibited by Company policy. Verbal abuse, racial/ethnic jokes, religious and age-related slurs, racial and/or sexual harassment, etc., which depend upon the use of degrading cultural and sex role stereotypes, violate Company policy. Violations of this policy will be grounds for disciplinary action, including discharge.

EQUAL EMPLOYMENT OPPORTUNITY FOR THE DISABLED, VIETNAM-ERA VETERANS, AND SPECIAL DISABLED VETERANS

The Company's continuing commitment to Equal Employment Opportunity includes an Affirmative Action Program for the disabled, Vietnam-era veterans, and special disabled veterans. This plan reflects our policy of hiring and promoting individuals based on ability and potential and without regard to those facts that have no bearing on the execution of job responsibilities.

The Company will take positive steps to employ and advance qualified individuals who are disabled, special disabled veterans, or Vietnam-era veterans.

Definitions

"A Disabled Individual" is any person who: (1) has a physical or mental impairment that substantially limits one or more of a person's major life activities; (2) has a record of such impairment; or (3) is regarded as having such an impairment.

A disabled individual is "substantially limited" if he or she is likely to experience difficulty in securing, retaining, or advancing in employment because of a disability.

A "Veteran of the Vietnam Era" is a veteran, whose active military, naval, or air service was during the period August 5, 1964 through May 7, 1975, who served on active duty for a period of more than 180 days and was discharged or released therefrom with other than a dishonorable discharge or was discharged or released from active duty because of a service-connected disability.

"Special Disabled Veteran" is a veteran who is entitled to compensation (or who but for the receipt of military retired pay would be entitled to compensation) under laws administered by the Veterans Administration for a disability rated at 30 percent or more, or rated at 10 or 20 percent in the case of a veteran who has been determined under Section 1506 of Title 38 U.S.C., to have a serious employment disability, or a person who was discharged or released from active duty because of a service-connected disability.

Enrollment

Enrollment in the Company's Affirmative Action Program for the disabled, special disabled veterans, and Vietnam-era veterans may be made upon request to the Human Resources Manager.

Information concerning an individual's status in the program will be kept confidential except to the extent necessary to provide special accommodations or emergency treatment. Participation is voluntary.

FIREARMS

The Company prohibits firearms on all Company premises, including associated garages and parking lots. Employees and others who enter Company premises with firearms in their possession, regardless of whether or not they are licensed or permitted by law to carry such firearms, concealed or otherwise, are in violation of this policy.

The Company is aware that some jurisdictions allow qualifying citizens to obtain permits to carry concealed weapons, including handguns, on public property, except where expressly prohibited. These permits, however, do not automatically confer the right to carry concealed weapons on private property.

The sole exception is for law enforcement officers whose official duties require carrying firearms.

Enforcement

Employees who violate this policy are subject to disciplinary action up to and including separation from the company. Others who are found violating this policy will be directed to leave the property at once and will be arrested by the police for criminal trespass if they refuse to do so.

Signs expressing this prohibition will be posted at all entrances to Company premises.

GENERAL BUSINESS

The ultimate expression of policy lies in how we carry out our business. We seek success by being innovative in every aspect of our business, by being sensitive and alive to the interests and concerns of others in society, and by working constructively with them to find solutions of mutual benefit.

Our policy is to be both competitively successful and a force for good. In everything we do, we want to be seen to be making a distinctive contribution and acting responsibly. We want others to see this in the approaches we adopt, in the relationships we develop, and in the actions we take.

The Company must be an integral part of the society in which it operates; it must meet a number of different expectations, particularly in respect to financial, social, and environmental issues. However complex our business becomes, there is no substitute for getting the simple things right, and consistently so.

Our general business policy focuses on five areas: ethical conduct; employees; relationships; health, safety, and environmental performance; and finance and control. Others will judge us by our performance in these five areas. What we state here is an aspiration, but also a determination. This policy document describes what the Company expects of its people and what society can expect of the Company.

We believe that wherever we operate, our activities should generate economic benefits and opportunities, our conduct should be a source of positive influence, our relationships should be honest and open, and we should expect to be held accountable for our actions.

We are committed to:

- Respect the rule of law, conduct our business with integrity, and show respect for human dignity and the rights of the individual wherever we do business.

- Develop employment practices that create a stimulating working environment in which diversity is valued.

- Create mutual advantage in all our relationships so that people will trust us and want to do business with us.

- Demonstrate respect for the natural environment and work toward our goals of no accidents, no harm to people, and no damage to the environment.

- Manage our financial performance to maximize long-term value for our shareholders.

We expect everybody who works for the Company to take responsibility for living up to these commitments. We recognize that these commitments may in some cases represent aspirations for the future rather than statements of today's reality. We will seek continual improvement both in our own performance and that of our business partners. We will endeavor to learn from our mistakes. We will be open about our actual performance, whether good or bad. Doing so not only enhances our accountability but also acts as a stimulus for improvement.

Our measures of success are:

- The extent to which we meet these commitments.

- The long-term value we create for our shareholders.

- The pride of our employees in their accomplishments.

- The satisfaction of our customers and all those with whom we do business.

- The way communities, both local and international, judge our activities.

Ethical Conduct

We will pursue our business with integrity, respecting the different cultures and the dignity and rights of individuals wherever we operate.

In our actions and our dealings with others, we will:

- Respect the rule of law.

- Promise only what we expect to deliver, only make commitments we intend to keep, not knowingly mislead others and not participate in or condone corrupt or unacceptable business practices.

- Meet our obligations and commitments, treat people according to merit and contribution, refrain from coercion, and never deliberately do harm to anyone.

- Act in good faith, use company assets only for furthering company business and not seek personal gain through abuse of position.

Ethical Conduct Expectations

Many ethical decisions involve dilemmas and require judgment in arriving at the best way forward. In cases of uncertainty, everyone working for the Company is expected to raise the issues with their management and colleagues to obtain clarification. However, in deciding whether or where to do business, it will be a precondition that we can implement our policy commitments in all our operations. We will:

- Respect the law in the countries and communities in which we operate. This will include competition and anti-trust laws and the Foreign and Corrupt Practices Act. Where the law is unclear or conflicting, we will take expert advice but will always seek to act in accordance with these commitments.

- Never engage in bribery. The Company's preference is not to make facilitating payments, but they can be made where needed to meet local custom and practice if they have been discussed with and approved by senior local management and are properly recorded in the accounts.

- Hold no secret or unrecorded funds of money or assets.

- Only give or accept gifts and entertainment that are for business purposes and are not material or frequent. Senior Managers will put in place local rules to cover the giving and acceptance of gifts and entertainment which reflect this expectation and local custom.

- Never accept gifts or entertainment during the process of a competitive bid.

- Avoid situations where loyalty to the company may come into conflict with personal interests or loyalties. If such a conflict does arise, it should be declared to more senior management in writing, who must make sure that the individual is insulated from any decision making or operation in the area of the conflict of interest.

- Not employ agents to carry out actions that conflict with these commitments. Fees to agents or consultants should be demonstrably commensurate with the services they are contracted to provide.

Any employee or contractor who feels under pressure to take action inconsistent with these commitments should discuss the issue with their management or Internal Audit, who will find an acceptable solution, respecting confidences and addressing any fears of retribution.

Employees

Everybody who works for the Company contributes to our success. Working together and drawing from our diverse talents and perspectives, we will stimulate new and creative options for our business. Collectively we will generate a more exciting and rewarding environment for work, in which everyone feels responsible for the performance and reputation of our company.

We commit to creating a working environment in which there is mutual trust and respect and where all employees:

- Know what is expected from them in their job.

- Have open and constructive conversations about their performance.

- Are helped to develop their capabilities.

- Are recognized and competitively rewarded for their performance.

- Are listened to and involved in improving their team's performance.

- Are fairly treated.

- Feel supported in the management of their personal priorities.

Employee Expectations

All employees can expect to know what is expected of them in their job. Supervisors will provide a clear view of the business aims and everyone's part in delivering them. Supervisors will help subordinates to get the information they need to do their job.

We will handle organizational change and job dislocations with care and sensitivity through a constructive dialogue, a sympathetic hearing, and provision of the maximum possible range of options. We will only outsource in-house activities if we believe that this will lead to better business in the long term.

Supervisors will give everyone in their team open and constructive feedback through face to face conversations. Supervisors will hold a formal conversation with every employee in their team at least once a year to review their performance and identify how it can be improved further. We will:

- Encourage individuals to formulate personal development plans and play an active part in shaping their future careers.

- Coach people in their development and make training accessible to all to build relevant skills.

- Use systematic selection and placement processes to make the best use of people's skills and abilities.

- Clearly explain the relationship between individual performance and reward so that all employees understand how they can share in the Company's success.

- Set base pay and benefits at competitive levels.

- Explicitly link annual individual and team awards to business performance.

- Recognize and reward contributions to innovation and creative change and the building of effective business relationships.

- Give exceptional rewards for exceptional performance.

- Encourage employees to become shareholders in the Company.

Everyone will have the opportunity to give feedback to supervisors to enable them to improve their leadership performance. Supervisors will:

- Initiate and encourage open and timely two-way dialogue with their teams on all issues relating to business performance.

- Use upward feedback and peer review processes to provide performance feedback.

- Expect everyone to network both within and outside the Company and to share knowledge, skills and experience across the Company.

- Deploy the diversity of talent, background, and perspective within the Company's workforce to work together to build innovative, high-performance teams.

- Ensure that leadership opportunities and development are open to all on merit.

- Establish a working environment that provides assurance of protection against any form of harassment or unlawful discrimination and against threats to the personal safety of employees.

Relationships

We believe that long-term relationships founded on trust and mutual advantage are vital to the Company's business success. Our aim is to create mutual advantage in all our relationships so that others will always prefer to do business with the Company. We will do this by:

- Understanding the needs and aspirations of individuals, customers, contractors, suppliers, partners, communities, governments, and nongovernment organizations

- Conducting our activities in ways which bring benefits to all those with whom we have relationships

- Fulfilling our obligations as a responsible member of the societies in which we operate

- Demonstrating respect for human dignity and the rights of individuals.

We will work to build long term relationships founded upon:

- High performance standards.

- Delivering on our promises.

- Openness and flexibility.

- Learning from others.

- Mutual interdependence.

- Sharing success.

In all our relationships, our guiding principle is working together for mutual advantage in delivering business objectives. We will work anywhere and with anyone provided that our commitments are not compromised. We will make others aware of our commitments and expectations. Our aims go beyond the purely commercial. We seek profitability but not at any price.

We respect cultural diversity and seek mutual benefit from working together with people with diverse experiences and cultural backgrounds. We will engage in dialogue with many different groups to promote understanding and seek new ways of conducting our business to greater mutual advantage. In addition:

- For Individuals

  - We will respect their rights and dignity.

  - We will act fairly and justly and not deliberately do harm to anyone.

- For Customers

  - We will provide high-quality goods and services meeting their needs.

  - We will deliver what we promise.

- For Partners, Contractors, and Suppliers

  - We will seek partners whose policies are consistent with our own.

  - We will make our contractors and suppliers aware of our own commitments and expectations and their responsibilities in implementing them.

- For Communities

  - Our aim is that countries and communities in which we operate should benefit directly from our presence, the wealth and jobs we create, the skills developed within the local population, the resources we invest, the products and services we provide, and our active participation in helping to meet society's needs.

  - Wherever we operate, we will strive to minimize any disruption to the environment arising from our activities.

- • We will work constructively with governments in the development of policy.

- • We recognize changing public expectations of the extent to which companies should put pressure on governments on human rights issues. We will seek to resolve any tensions or conflicts arising between international expectations and national or local practice in a sensitive manner, using independent experts and advisers where appropriate.

- • For Nongovernmental Organizations

  - • We will seek to create mutual understanding and build constructive relationships with nongovernmental organizations who have a genuine interest in our business and concerns about its impact upon individuals, society, and the environment.

- • For Media

  - • We will seek to form a constructive and productive relationship with all aspects of the media: television, radio, newspapers, and the Internet.

- • For Trade Bodies

  - • We will seek to influence trade bodies for the mutual benefit of the industry and society.

- • For Employee Representative Bodies

  - • We will seek to work in good faith with trades unions and other bodies that our employees collectively choose to represent them within the appropriate local legal framework.

Health, Safety, and Environmental (HSE) Performance

Everybody who works for the Company, anywhere, is responsible for getting HSE right. Good HSE performance is critical to the success of our business. Our goals are simply stated - no accidents, no harm to people, and no damage to the environment. We will continue to drive down the environmental and health impact of our operations by reducing waste, emissions, and discharges and using energy efficiently. Wherever we have control or influence we will:

- • Consult, listen and respond openly to our customers, neighbors, and public interest groups.

- • Work with our partners, suppliers, competitors, and regulators to raise the standards of our industry.

- • Openly report our performance, good and bad.

- • Recognize those who contribute to improved HSE performance.

- Work with our partners, suppliers, competitors, and regulators to raise the standards of our industry.

- Openly report our performance, good and bad.

- Recognize those who contribute to improved HSE performance.

Integrity Assurance Program (IAP)

The Company's IAP sets out the approach we intend to take in identifying and managing safety, health, environmental, and operational risks. Application of IAP is mandatory and use of the terminology within it is required. Every operation must meet or exceed IAP standards. In all our activities and operations, we will:

- Comply fully with all legal requirements and meet or exceed the expectations set out in the IAP wherever we operate.

- Provide a secure working environment by protecting ourselves, our assets, and our operations against risk of injury and loss or damage from criminal or hostile acts.

All our employees and contractors will be well informed and well trained. Our managers must regularly provide assurance that the processes they have in place are working effectively. While everyone is responsible for HSE performance, managing HSE risk is a line management responsibility. We will:

- Openly report our performance and consult with people outside the company to improve our understanding of potential HSE issues associated with our operations.

- Encourage third parties working on our behalf and others in our industry to operate to high standards.

- Assure ourselves that our contractors' management systems are compatible with our commitment to HSE performance.

The IAP comprises a set of expectations that outline the Company's requirements for the management of safety and accident prevention, plant and equipment integrity, pollution prevention, energy conservation, occupational and environmental health, physical security, and product stewardship. Senior Managers are accountable for putting management systems and local processes in place to implement the following expectations.

Management Leadership, Commitment, and Accountability

We will put in place systems and processes to manage the integrity of our design, construction, and operational activities. Our managers will take the lead by establishing goals and objectives, ensuring programs are adequately resourced, designating accountabilities, and demonstrating their commitment through personal involvement.

Risk Assessment and Management

We will regularly identify the hazards and assess the risks associated with our activities and take appropriate action to prevent, or reduce the impact of, potential incidents or accidents.

Facilities Design and Construction

We will enhance the inherent safety and security of our plant and equipment, and minimize environmental and health risks, by using sound standards, procedures and management systems for the design, procurement, construction, and start up of our facilities.

Operations and Maintenance

We will operate within established parameters to deliver good health, safety, security, and environmental performance. We will reduce the environmental impact of our activities. Risks associated with nonroutine operations will be properly managed. Facilities that are no longer required will be responsibly decommissioned with due care for the environment.

Management of Change

We will evaluate and manage changes to processes, equipment, organizations and people to ensure that health, safety, security, and environmental risks remain at acceptable levels. We will comply with changes to laws and regulations and take account of new scientific evidence relating to health and environmental effects.

Information and Documentation

We will maintain up-to-date information on the design and operation of our processes and facilities; properties of materials handled; potential health, safety, and environmental hazards; and regulatory requirements.

Personnel and Training

We will carefully select, train, and regularly assess the competence of personnel to sustain operations that are healthy, safe, secure and environmentally sound and that conform to laws and regulations.

Working with Contractors and Third Parties

We will assess the capability of those who work on our behalf to operate to agreed standards and monitor their performance. We will work with contractors, suppliers, partners, and other third parties to encourage a responsible and effective approach to HSE issues within our industry.

Incident Investigation and Analysis

We will report and investigate incidents and near misses and follow-up as necessary to improve our performance. We will share and learn lessons from such incidents and use the information to take corrective action and prevent recurrence.

Community Awareness and Emergency Preparedness

We will have emergency plans in place together with appropriate equipment, facilities, and trained personnel to protect the public, the environment, and those working for us in the event of an accident or an incident. We recognize the importance of community awareness in maintaining public confidence in the integrity of our operations.

Operations Integrity Assessment and Improvement

We will regularly measure our HSE performance and set targets for continuous improvement. We will regularly assess the implementation of these expectations to assure ourselves that appropriate management processes are in place and working effectively; we will involve third parties in this process where appropriate to provide external perspectives.

Customers and Products

We will evaluate the health, safety, and environmental hazards associated with our products and assess the consequential risks from supply through to disposal. Advice will be communicated to help users and others handle our products safely. Systems will be established to collect and review any reported adverse effects and to respond to requests for emergency HSE information.

Finance and Control

The Company commits to maximize long-term shareholder value. To deliver this commitment we need excellent standards of planning and control. Our understanding of risk and management of financial matters must be carried out to the highest professional standards. We will do this by:

- Preparing plans and setting clear business performance targets.

- Challenging plans and targets and monitoring progress against them.

- Ensuring that investments of whatever type are properly evaluated and approved and that expenditure (both revenue and capital) is authorized.

- Understanding and managing the risks and ensuring that objectives are met efficiently with sound control processes.

- Producing financial reports that are reliable, accurate, and timely and ensuring that all transactions are properly handled and reported and that assets are financially safeguarded.

Financial Planning, Performance Contracts, and Monitoring

Annual performance contracts and medium-term plans will be prepared for all Business Units and service functions and agreed on by their respective Senior Managers. The degree of risk to achieving the targets set will be appraised realistically. Progress against these targets will be measured and reported accurately and monitored through quarterly performance review meetings.

Management of Risks

The key risks to the achievement of any objective will be understood and managed. Adequate controls will be maintained to give reasonable assurance that operations are effective and efficient, financial results are timely and reliable, assets are safeguarded, and laws and regulations are complied with.

Authorities

Delegated financial authority should be given to individuals best able to exercise these authorities. Staff at all levels will make decisions only within the authority delegated to them and within their competence to do so.

Independent Review

All activities will be subject to independent review at a frequency determined by risk. The extent of independent review will be determined by the internal and external auditors. Unrestricted access to staff and documents will be provided (subject to legal constraints) to Internal and External Audit on request.

Development and Deployment of Financial Staff

Processes will be put in place to ensure that staff are trained and obtain the appropriate experience and are deployed in appropriate posts. The appointment of controllers or more senior posts will require the approval of the Chief Financial Officer.

Clear Understanding of Roles

Business Unit leaders, controllers, and functional team members will ensure they have a clear understanding of their responsibilities.

Policy Implementation

These policy commitments apply to all our business operations and our dealings with all those with whom we do business. Everyone in the Company is held accountable for implementing these commitments and for raising with their management any issue where they are in doubt about the correct course of action they should take. Senior Managers are responsible for aligning the policies regionally to take account of local legislation and practice.

Willful or careless breach or neglect of these commitments will be treated as a serious disciplinary matter.

Assurance

Policy assurance in the Company means people being sure about how effectively the policies are being implemented so that they can confidently assure others based on their own knowledge and experience. Each individual's knowledge and experience must be reinforced through rigorous and objective processes that measure performance and identify knowledge gaps that need to be addressed.

Primary accountability for providing assurance in all aspects of performance lies with the line, and line managers are accountable to their Senior Managers for providing assurance on compliance.

Assurance is generated by a number of activities and processes that need to be tailored to fit the particular circumstances of a business or functional unit and integrated into its overall management process.

Assurance activities and processes fall into three broad categories:

- Performance measures to demonstrate that the policies are being implemented in practice. These can be hard measures, such as HSE measures or staff survey results, or soft measures, such as the quality of important relationships or the level of staff awareness of the ethical dilemmas they face.

- The internal processes for implementing each of the policies, monitoring performance, and reporting gaps at all levels.

- External support and challenge by functional experts and independent reviews. These promote better understanding of external perceptions and potential risks to performance or reputation and facilitate the sharing of experience to improve internal processes and performance.

HARASSMENT

It is the policy of the Company to provide a workplace free of harassment of employees by other employees, including supervisors. Harassment, whether based on sex, race, color, religion, age, national origin, handicap, or veteran status, is discriminatory and unlawful. Harassment is considered an act of misconduct and may subject an individual to disciplinary action. All supervisors and managers are responsible for implementing and monitoring compliance with this Policy.

Harassment is defined as unwelcome or unsolicited verbal, physical, or sexual conduct that substantially interferes with an employee's job performance or that creates an intimidating, hostile, or offensive working environment. Examples of harassment are:

- Verbal harassment, e.g., derogatory or vulgar comments regarding a person's race, sex, religion, ethnic heritage or physical appearance or threats of physical harm.

- Visual harassment, e.g., demeaning or derogatory posters, cartoons, photographs, graffiti, drawings, gestures or leers or distribution of written or graphic material having such effects.

- Physical harassment, e.g., hitting, pushing, or other aggressive physical contact or threatening to take such action.

- Sexual harassment, e.g., unwelcome or unsolicited sexual advances, demands for sexual favors, or other verbal or physical conduct of a sexual nature.

Any person who feels he or she has been harassed or who witnesses harassment can report, without fear of reprisal, such incident to his or her supervisor or manager, or any member of management, or the Human Resources Manager. The Human Resources Department is responsible for promptly investigating and resolving complaints of sexual harassment. Confidentiality will be maintained.

HEALTH, SAFETY, AND THE ENVIRONMENT

The Company has long regarded the safety and health of its employees as core values. In addition are extensive local and national laws designed to promote a safe workplace. These laws are to be strictly enforced. Any incident that leads to the serious injury or death of an employee is likely to be thoroughly investigated by governmental agencies. Extensive and continuous training and regular safety audits are essential for understanding and complying with safety laws.

In recent years, governments at all levels and in many countries have enacted very strict laws in the environmental area. Moreover, enforcement authorities have shown a strong tendency to enforce criminal laws against corporations and their employees for serious environmental offenses. Environmental laws govern nearly every aspect of the Company's operations, especially those causing emissions of materials to air, land, or water. Many incidents such as accidental releases and spills, or newly acquired information indicating that chemicals may pose a health threat of toxins must be reported to governmental agencies. Also, many governments require advance notification before the Company manufactures or imports new chemicals.

In addition to complying with applicable environmental laws and regulations, the Company has a long-standing policy on safety, health, and the environment.

It is the Company's policy to conduct global operations and businesses in a way that will protect the environment and the safety and health of our employees, our customers, our communities, and our contractors. In addition to complying with applicable laws, we should continuously strive to make improvements in the following key areas:

- Designing, building, and managing our facilities to ensure they are operated safely and are acceptable to the community.

- Preventing hazardous waste generation and emissions at the source and reusing and recycling to minimize the need for disposal.

- Eliminating environmental incidents, including inadvertent releases, leaks, and spills.

- Making, using, handling, and disposing of our products safely and working with our customers, distributors, and contractors so that they apply similar principles in their handling of our products.

- Integrating excellence in health, safety, and environmental performance as a core value at all levels and for every employee.

- Committing adequate resources to train employees and sustain our commitment to health, safety, and environmental performance.

- Seeking and responding to public values and concerns about the impact of our operations on health, safety, and the environment.

INFORMATION SECURITY

Sensitive information has value and will therefore be protected. Sensitive information includes:

- Proprietary business and technical information.

- Personal data concerning applicants, employees, and former employees.

- Proprietary information of suppliers provided under contractual agreement.

Sensitive information will be assigned one of three classifications. The classifications are Company Restricted, Company Confidential, or Company Personal.

Sensitive information will be protected at all times and in all forms. Access to or knowledge of sensitive information will be based on need to know, following from assigned job tasks. Protection measures will include avoiding careless talk, maintaining a clean desk, controlling unauthorized disclosure to outside parties, and avoiding unnecessary distribution internally.

Classification System

The Company's classification system evaluates information and determines which classifications are to be applied. The classifications are:

- Company Restricted is information that the unauthorized disclosure of which could cause serious damage to Company operations. This is the highest Company classification. Its use, and the access to information so classified, must be strictly limited.

- Company Confidential is information of such value or sensitivity that its unauthorized disclosure could have a substantially detrimental effect on Company operation.

- Company Personal is information that an originator determines should be limited in its disclosure.

Information owners (i.e., the senior functional managers responsible) and originators of information are responsible for assigning the appropriate Company classification.

Declassification will be carried out in the manner prescribed by the Company's information security standards.

Handling and Marking

Classified information in documents, electronic form, or both will be marked, distributed, copied, mailed, hand carried off premises, stored, and destroyed only in accordance with prescribed Company standards, which are specified in the information security standards.

Protective Measures

Awareness

Programs will be implemented to ensure that all employees are advised of their responsibility for protecting Company classified information. All employees will read and sign the Company's confidentiality agreement.

Careless Talk

Careless talk about Company plans, strategies, and so forth will be avoided both at and away from the job. Under no circumstances should there be any discussion with outsiders of sensitive Company information.

Clean Desk

All Company employees must adhere to clean desk practices. During nonbusiness hours or when a workplace is unattended, sensitive information will be secured in accordance with the Company's information security standards.

Disclosure of Information to Outside Parties

If, in the course of business, consultants, contractors, and other outside parties must have access to Company classified material, they must sign a confidentiality agreement. They are to receive only such information as is necessary to comply with their contract.

Publications

Although publication of scholarly or research material is permitted after required clearances have been obtained, Company proprietary information must not be compromised in such material.

Public Disclosure

Press Relations

The Company's Public Affairs department is solely responsible for dealings with the press. The significance of information to be released must be carefully assessed by the originators beforehand.

Release of Financial Information

Financial information, other than published financial statements, is sensitive information and may not be released to outside agencies, individuals, and foreign subsidiaries unless such release is approved by an officer of the Company.

Legal Affairs

Inquiries with respect to the Company's legal affairs should be referred promptly to the general counsel. Legal affairs, such as proposed or ongoing litigation, proceedings before regulatory agencies, and governmental investigations, can be highly sensitive and therefore must not be discussed outside the Company.

Speeches and Publications

Wherever the author of any speech, article, presentation, or statement, or participant in a panel discussion, outside education program, or other activity intended for public release, will be identified with the Company, or if the content mentions the Company or discusses any Company matters whatsoever, the following clearance must be obtained before publication, delivery, or participation:

- For nontechnical material, clearance must normally be granted by a department manager, general counsel, and the cognizant manager of Public Affairs.

- For technical material or material that refers to current or future products, research plans, or programs, additional approvals are required from general counsel.

Electronic Information

The unique characteristics and inherent security risks of electronic forms of information make enhanced security essential.

Information Technology Manager

This individual will:

- Develop and revise policies and procedures for safeguarding information.

- Prepare training programs.

- Provide guidance and leadership in resolving information management problems.

- Ensure the establishment of a security coordinator network.

- Perform staff visits and reviews.

- Ensure internal auditing of operating units for conformance to this policy.

Operating Groups

These groups will:

- Develop, publish, and implement information control plans to achieve adherence to policy.

- Initiate policies, standards, and procedures that meet local requirements.

- Obtain review and concurrence of information management implementation plans by the Information Technology Manager.

- Conduct operating unit compliance reviews.

- Identify and correct problem situations.

- Report significant security breaches to the Information Technology Manager.

Managers, Supervisors, and Employees

All individuals will:

- Ensure adherence to policy and related procedures.

- Protect Company classified material in accordance with established policies and procedures.

- Ensure that security indoctrination is provided to employees and contract and temporary personnel assigned to the organization.

- Designate IT Security Representatives as needed.

- Monitor implementation of information security regulations and programs.

IT Security Representatives

These persons will:

- Be fully conversant with security policies and guidelines.

- Provide counsel to their management on security matters.

- Carry out tasks and programs as set forth in the security coordinator guide and perform special assignments as required.

INTERNET

The Internet is a valuable source of information, an important communication tool, and an important facilitator of electronic commerce. The purpose of this Policy is to protect employees and the Company from legal exposure and to protect the Company's reputation. This Policy is not meant to discourage the proper use of the Internet. Where the Policy is not explicit or where there may be any questions about the appropriateness of an Internet site, the employee will inquire with a supervisor or manager before accessing the site. Accessing or distributing inappropriate or offensive material damages the workplace environment and may harm the Company's reputation.

Internet access is provided for business purposes only. Limited occasional or incidental personal nonbusiness use is understandable and acceptable where such personal use is conducted with a sense of responsibility. The privilege must not be abused. User conduct is subject to all Company policies as well as statutory legislation.

Any employee found to be abusing the privilege of Company-facilitated access to electronic media and services will be subject to disciplinary action, up to and including termination. Any contractor performing work for the Company found to be in violation will be barred from the Company premises and facilities at the Company's sole discretion.

Violation of statutory regulations may result in personal liability.

Guidelines

The following guidelines apply:

- Employees must restrict their use to those systems which they are authorized to access. Employees should be aware that all access to Internet sites is monitored, including individual use.

- Employees are expected in their Internet use to protect the Company's reputation and to eliminate potential legal liabilities.

- Any information an employee views, downloads, or distributes must conform to Company policy. Viewing, downloading, or distributing obscene or abusive material is strictly prohibited.

- An employee may not advertise or participate in any illegal activities related to the Internet.

- Applicable copyright laws must be respected.

- Employees should not totally rely on information obtained from the Internet without verification.

- Communication over the Internet should be considered not secure except where encryption is provided. Sensitive or confidential information should not be communicated using the Internet.

Categories of Use

Internet activity falls into four categories:

- **Business use**. Examples include industry reports, economic information, business news, and technology data.

- **Non-business but acceptable use**. Examples include news, weather, and other uses of a responsible nature.

- **Inappropriate use**. Examples include large-volume downloads, games, audio, chat sites, movies, excessive time, Web-based e-mail.

- **Misuse**. Examples include pornographic or adult-oriented sites, racist sites, gambling, hacking, sites promoting violence, and illegal software.

Disciplinary action will be taken where usage falls into either of the latter two categories.

INVESTIGATIONS

The policy of the Company is to thoroughly investigate crimes committed against Company interests, vigorously prosecute offenders, and obtain restitution.

Controls will be in place in business affairs that are susceptible to crime, such as fraud in awarding contracts and in making purchases, especially where large sums are involved. Multiple approvals, segregation of authority, and audit trails are examples of controls designed to prevent and detect irregularities.

The Corporate Security Manager and the managers of Audit, Information Technology, Legal, and Procurement are required to confer and collaborate so as to look for the indications of fraud-related crime and to conduct investigations when warranted.

Implementation

Crimes will be investigated and, where appropriate, legal and/or disciplinary action taken against offenders to include civil and/or criminal prosecution.

Depending upon the nature and seriousness of the offense, the initial investigative action will be to confer with the relevant business unit managers concerning strategy, tactics, the acquisition of in-house and external resources, and other actions that may be appropriate.

Confidentiality will be observed and the number of people who have knowledge of the case will be restricted to those with a legitimate need to know.

The following principles apply:

- Allegations and initial findings should be reviewed with Company counsel.

- If the decision is made to proceed with a formal investigation, the investigator will comply fully with the applicable law.

- Collect and safeguard evidence. Since much of the work product associated with a thorough investigation will involve documentary evidence, originals should be obtained. Originals will be the standard expectation at trial. Chain of custody will also be an issue at trial.

- Persons familiar with the matter will be asked to submit voluntarily to interviewing and provide written statements. Care must be taken by the interviewer in order to avoid later claims of harassment, false imprisonment, and intimidation. A poorly executed interview can place the investigation and the Company in jeopardy.

The Corporate Security Manager will draft a final report of investigation for review by in-house legal counsel. In addition to citing the facts of the case, the report should contain recommendations to management for preventing recurrence.

POLITICAL CONTRIBUTIONS

Employees may not make any contribution of Company funds, property, or services to any political party or committee or to any candidate for or holder of any office of any government. This policy does not preclude, where lawful:

- The operation of a political action committee.

- Company contribution to support or oppose public referenda or similar ballot issues.

- Political contributions that have been reviewed in advance by members of Company management charged with responsibility in this area.

No direct or indirect pressure in any form is to be placed on employees to make any political contribution or participate in the support of a political party or the political candidacy of any individual.

PROTECTION OF ASSETS

Company assets are to be protected and to be used for authorized purposes only. Employees must comply with security programs that safeguard company assets against theft, damage, and unauthorized use.

Internal Controls

The Company has established accounting control standards and procedures to ensure that assets are protected and properly used and that financial records and reports are accurate and reliable. Employees share the responsibility for maintaining and complying with required internal controls.

Reporting Integrity

All Company financial reports, accounting records, research reports, sales reports, expense accounts, time sheets, and other documents must accurately and clearly represent the relevant facts or the true nature of a transaction. Improper or fraudulent accounting, documentation, or financial reporting is contrary to Company policy and may also be in violation of applicable laws. Intentional accounting misclassifications (e.g., cost versus capital) and improperly accelerating or deferring expenses or revenues would be examples of unacceptable reporting practices.

Electronic Information

Company data transmitted and/or stored electronically are assets requiring unique protection. Corporate standards for the protection of electronic information have been adopted and are available through line management. Each data user throughout the Company is responsible for compliance with the standards and related procedures.

SECURITY

The Company will provide for employees and contractors a secure working environment through proactive security measures designed to protect people, assets, and operations against the threats of injury and loss or damage by criminal, hostile, or malicious acts.

The security threats facing the Company will be regularly assessed and properly managed.

Employees will comply with security measures and report security infractions to supervisors or managers. Security is an integral function of line management.

Responsibilities

Each business management is assigned full responsibility for the security of its operations and is required annually to provide assurance upward that security threats are being properly managed.

Where a management is legally accountable for the Company's local security performance, it must ensure that the business operates in accordance with local legal requirements.

The Corporate Security Director is responsible for providing advice on strategic security issues.

Minimum Expectations

With Corporate Security guidance, business management will ensure that:

- Security risks are reviewed regularly and at least once a year.

- Security measures are based on sound assessments of risk, are appropriate to offset the risks, and are cost effective.

- On an ongoing basis, employees are made aware of security risks and of their personal responsibilities to maintain security.

- The need for security measures will be considered at the earliest stage of new projects, such as renovation or construction of Company facilities.

- Security resources are allocated, that security responsibilities are being met, and that upper management is assured of the adequacy of the security program.

- At a frequency of not less than once every three years, the business will schedule through the Corporate Security Department a comprehensive evaluation of the security program.

- Serious security violations will be reported upward and investigated and legal and/or disciplinary action taken against offenders. The Corporate Director of Security will devise a rating scheme for determining the seriousness of violations. The rating factors will include extent of personal injury, extent of material loss or damage, and impact on reputation.

SEXUAL HARASSMENT

The Company prohibits any form of sexual harassment of any employee by any person, including management, employees, and vendors.

Sexual Harassment Defined

The term sexual harassment includes, but is not necessarily limited to, unwelcome sexual advances, requests for sexual favors, and other verbal or physical conduct of a sexual nature. Sexual harassment can take the following forms:

- Sexual conduct that unreasonably interferes with another person's work performance or creates an intimidating, hostile, or offensive work environment

- Personnel decisions (e.g., promotion, salary adjustments, evaluations, and discipline) made by a supervisor on the basis of an employee's submission to or rejection of sexual advances.

- Submission to sexual conduct as an explicit or implicit term or condition of an individual's employment.

Prohibitions

Any verbal or physical conduct constitutes harassment when this conduct:

- Has the purpose or effect of creating an intimidating, hostile, or offensive working environment.

- Has the purpose or effect of interfering with an individual's work performance.

- Otherwise adversely affects an individual's employment opportunities.

Responsibilities

Each supervisor has a duty to maintain his or her work area free of sexual harassment. This duty includes discussing this Policy with all employees and expressing disapproval of harassing behavior. It also includes explaining applicable complaint procedures and potential discipline for violations and assuring employees that they are not required to endure insulting, degrading, or exploitative sexual treatment.

No company supervisor will threaten or insinuate, either explicitly or implicitly, that an employee's refusal to submit to sexual advances could affect the employee's employment, evaluation, wages, advancement, assigned duties, shifts, or any other condition of employment or career development.

Any person who believes that he or she is being sexually harassed should politely but firmly confront the individual doing the harassing and request that the person cease the unwanted, unwelcome, or offensive behavior. Any employee who feels that he or she has been subjected to sexual harassment should immediately contact his or her supervisor or manager as provided for under the company's regular complaint procedures or may immediately contact his or her supervisor, manager, the Human Resources Manager, or any member of management.

Any supervisor or manager who becomes aware of any incident of sexual harassment should immediately contact the Human Resources Manager.

The Human Resources Manager is responsible for maintaining procedures that facilitate the prompt and thorough investigation and review of all sexual harassment complaints. All actions taken to resolve complaints of sexual harassment through internal investigations will be conducted with sensitivity and discretion. No retaliation against an individual complaining of sexual harassment, or anyone providing information in the investigation of such a complaint, will be tolerated.

Enforcement

The Company will strictly enforce its sexual harassment policy. A violation of this policy by any employee, especially those who perform in a supervisory/managerial capacity, shall subject that employee to disciplinary action, up to and including termination.

All personnel, including management and supervisory personnel, will be informed of this policy through management meetings, bulletin board notices, company publications, and other appropriate forums.

SMOKING

The Company accommodates the personal preference of smoking and nonsmoking employees, contractors and visitors. To improve the health of employees, smoking cessation is encouraged, and in situations where conflicts between smokers and nonsmokers arise, preference will be given to accommodating the nonsmoker.

Implementation

All employees, contractors, and visitors will be expected to abide by this Policy, and supervisors are expected to implement appropriate rules within their areas of operation. Smoking is prohibited in:

- Any area in which a safety or fire hazard exists, as determined by local management. Such areas include computer rooms and storage areas.

- Any common areas designated as nonsmoking, such as elevators/lobbies, stairwells, lofts, hallways, copier/kitchen rooms, coffee bars, workrooms, file rooms, restrooms, libraries, and cafeteria.

Supervisors and managers of work areas shared by smokers and nonsmokers are to undertake reasonable efforts to separate the two groups, taking into account business necessity, air flow and ventilation, and physical impediments. Entire floors or work areas may be designated as nonsmoking by the senior manager having authority over and responsibility for the space.

SPECIAL PROJECT SECURITY

In addition to the sensitive information generated, processed, and held in the normal business routines of the Company, there exists a category of especially sensitive information related to Special Projects. A Special Project is a Company endeavor with a clear beginning and end and a predictable duration that involves sensitive information the release of which could cause serious damage to the interests of the Company. In terms of dollars, serious damage begins at the $10 million level. Examples of Special Projects include construction and renovation of research and development facilities; new product development; acquisition and divestment; litigation; major reorganization; shifts in business strategy; matters that have high political, legal, or reputation sensitivity; and matters that have a potential impact on the Company's share price. The Company requires full protection of Special Project Information (SPI).

Potential Negative Outcomes

Among the negative outcomes that can follow from the unauthorized disclosure of SPI are:

- Loss of market share.

- Loss of critical technology.

- Higher than necessary fees paid to contractors.

- Weakened position in matters undergoing negotiation or litigation.

- Reduction of share values.

- Damage to reputation.

- Loss of confidence by government leaders.

Threats

Experience has shown that some organizations will make extraordinary attempts to acquire SPI. These attempts have included:

- Subversion of project staff and support staff, many of whom have considerable access to sensitive information.

- Theft of sensitive information as a result of gaining unauthorized access to document waste, filing cabinets, and unattended proprietary materials.

- Theft of sensitive information stored and transmitted on computer and telecommunications systems, such as fax and telephone.

Information has been leaked by carelessness such as:

- Sharing of information with others whose need to know the information is questionable.

- Discussing information in public places, such as hotel lobbies, bars, and aircraft.

- Leaving sensitive papers in waste baskets, printers, fax machines, and photocopiers.

- Improper setting of information technology access controls so that passwords are ineffective and protection against unauthorized access is insufficient.

Protection of SPI

The sensitivity of SPI and the threats to it exceed the norm. The simplest assessment of risk dictates that security measures must be used that effectively resist a determined and capable attacker. The Company's minimum standards for security of information apply but must be supplemented by stronger measures, for example:

- Agree on a Project Security Plan, developed through the collaboration of the Special Project Manager, the Security Manager, and the IT Security Coordinator.

- Implement procedures that:

  - Limit the access to SPI to a core group of cleared individuals.

  - Prohibit removal of SPI from a restricted area that is itself inside an access-controlled area.

  - Require SPI to be stored in high-security, fireproof containers when not in use.

  - Require SPI destruction to be witnessed and documented by a member of the core group.

  - Put into place for SPI protection all reasonable electronic information security measures, such as passwords and firewalls.

  - Provide initial and refresher training to all project staff concerning the security of SPI.

- Validate the Project Security Plan by periodically reviewing the performance of the Corporate Security Department and Internal Audit Department.

Elements of the Project Security Plan

The Project Security Plan will be the guiding document for the protection of SPI. It will reflect the perceived and agreed risks and the agreed security measures to counter the risks. The Plan will be shared by all involved so that a fit-for-purpose and balanced approach can be taken to safeguard SPI. The plan will:

- Assess the specific risks and threats to SPI. For example:

  - Identify likely adversaries.

  - Evaluate the methods and capabilities of adversaries.

  - Identify possible attack schemes of adversaries.

  - Estimate probable success of attack.

  - Estimate loss that may result from attack.

  - Identify appropriate countermeasures.

  - Match the cost of countermeasures against the estimated probable loss.

  - Develop a timetable for implementing countermeasures.

  - Develop a scheme for evaluating the cost-effectiveness of countermeasures.

- Assign specific accountability to special project staff.

- Identify resources required for Plan implementation; e.g., identify employees and outside contractors who are qualified and available to perform electronic eavesdropping analyses. Ensure that the expertise of the anti-eavesdropping technician is at a high level and that the equipment used is the best available.

- Declare a classification for SPI that is higher than the highest classification used for the Company's non-project-sensitive information. The classification descriptor will be "SPI" followed by a code word, for example: "SPI Groundhog" or "SPI Roma."

- Identify the security measures that will be applied to the modes through which SPI is transmitted, such as from person to person; over the telephone; by fax, Email, and mail; and between computers.

TRAVEL AND ENTERTAINMENT

Travel and entertainment should be consistent with the needs of business. The Company's intent is that an employee neither lose nor gain financially as a result of business travel and entertainment. Employees are expected to spend the Company's money as carefully as they would their own.

Employees who approve travel and entertainment expense reports are responsible for the propriety and reasonableness of expenditures and for ensuring that expense reports are submitted promptly and that receipts and explanations properly support reported expenses.

U.S. SENTENCING GUIDELINES

Compliance Is Mandatory

The Company and each of its subsidiaries will establish and maintain an effective compliance program that conforms to the standards established in the Sentencing Guidelines promulgated by the U.S. Sentencing Commission. The program will be designed, implemented, and enforced with the purpose of being effective in preventing and detecting criminal conduct.

Due Diligence

The Company will exercise due diligence in attempting to prevent and to detect criminal conduct by its employees and agents. To those ends the Company will establish and maintain the policies and practices set forth as follows:

- The Company will determine the likelihood that there is a substantial risk that certain types of criminal offenses may occur.

- The Company will establish and maintain compliance standards and procedures to be followed by its employees and agents that are reasonably capable of reducing the prospect of criminal conduct.

- Specific high-level individuals within the Company shall be assigned overall responsibility to oversee compliance with such standards and procedures. Business unit heads are hereby assigned such responsibility for their respective operations.

- The Company will not delegate substantial discretionary authority to any individual it knows, or through the exercise of due diligence should have known, had a propensity to engage in illegal activities.

- The Company will take reasonable steps to communicate effectively its standards and procedures to all employees and other agents.

- The Company will take reasonable steps to achieve compliance with its standards. Such steps can include the use of monitoring and auditing controls designed to detect unlawful conduct by employees and agents and hot lines and other mechanisms or processes that allow anonymous reporting and reporting that is free of retribution or fear of retribution.

- The Company will consistently enforce its standards through appropriate disciplinary mechanisms, including, as appropriate, discipline of individuals responsible for the failure to detect an offense.

- If a criminal offense is detected, the organization will take all reasonable steps to respond appropriately to the offense and to prevent similar offenses.

- Each division and subsidiary will establish one or more committees to assist the business unit head in the implementation and enforcement of this program.

WORKPLACE VIOLENCE

The Company is committed to maintaining a safe and secure workplace. Conduct of any type that threatens or manifests violence in any form or at any magnitude is unacceptable and will not be tolerated.

Unacceptable Conduct

- Making threats in any form, verbal or otherwise.

- Making unwanted physical contact with another, even when minor.

- Stalking.

- Carrying a lethal weapon onto the premises. Lethal weapons include all items designed to kill or that have killing power, such as firearms, hunting knives, and explosives.

Actions

- The Human Resources Manager will ensure that each job applicant will be screened for a history of violent conduct and that where such conduct is indicated the applicant will not be selected for employment.

- The Human Resources Manager and the Procurement Manager will ensure through contract language and administration that contractor employees undergo screening for violent conduct to at least the same extent such screening is used in the selection of regular employees.

- The Human Resources Manager will provide training to supervisors and managers in how to identify the indicators of potential violence, how to refer apparently troubled employees to treatment professionals for diagnosis and counseling, how to follow up on referrals, how to document such matters, and how to respond when workplace violence occurs.

- The Human Resources Manager will ensure that HR staff are trained in how to conduct termination interviews and other person-to-person transactions that carry a potential for violence.

- The Security Manager will develop and implement procedures for:

  - A quick response by security officers and the police to incidents of violence.

  - Assisting HR staff when requested in situations that might lead to violence.

- Canceling the access privileges of terminated employees.

- Extra vigilance in preventing access to a terminated employee who indicated a potential for violence.

Indicators of Violence

- A history of depression.

- A history of hurting living things.

- An elevated frustration level.

- Evidence of personality disorder.

- A pattern of pathological blaming.

- Chemical or alcohol dependence.

- Strange, bizarre, or threatening behavior.

- Behavior suggestive of distress.

- Vocalizing violent intentions.

PLANS

plan *n*, a detailed formulation of a program of action.

ACCESS CONTROL

The purpose of access control is to provide a safe and secure work environment for employees, contractors, and visitors. Access control is specifically directed toward preventing harm to people, preventing the loss of assets, and preventing disruption to operations from criminal, hostile, or malicious acts. Controls will be carried out through an integrated and harmonious arrangement, for example:

- Barriers, such as fencing and walls.

- Physical and mechanical safeguards, such as vaults, safes, and locks.

- Personnel, such as security officers at entry points.

- Written procedures, such as those that guide persons charged with access control tasks.

- Electronic systems, such as those that detect unauthorized attempts at entry or that open door locks upon recognition of an authorized key card.

Controls will be arranged in layers of protection, and with a variety of control mechanisms, for example:

- Entry through the outer perimeter fence of the facility can be controlled by an electronically operated gate. The gate opens upon presentation of a key card or by a switch operated by a security officer at the security control center within the facility. Communication between the gate and the security control center can be via intercom, telephone, CCTV, or any combination thereof.

- The road from the outer perimeter fence can lead to a gatehouse covered by a security officer who examines the identification cards of vehicle occupants before lifting a gate arm.

- The entering individual can next encounter a numeric key pad at the entry door of the building where he or she works.

- The individual can next be required to insert his key card into a slot in the elevator cab.

- When exiting the elevator, the individual can be buzzed through a locked glass door by a receptionist.

- The individual goes to his or her office and uses a mechanical key to enter.

BOMB THREAT

This Plan applies to bomb threat incidents at the Company's home office. It is based on requirements of the applicable fire code and law enforcement guidelines.

Receipt of the Threat

Guidance to employees who receive telephone bomb threats will be provided in a Bomb Threat Checklist.

A bomb threat is rarely made in person and is sometimes transmitted in writing. A bomb threat made in writing should be handled carefully, touched by as few persons as possible, and the envelope or any other accompanying materials retained and preserved. Observing these simple precautions can be extremely helpful to a post-incident investigation.

A probability exists that a bomb threat against the building will be made to another party, such as the police department or fire department. If this should occur, the initial notice would come from the police department by telephone or in person. This initial notification might be supplemented by a police patrol being sent to the building to stand by to render possible assistance.

The Initial Response

Receptionists and certain secretaries will be trained to call the Security Control Center upon receipt of a bomb threat call. The objective is to begin implementation of this Plan as rapidly as possible.

When the Security Control Center receives, or is informed of a bomb threat, the following initial actions will be:

- Notify the Building Manager or Assistant Building Manager.

- Notify the Security Supervisor.

Evaluation

Evaluation of a bomb threat will be made by the Building Manager or Assistant Manager. Evaluation will be made on the basis of all facts available at the time. Many of the available facts will be obtained from the person who received the bomb threat. Evaluation is the process of judging the credibility of the threat. When a threat is judged to be false, the evaluator may elect to take no action. An example might be a bomb threat made by a child over the telephone. When a threat is judged to have possible credibility, one of three decisions will be made:

- To search without evacuation.

- To evacuate, partially or fully, and then search.

- To evacuate and not search.

When a threat is judged to have no credibility at all, the decision will be to take no action.

Evacuation Options

If a credible bomb threat is received and if the decision is not to evacuate, the Building Manager will make a public address announcement to the effect that:

- A bomb threat has been received.

- There is no reason to believe that anyone is in danger.

- The decision has been made to not evacuate.

- Any person in the building who wishes to leave may do so.

If the decision is to evacuate, the announcement will include brief instructions to employees to:

- Take with them any personal belongings (particularly purses, briefcases, and lunch boxes).

- Make a quick visual surveillance of their immediate work areas for the purpose of detecting suspicious objects.

- Report their suspicions to the security officer in the lobby as they exit the building.

The decision to evacuate will take into consideration the location of a suspect bomb relative to the fire stairwells. If a suspect bomb is believed to be in or near a stairwell, the evacuation announcement will direct evacuees away from the danger zone.

Total evacuation will not be an automatic response. Partial evacuation would be an appropriate response in those instances where the bomb threat caller mentions a specific location.

Communications

There have been very few recorded instances of explosive charges triggered by radio frequency energy. Generally, therefore, it is considered that the use of hand-held radios to assist in search procedures is not a serious hazard. However, operate a hand-held radio beyond a radius of ten feet from the suspicious object. If in doubt, use the telephone as the primary means of communication.

Suspicious Object

If a suspicious object is found, the finder will call the Security Control Center without delay, ensuring first that the suspect device is not touched or moved by another searcher or an uninformed bystander. The following actions will take place after the discovery of a suspicious object:

- The Security Control Center will notify the Building Manager and the Security Supervisor. The Building Manager or the Security Supervisor will ask the police to take command of the situation with respect to handling the suspect bomb.

- Depending on the circumstances, a partial or full evacuation will be implemented immediately.

- The Security Control Center will ensure that the fire department has been notified and that first aid supplies have been readied for possible use.

The police may ask for help when a suspicious object is found. This help might be to:

- Place calls to the bomb disposal unit or other emergency response agencies.

- Open doors to dissipate a possible blast effect.

- Confer with knowledgeable employees to learn of other possible hiding places where a secondary device could be concealed.

- Question employees who may be able to account for the object being in fact an innocent object.

Floor Wardens

Floor Wardens will perform their established functions with respect to evacuation but will not be used to search or perform other actions directly related to the bomb threat.

The assembly locations will be the same as those for fire emergencies. Floor wardens can be used to ascertain who is missing from each floor and to issue instructions to assembled employees.

Coordination

The Security Control Center will serve as the focal point of telephone communications during a bomb incident. At the earliest possible moment following the initiation of a bomb incident, the Building Manager and the Security Supervisor will proceed to the Security Control Center to coordinate management of the incident.

If the Security Control Center is within the danger zone posed by the bomb, all personnel in that area will evacuate to the assembly area. Before leaving the Security Control Center, the telephones will be placed on call forwarding to the office of the Building Manager. The Building Manager and the Security Supervisor will proceed to the Building Manager's office to coordinate management of the incident from that location.

Police Involvement

Depending on the nature of the threat, the police will decide what other notifications are appropriate with respect to the fire department, paramedics, and bomb disposal unit. The principal functions of the police will be to:

- Provide guidance to the Building Manager.

- Conduct certain limited searches of areas surrounding a suspect device.

- Dispose of suspect devices.

Bomb Threat Checklist

If you receive a bomb threat telephone call, use the checklist and follow this guidance:

- Be calm. Be courteous. Listen carefully. Do not interrupt the caller.

- Get as much information as possible from the caller, but avoid the impression you are working from a checklist. If possible, alert your supervisor while the caller is on the line. Take notes, try to get the caller's remarks word for word.

It is very important to obtain answers to these questions:

- "When is the bomb going to explode?"

- "Where is the bomb right now?"

- "What does the bomb look like?"

- "What is the bomb made of?" (Obtain details about its parts.)

- "What will cause the bomb to explode?"

- "Who placed the bomb? Why?"

- "What is your name? Where are you now?"

NOTE: TRY TO KEEP THE CALLER TALKING. IF NECESSARY, PRETEND DIFFICULTY WITH YOUR HEARING. TRY TO WEAVE THESE GENERAL QUESTIONS INTO THE CONVERSATION:

- "What did you say? I'm sorry, I didn't understand what you said."

- "How do I know this is not a joke?"

- "What group do you represent?"

- "Why are you doing this?"

Notify your supervisor and the Security Control Center immediately. Discuss the incident only as needed. Fill in the lines below.

Call received by:

Time call began: Time call ended:

Caller's remarks, word for word where possible:

_____

_____

_____

_____

_____

_____

_____

_____

Describe background noises:

_____

_____

_____

_____

Describe the caller in terms of voice (e.g., accent, stutter, lisp), approximate age, emotional condition (e.g., angry, calm, incoherent, precise), and any other peculiar characteristic:

_____

_____

_____

_____

_____

_____

_____

_____

_____

_____

_____

_____

_____

_____

_____

_____

_____

_____

_____

_____

BUILDING EMERGENCY

This Plan involves people, equipment and procedures. By far, the first is predominant. People are the essential elements, and in fact, the other two have no value without people. Although many parts of this Plan relate to equipment, such as the fire detection and alarm system, and procedures, such as evacuation, the critical key and driving force of the Plan is the people component.

Set forth are organized, planned, and coordinated actions to be followed with respect to various emergency events: fire, severe weather and natural disasters, medical emergencies and fatalities, bomb threats, and civil disturbances.

This Plan is both a planning tool and a crisis control tool. On one hand, it requires preparation and readiness, and on the other hand, it assigns response obligations to specific persons or units.

Note three significant characteristics. First, the core of the Plan is founded on procedures co-developed with the fire department (per fire code) and the Property Management Office. Second, the Plan has been and continues to be evolutionary. Third, it encompasses a wide variety of contingencies.

Detection and Alarm Components

The major components of the fire detection and alarm system are:

- Fire Command Center

- Fire Alarm (Manual) Pull Stations

- Ionization Detectors

- Air Handling Devices

- Alarm Horns and Voice Communication Speakers

- Elevators and Emergency Signs

- Firefighters' Telephone System

- Sprinkler System

- Emergency Generator System

Fire Command Center

The Fire Command Center serves as a central location for the fire alarm system and houses panels with indicator lights showing the areas of activated equipment by floor. Also located here is the microphone for voice communication throughout the building which can be activated selectively to floors, stairwells, and elevator cabs. All components of the fire alarm system are connected to the standby or emergency generator power system.

Fire Alarm (Manual) Pull Stations

Fire alarm (manual) pull stations are mounted on the walls by the stairwell doors on each floor. Pulling a manual station will sound the fire alarm on the floor where the alarm is pulled, as well as the floors immediately above and below that floor.

Ionization Detectors

An ionization detector reacts to smoke and invisible gases. At least six such detectors are located on each floor:

- Two in the passenger elevator lobby.

- One at each of the two stairwell entrances.

- One in each of the two mechanical rooms.

When an ionization detector activates, a signal is registered at the alarm panel in the Fire Command Center.

This initial signal will not trigger an alarm (i.e., horn and flashing exit signs) unless two or more detectors on the same floor go into active status at the same time. However, the alarm will automatically go into effect if within three minutes there is no human intervention at the alarm panel. This alarm, consisting of a horn and flashing exit signs, will sound on the affected floor, plus the floor above and below.

The purpose of the three-minute delay is to allow time for the building management staff (called the Fire Brigade) to go to the floor covered by the activated sensor and make an on-scene evaluation. If a fire condition is confirmed, an evacuation announcement will be made on the public address system. If a fire condition is not present, the announcement will so indicate.

Air Handling Devices

Certain equipment will automatically start up or shut down upon an alarm device activation:

- Stairwell pressurization fans will start.

- Toilet exhaust fans will start.

- Outside air fans will start.

- Air handling units on the affected floor will shut down.

- Relief fans will shut down.

Alarm Horns and Voice Communication Speakers

An alarm horn and a voice communication speaker are located next to every stairwell door on all floors. Speakers are also in the penthouse, the control plant, in both stairwells at every third floor, in the elevator cabs, and at various locations where an alarm sound might be muffled (such as within a sound-treated conference room).

Voice communication originating from the Fire Command Center will override the alarm horn on floors selected for communication. The horn will continue to sound in areas not selected for voice communication. Upon completion of voice communication, the horn will resume. The exit lights will flash on floors where alarm horns are sounding.

Elevators and Emergency Signs

Whenever two smoke detectors are activated in an elevator lobby, an interlock circuit provides for all cars serving that lobby to return to the ground floor. An emergency sign stating "In an Emergency, Use Exit Stairs" is located behind the call button panel in each elevator lobby and will illuminate whenever two smoke detectors in the same elevator lobby are activated.

During power outage, the emergency generator system will operate one elevator in each bank of four.

Firefighters' Telephone System

Portable telephone units are stored in the Fire Command Center so that the firefighters can . from each floor to the Fire Command Center. Telephone jacks are on the elevator lobby call button panels in every floor lobby and at both stairwell doors on every floor.

Sprinkler System

The building is equipped with heat-activated water sprinkler heads. The panel in the Fire Command Center will alarm and indicate the affected floor.

Sprinkler pipes on each floor have valves that remain in the open position. If a valve is closed for any reason, the panel in the Fire Command Center will indicate this condition.

Emergency Generator System

The Emergency Generator System automatically starts up in the event of a power outage. This system provides electrical service for a number of critical functions including the stairwell lights, exit signs, lights in the elevator lobbies, and the Fire Command Center.

Emergency Equipment

First-aid kits, oxygen resuscitators, fire extinguishers, and emergency bottled water are in the coffee/copy areas on each floor. Additionally, fire extinguishers are near each of the two fire stairwell exits on every floor and in computer and equipment rooms. Additional emergency equipment such as portable PA systems and stretchers are kept on standby status in the Security Control Center.

Management of a Fire Emergency

During a fire emergency, the fire detection and alarm system is monitored and operated by building management staff. The senior building management employee present will assume the function of Fire Director. This function, however, is immediately subordinated to the first arriving unit of the fire department.

In the early stages of a fire emergency, before the fire department arrives on the scene, the authority to order an evacuation resides with the Fire Director, Floor Wardens, and Security Officers.

Floor Wardens

Two or more employees on each floor are designated as Floor Wardens. A Floor Warden has these overall responsibilities:

- Educate co-workers concerning individual responsibilities for fire prevention, reduction of safety hazards, how to report a fire, how to evacuate, and where to assemble following evacuation.

- To prevent, report, and correct fire and safety hazards through daily inspection of the floor.

- To exercise leadership during an evacuation by directing co-workers down stairwells and insuring that no one has been left behind.

- To provide first-responder medical assistance to persons who are in need of CPR or First Aid.

The Floor Wardens are trained by and receive certification from the fire department. They are also trained and certified in CPR and First Aid.

In preparing to deal with a fire emergency, a Floor Warden will:

- Know the locations of the fire stairwells and the pull stations on the floor.

- Study the floor diagram that shows the most direct routes to the fire stairwells and ensure that the diagram is posted on the bulletin board in the coffee/copy rooms.

- Obtain volunteers on the floor who will direct employees away from the elevators and down the fire stairwells.

- Inform every new person on the floor concerning what to do in case of an emergency.

- Keep a list of the persons on the floor so that they can be accounted for immediately after an evacuation.

- Identify persons with medical conditions, such as asthma or pregnancy, who may need help during an evacuation. Arrange in advance with someone on the floor to provide the needed help. Inform Security of any handicapped persons.

- Be alert on the floor for fire hazards, e.g., overloaded electrical circuits, unattended cooking appliances, and materials blocking stairwell doors.

In responding during a fire emergency, a Floor Warden will immediately look through the entire floor for fire conditions, starting with the coffee/copy rooms, since these are the places where fire is most likely to occur.

If a search of the floor reveals fire conditions (i.e., visible flame or smoke), the Floor Warden will pull a pull station, report the fire by calling the fire department and the Fire Director, check the stairwells to ensure they are free of fire or smoke, and begin evacuation immediately. When the floor is completely evacuated, the Floor Warden will notify the Fire Director.

Employees will be directed away from the elevators unless specifically directed by the fire department to do otherwise.

If a search of the floor does not reveal fire conditions, the Floor Warden will wait for the arrival of the Fire Brigade from the building management office. The Fire Brigade will double-check the floor to validate that the initial search was thorough. When this has been done, the building management office will make an announcement over the loudspeaker.

A Floor Warden does not have to wait for an evacuation announcement to be made over the loudspeaker to begin evacuation. If fire conditions are present on the floor, the Floor Warden will immediately begin instructing people to leave via the stairwells.

During an evacuation, the Floor Warden will make a final search of the floor to ensure that no one has been left behind. Rest rooms, conference rooms, and closed offices will be checked.

Security Officers

Security officers are on duty 24 hours per day throughout the building and at the Security Control Center. Annunciation devices in the Security Control Center will alert officers to report fire conditions and location. The response will be as follows:

- One or more officers will proceed without delay to the affected floor for the purpose of assisting/backing up the Floor Wardens in the performance of their duties.

- The findings of the on-scene officers will be reported immediately to the Fire Command Center.

If an evacuation is ordered, the Security Officers will:

- Assist the Floor Wardens in guiding people from the building.

- Provide traffic control as may be needed to move firefighting apparatus into close proximity to the building.

- Serve as a communications link between Floor Wardens at the assembly area and the fire department.

If a fire alarm occurs during other than normal working hours, the Security Officers perform the functions of the Fire Brigade, i.e., determine the cause for the alarm and respond accordingly.

Individual Employees

The Floor Wardens educate employees on an on-going basis to assure that everyone will know what to do in the event of an evacuation. The employee will:

- Upon hearing the alarm, listen for and follow instructions given over the public address system or by Floor Wardens, building management staff, and Security Officers.

- Use the nearest stairwell for evacuation, unless otherwise directed.

- Not run and not smoke.

- Remain calm. Keep talking to a minimum.

- Obtain any needed assistance by seeking the help of a fellow employee, a Floor Warden, a Security Officer, or a building management employee or by calling the Security Control Center.

- Once out of the building, proceed directly to the designated assembly area in the garage and stand by for instructions.

Training and Drills

Floor Wardens and Security Officers will be trained in:

- CPR.

- Basic First Aid.

- Operation of ABC fire extinguishers.

- Operation of oxygen resuscitators.

Floor Wardens will receive refresher training at quarterly meetings conducted by the Fire Director.

Security officers will receive training in the post orders and special instructions that relate to building safety at time of hire and periodically as part of regularly conducted refresher and advanced training.

Security officers will engage in fire response drills and conduct tests of detection and annunciation equipment on a regular on-going basis. Such drills and tests will be conducted during other than normal working hours.

Fire drills for the benefit of Floor Wardens, Security Officers, the Fire Brigade, building management, and all occupants will be conducted at a frequency of at least one every three months. The nature of the drills will be specified by the fire department.

Severe Weather Emergencies

The Security Control Center monitors local weather conditions 24 hours per day, year round. Monitoring is done by a Weather Alert Scanner which is locked onto the National Weather Service broadcast frequency. The Weather Alert Scanner receives and announces NWS alerts automatically, without the need for human intervention.

Definitions

"Tornado" means a violent local storm with whirling winds of speed that can reach 200-400 miles per hour. A tornado appears as a rotating, funnel-shaped cloud that extends toward the ground from the base of a thundercloud.

"Severe Thunderstorm" means a storm with the possibility of frequent lightning, damaging winds of greater than 50 miles per hour, hail ¾ inch or more in diameter, and heavy rain.

"Tropical Storm" means a storm of tropical origin having winds near the center greater than 38 miles per hour (33 knots) but less than 74 miles per hour (64 knots).

"Hurricane" means a violent storm originating over tropical waters with winds near its center reaching 74 miles per hour (64 knots) and higher.

"Hurricane Advisory" means warning information concerning where the tropical storm or hurricane is located, how intense it is, where it is moving, and what precautions should be taken.

"Hurricane Watch" means an announcement is issued by the U.S. Weather Bureau to the public and all other interests via press and radio and television broadcasts whenever a tropical storm or hurricane becomes a threat to the coastal area. This announcement is not a warning; it indicates that the hurricane or tropical storm is near enough that everyone in the affected area should listen for subsequent advisories and be ready to take precautionary action in case hurricane warnings are issued.

"Severe Thunderstorm Watch" means an announcement indicating the possibility of tornadoes, thunderstorms, frequent lightning, hail, and winds of greater than 75 mph.

"Tornado Watch" means an announcement indicating that conditions are such that tornadoes are expected to develop.

"Tornado Warning" means an announcement indicating that a tornado has actually been sighted in the area, or is indicated by radar.

"Flash Flood Watch" means an announcement indicating that conditions are favorable for flash floods and rapidly rising waters (rivers, bayous, street flooding, etc.).

"Flash Flood Warning" means an announcement indicating that conditions exist or are imminent for flash floods.

Response Procedures

Should a severe weather condition threaten normal business operations, the decision to cease normal operations will be made by the senior executive present.

Should this decision be made, employees will be immediately notified.

In offices with exterior windows, employees will be told to take these actions prior to leaving the premises:

- Remove all loose items from the tops of desks, credenzas, cabinets, shelves, and window ledges.

- Put the blinds down and turn slats to shut position.

- Secure all company records and lock all file cabinets.

- Cover open shelving with plastic.

- Move artwork and personal items to interior space.

- Disconnect all electrical office equipment.

- If possible, move computer hardware away from windows to interior spaces.

Should a weather condition be so imminent as to make evacuation risky, employees will be told to:

- Close all doors to exterior offices.

- Move quickly to the core of the building for shelter, i.e., the center-most corridors and rooms.

- Sit down and put heads between knees.

- Remain in a safe area until directed to resume normal activities.

If the decision to close the offices is made prior to the normal opening time, an announcement to that effect will be aired on local radio stations or employees can obtain a tape-recorded message by calling the Company's switchboard.

Other Natural Disasters

It is anticipated that dangers associated with flooding can be managed through application of the procedures for the wind-related emergencies just described.

Because earthquakes cannot be accurately predicted, the response actions under this Plan will conform to guidance provided by governmental agencies charged with managing and responding to such major disasters.

Medical Emergency

If an accident or illness of an employee or visitor takes place, a call is immediately made to the Security Control Center. The caller will be asked to provide the following information:

- The name and extension of the caller.

- The name, sex, and approximate age (if known) of the victim.

- The nature of the injury or illness. Is the victim:

  - Conscious?

  - Breathing without assistance?

  - Bleeding?

- The exact location of the victim.

The caller will be told to not move the victim and, if possible, to have someone meet responding personnel in the corridor to lead them to the victim's location. The Security Control Center will:

- Summon first responder employees.

- Dispatch an officer to assist.

- Call the Emergency Medical Team (EMT) if the injury or illness is serious.

A serious injury or illness is any physical condition that is life-threatening and requires the immediate attention of a medical professional. Examples include unconsciousness, absence of breathing or pulse rate, uncontrolled bleeding, and severe chest pain.

The nature of assistance given by first responder employees is directed at stabilizing the victim's condition until the arrival of an EMT who will assume responsibilities for the victim's care and transport to a medical facility.

A minor injury or illness is a physical condition that requires diagnostic review or simple treatment by a medical professional. Examples include suturing, taking x-rays, and administering relief medication.

Reporting Requirements

All illnesses and injuries that occur on the job must be reported by the victim's supervisor. The Security Control Center will contact the supervisor in the immediate aftermath of the incident to provide the forms and guidance for preparing/submitting the required report.

Fatalities

The first responder (whether a Floor Warden or Security Officer) to a report of a fatality will not assume that the victim is in fact dead. First responder care will be administered to the victim to the extent possible until the arrival of an EMT.

The EMT will transport the victim to a hospital where a physician will determine condition of life.

The scene of a fatality should not be disturbed in the event that a formal investigation may be required to determine cause of death or culpability.

Because a fatality is likely to generate news media interest, Security will notify the public affairs representative without delay and will refer all news media inquiries to Public Affairs.

Injuries to more than one person in a single incident are also likely to attract news media interest. An incident of this type will be similarly reported to Public Affairs.

Civil Disturbance

Civil disturbances can range from mildly disruptive activities, such as peaceful picketing, to violent and uncontrolled events, such as rioting and looting.

It is not likely that an office location will be the scene of significantly disruptive civil activity. It can be expected, however, that the diverse and international nature of the Company's business interests will periodically come into conflict with the interests of groups that would resort to picketing, public demonstrations, and similar activities.

Such opposition in most cases can be anticipated and countermeasures put into place to minimize disruption of work operations. The Security Department will provide specific guidance to employees in advance of activities that have been announced by opposition groups.

If a civil disturbance occurs in an area not immediately surrounding the building, employees will be instructed to travel around the affected area. The best sources of information for determining the affected area and safe travel routes will be local TV and radio broadcasts.

If a minor disturbance, such as picketing or a peaceful rally, occurs at the building employees will be instructed to enter or leave the building through whatever door provides minimum exposure to demonstrators and to avoid any contact and communication with demonstrators.

If a major disturbance occurs at the building, the police will be called and asked to restore public order. If the disturbance occurs while employees are in the building, guidance will be provided via the intercom system. Employees at home can obtain guidance by calling the switchboard operator.

The Security Department, in concert with the Property Management office, will monitor disturbance situations and communicate with the police and other emergency response agencies as required.

BUSINESS CONTINUITY

This business continuity plan (BCP) is an administrative mechanism for facilitating a quick and coordinated return to the essential business operations of the Company during the immediate aftermath of a disaster or catastrophic event impacting corporate headquarters. The BCP complements and is a follow-on to contingency plans already in place, e.g., Fire Protection Plan, Bomb Threat Plan, and Severe Weather Plan. The BCP picks up where those plans end.

This Plan takes into account the Company's heavy dependence on information, e.g., leading edge software, computer technology, and telecommunications. The type of catastrophic event hypothesized will have a severe impact on computer programs and telecommunications services, which in turn will severely impact critical business functions. For this reason, the Information Technology Department (IT) will be a major player in the implementation of the BCP.

The critical business functions have been identified by the managers responsible for their discharge during the extraordinary circumstances present in a post-disaster scenario. The BCP places upon these managers an individual responsibility for developing procedures within their units that:

- Assess the degree of loss of critical functioning.

- Notify key people.

- Deploy resources needed to restore critical functioning.

Key points in such procedures will vary from manager to manager, but may include a mission statement, scope, decision-making responsibilities, assignment of key tasks, resources required, a process for communicating with employees immediately following an event, a list of persons to be notified, the composition of recovery teams, recovery priorities, working interrelationships, work flow diagrams, decision trees, and training. Each set of procedures will be attached to the BCP, which managers will keep ready for use as needed.

Assumptions

The BCP assumes that:

- Some catastrophic events, such as a nuclear explosion, will be so severe as to fall outside the scope of the BCP.

- The catastrophic event impacting corporate headquarters is likely to be a wind storm, such as a hurricane or tornado, more so than other business-disrupting events, such as major fire, earthquake, bomb, civil unrest, or labor strike.

- The time required to bring corporate headquarters back to normal operating routines will take not less than two days and not more than thirty days.

- Temporary working space, equipment, data, supplies, and vendor services needed to carry out critical functions will be available within forty-eight hours following the event. This assumption recognizes that when other companies are impacted by the same event (e.g., a hurricane), extraordinary demands will be placed upon the community's business services infrastructure, thereby placing the Company into competition with other companies for needed facilities, equipment, supplies, and services. Advanced planning and preparation by service groups, such as IT and building management, will be essential.

- Key employees will be available to implement the BCP. Recognition is given, however, to delay that might result from the need of all employees to first attend to the needs of their families should the catastrophic event extend into the community at large.

Objectives

The objectives of the BCP are to:

- Restore the most critical of all critical functions within two days.

- Restore all or most all of the critical functions within seven days.

- Restore all business functions within thirty days.

Business Continuity Team

The BCP establishes a team consisting of representatives from the following business activities:

- Executive

- Information Technology

- Real Estate

- Procurement

- Human Resources.

The business continuity team is further supported by associates from:

- External Affairs

- Security

- Health and Safety.

The business continuity team and the supporting associates will develop, like the managers of critical functions, sets of procedures that spell out roles and responsibilities.

CIVIL DISTURBANCES

The Company recognizes that civil disturbances can range from mildly disruptive activities, such as peaceful picketing, to violent and uncontrolled events, such as rioting and looting. This Plan relates only to the Corporate headquarters, and is intended to cover a limited range of possible scenarios, although not in specific detail. The concept will be to anticipate that, given the location of the headquarters, the business activities transacted there, and the public profile of the Company, there will always be the possibility of civil disorder. This plan anticipates disorder resulting from widespread civil disruption and from specific protest activities of interest groups.

Assumptions

- It is not currently assumed that the corporate headquarters will be the scene of significantly disruptive criminal activity arising from a breakdown in the social order.

- It is currently assumed that the diverse and international nature of the Company's business interests will periodically come into conflict with the interests of groups that would resort to picketing, public demonstrations, and similar activities.

- It is assumed that opposition to the Company in most cases can be anticipated and countermeasures put into place to minimize disruption of work operations.

Responsibilities

The Security Manager will:

- Network with fellow security professionals, industry peers, law enforcement officials, and representatives of intelligence-gathering organizations for the purpose of learning of possible civil disturbance threats.

- Develop and implement procedures that guide security officers in how to respond to civil disturbances.

- Provide training and practice to security officers, and other emergency response employees, in how to respond to civil disturbances.

- Coordinate the Company's response actions with those of other emergency response organizations, such as the police and fire departments, and ambulance service.

When a civil disturbance is predicted, the Property Manager at corporate headquarters will:

- Acquire and lay aside stores and supplies to support security officers and others whose duties require them to remain on site during the disturbance. Such stores and supplies would include, for example, food, water, and first aid supplies.

- Ensure that emergency devices and equipment, such as emergency power generators and the noninterruptible power system, are in good working order.

- Remove from around the building any materials that might be used in a violent way by demonstrators.

The Public Affairs Manager will:

- Script and deliver public announcements to the news media as needed.

- Arrange with local radio and television organizations to provide messages to employees concerning when it is safe to return to work.

General

If a civil disturbance occurs in an area not immediately surrounding the building, employees will be instructed to travel around the affected area. The best sources of information for determining the affected area and safe travel routes are local TV and radio broadcasts.

In the event of a minor disturbance, such as picketing or a peaceful rally, employees will be instructed to enter or leave the building in a manner that provides minimum exposure to demonstrators.

COUNTRY EVACUATION

The purpose of this plan is to provide for an orderly evacuation from overseas locations of Company employees, their dependents, and others when conditions or events pose a threat to their safety and well-being.

Responsibilities

The senior manager of each overseas location is responsible for the development of detailed evacuation procedures in line with this plan and appropriate for the overseas location.

The corporate security manager is responsible for providing guidance and support to the senior manager in preparing procedures commensurate to this plan.

Authority

When communication cannot be made between the senior manager and the corporate office, the senior manager is authorized to initiate and carry out an evacuation. This decision-making authority includes:

- Deciding when conditions are impacting or threatening to impact the safety and well-being of the workforce.

- Giving the order to evacuate.

- Expending Company funds as necessary to effect the evacuation.

- Making other decisions as may be required in the circumstances.

General

The life-threatening conditions anticipated by this plan include:

- War or major military action.

- Terrorism.

- Insurrection.

- Civil disorder.

- Natural disaster.

It often happens that life-threatening conditions arise incrementally, almost imperceptibly, thereby making difficult the senior manager's task of threat recognition. The signs of approaching threat include a decline in the provision of local services, shortages in goods, capital flight, increased government travel restrictions, decreased internal security, and a souring of attitudes among established contacts.

Although U.S. Embassies and Consulates monitor threat conditions and issue advisories, the Company considers it prudent to monitor on its own and develop the means to act on its own in effecting evacuations.

Conducting a safe and efficient evacuation in a destabilized overseas environment relies upon prior planning, analysis of potential security threats, and timely decision making.

Preplanning

The senior manager should:

- Encourage employees and their families to register with the U.S. Embassy or Consulate, or if one is not present, with an embassy representative. Employees with other nationalities should register with the embassy of their country when available.

- Maintain an on-going liaison with the U.S. Embassy or Consulate.

- Ensure that personnel files and other information required for evacuation are current and available for use on short notice.

- Communicate evacuation procedures to all affected employees.

- Establish a system for communicating with employees during a time of heightened danger.

- Maintain a dialogue with representatives of other companies so that threat information can be shared. If appropriate, establish mutual aid arrangements.

- Account for affected staff, for example, by keeping up-to-the-minute records on passports, visas, and vaccination certificates.

- Ensure the protection or planned destruction of sensitive documents. Where practical, original documents should be stored at the corporate office. Duplicate or backup files on technical data should be stored outside the country as well. Provision should be made for the destruction of sensitive data that cannot be left behind, by either burning or shredding.

- Ensure that sufficient funds are readily available to finance evacuation activities.

- Instruct the potentially affected parties to maintain updated household goods inventories (with photographic documentation) that can be handcarried out upon evacuation.

- Establish procedures for packing, labeling, and shipping employee possessions.

- Identify local staging areas and embarkation points, and prepare preliminary security plans calculated to minimize exposure of evacuees to danger.

- Identify primary and alternate modes of travel out of the foreign location; develop and maintain contacts with and commitments from carriers and agents; and consider using local national employees as drivers and translators.

The Evacuation Scenario

Evacuation is likely to evolve in three stages.

Alert Stage

This stage is characterized by routine collection and assessment of information about threat events in progress. The need to evacuate is considered, and prudent preparations are initiated.

Affected personnel and dependents are advised to apply common sense and due caution. They are also told to:

- Reduce movements, avoid incidents, avoid attention, and stay away from politically volatile areas and potential terrorist or military targets.

- Maintain in their homes a minimum two-week supply of essential food, medicines, flashlights, battery-operated radios, and bottled drinking water.

- Refuel personal vehicles frequently so the tank is always at least 3/4 full. Depending on circumstances, additional gasoline reserves may also be stored in safe metal containers at the employee's house.

- Update household goods inventories.

- Keep at hand travel documents.

The senior manager obtains situational updates from all sources available (e.g., the radio, television, the Internet, and the U.S. Embassy or Consulate); reviews travel options (e.g., transportation modes, primary and alternate destinations, temporary lodging, and cash for travel); keeps local vehicles available for short-notice deployment; meets periodically with affected employees to review current events and trends; sets up a rumor control procedure; assembles and assigns cellular phones to personnel critical to carrying out an evacuation; and establishes evacuation priorities:

- Priority One: Dependents

- Priority Two: Personnel not involved in operating the evacuation

- Priority Three: Remaining personnel

Partial Evacuation Stage

In this stage, conditions have deteriorated to a point requiring an evacuation of Priority One and Two personnel. The options that were considered in the Alert Stage are now exercised:

- Evacuees are moved out by commercial or chartered aircraft, boats, private vehicles, and other transportation modes.

- Personnel assigned to effect the evacuation provide ground travel to airports, rail stations, docks, and border crossing points; and coordinate communications and handle requests for assistance.

- Removal or destruction of records is initiated.

Full Evacuation Stage

The senior manager takes these actions:

- Ensures that all sensitive company documents are accounted for or destroyed, as appropriate.

- Issues notices as required by any contracts in effect at the time of the evacuation.

- Delegates authority to designated individuals to carry out the Company's business in the absence of evacuated personnel.

- Informs the U.S. Embassy or Consulate and appropriate host country officials of evacuation plans.

- Arranges for the protection of personnel for whom the company has either a legal or moral obligation to protect.

It is important to note that if the threat is from local authorities or the general public, the senior manager may decide to maintain a low profile by instructing personnel to remain indoors. The risk of harm is greater when moving about than when out of sight. Waiting for the situation to stabilize may be less dangerous than fleeing. Along these lines, the senior manager may decide to maintain the low profile at the pre-selected primary or alternate staging areas.

Stand Fast

Stand Fast is a special readiness option not amounting to an evacuation. It can be implemented in a threat situation when an evacuation is not considered prudent following a sudden and unanticipated event, such as a coup. In a Stand Fast, operations may slow down or be suspended. Employees and their dependents remain in their quarters awaiting further instructions. The families are sustained by liquids, canned foods, medicines, and staples that have been set aside to support them during emergencies.

Departure Kit

The departure kit is a collection of items kept available for use in an emergency situation. The kit is in two parts. Part One consists of sustenance items and equipment. Part Two contains vital personal papers and a departure checklist.

Part One

- A two-week supply of food, water, and fuel.

- First aid kit and an adequate supply of necessary medicines.

- Flashlight with fresh batteries and/or candles.

- Matches, preferably waterproof and windproof.

- Battery-operated short-wave radio with fresh batteries.

- One blanket and/or sleeping bag for each family member.

- Clothing and personal effects not to exceed 66 pounds.

- Street and road maps of the surrounding areas.

Part Two

- Passports.

- Cash in U.S. dollars and traveler's checks sufficient to cover incidental expenses for at least three days of travel. Sufficient currency in small denominations to take care of incidental expenses while en route to a safe haven.

- International certificates of vaccination.

- Host country identification papers.

- An inventory of household effects.

- Essential personal papers, e.g., birth certificates and marriage license.

Transportation Checklist

- Investigate the frequency and normal capacity of commercial flights, trains, and ships leaving the troubled location.

- Identify the most logical options for assembly and movement of evacuees to the departure or embarkation location while maintaining the best security posture possible. As a rule, it is preferable to assemble evacuees at a secure location other than the embarkation point and then to move them to the embarkation point in groups sized to the transport capacity and on a schedule calculated to minimize the exposure of evacuees and the means of transport at the embarkation point. This procedure could aid in the security and effectiveness of the operation, but be aware that circumstances may prevent a phased movement.

- Determine the most appropriate sites at which to assemble potential evacuees in anticipation of moving them to points of embarkation. If long-term, plans should consider shelter, security, food, water, and sanitation needs. The senior manager should appoint a responsible individual to document and list evacuees and to control movement to the embarkation point. The security risks of assembling in one place versus those of remaining in individual homes until departure or the risk of having employees making their way independently to embarkation points should be considered.

- In selecting assembly points and routes, be aware of potential choke points, bridges and areas that could be congested, and identify alternate routes if possible. Maps should be developed for each route.

- If overland movement out of the country is a possibility, define the circumstances under which overland transportation would be considered and special precautions that might be necessary.

- Anticipate the degree of support or problems that might be offered by the host government in an evacuation situation. Identify contacts and develop procedures that could be helpful with exit formalities. Investigate any departure problems for employees in connection with in-country taxes and any other business-related departure requirements.

- Consider what assistance should be asked of the host government for security of assembly areas, convoy routes, and embarkation points if appropriate. Assign liaison responsibilities to appropriate company representatives who may serve as liaisons to the host government for the aforementioned purposes.

- Details such as assembly, timing of movements, and aircraft schedules should be protected from unauthorized disclosure. A means of secure communications should be developed.

- Inquiries received from the media regarding a planned evacuation or one in progress should be referred to the senior manager. Speculative reasons for the evacuation could be harmful to the evacuation and the Company's relationship with the host government.

- As evacuees depart the embarkation point by aircraft, vehicle or ship, the designated coordinator should inform the Company of the following:

  - Estimated time of arrival and related details.

  - Names of evacuees.

  - Names of evacuees requiring assistance with onward transportation.

  - Names of evacuees who will stay at point of arrival and need arrangements for lodging, etc.

  - Medical assistance needed.

EXTORTION

This Plan does not cover extortion by type, e.g., kidnap or product tampering. It deals with the demands of the extortionists and the Company's appropriate responses.

The Demand

Extortionists often make unrealistic demands, such as immediate payment of an enormous sum. While they may be driven by greed, they rarely expect the demand to be met in its entirety or immediately. They cannot help but realize that the victim company does not keep large sums on hand for the express purpose of meeting the demands of criminals, and that since time is required to obtain even modest sums, it is to their advantage to be patient even when their communications indicate the opposite.

The Response

The person receiving a telephone demand should attempt to collect as much information about the extortionists as possible. Ask questions like:

- "What is the name of your group?"

- "Why are you doing this?"

- "How can I get back to you on this?"

The person receiving the call should:

- Listen carefully for the accent, speech pattern, emotional state, and intelligence level.

- Take note of background noises that may indicate the origin of the call.

- Make clear that nothing can be done until approval is received from a higher level.

- Do not imply that there can be "no deal."

- Bear in mind the caller may have inside knowledge of the company. Do not underestimate this factor.

- Do not volunteer information, but if questions are asked, answer them factually and truthfully.

- Immediately report the demand upward.

NOTE: If the extortion attempt credibly threatens death or serious physical violence, the prudent course may be to make an immediate payment. If there is only a small amount of cash on hand, show it to the extortionist and offer it.

Think Ahead

With a possible extortion demand in mind, the senior manager should review cash withdrawal levels to ensure that if forced to go to a bank (either at gunpoint or when a third party is being held hostage), the amount withdrawn will not exceed a certain amount on any one day. Communicate this procedure in writing to the bank; keep the written communication on hand to be shown to the extortionist. (Note: The office copy can be drafted to show a lower withdrawal figure than is actually the case.) The approving individual should be someone at a higher level in the Company so that the bank's procedure will prevent the extortionist from forcing the local senior manager into making the withdrawal.

FIRE EMERGENCY

This Plan is the product of collaboration between the Fire Marshal's Office of local municipal government, the Property Manager of the Company's headquarters building, and the Company's Security Manager.

This Plan also takes into account the building's fire detection and suppression system, a system that includes pull stations, ionization detectors, overhead sprinklers, fire extinguishers, alarm horns, voice speakers, pressurization fans, firefighters' telephones, and an emergency generator for backup power.

Responsibilities

The Property Manager will:

- Establish and maintain a Floor Warden Program that provides:

  - Four Floor Wardens per floor.

  - Initial training and certification of Floor Wardens in fire evacuation of a high-rise building, the use of hand-held fire extinguishers, the administration of CPR and first aid, the operation of oxygen resuscitation equipment, and the risks of blood-borne pathogens.

  - Refresher training and renewal of certification of Floor Wardens in the above subjects, plus other subjects of current concern.

  - Drills and practice with a frequency of not less than once every 6 months.

- Establish and maintain a Fire Control Brigade consisting of building engineer staff. The Fire Control Brigade will be trained in and prepared to:

  - Determine the presence or absence of fire conditions that have been reported by the electronic sensing devices of the fire detection system.

  - Operate hand-held fire extinguishers and the stand-pipe fire extinguishing system.

  - Assist Floor Wardens in the evacuation of the building.

  - Operate (i.e., shutdown or turn on) the building's built-in fire control and suppression equipment (such as dampers that channel smoke out of the building and fans that pressurize fire exit stairwells).

- Develop procedures for Security Officers to follow in a fire emergency. Such procedures will guide Security Officers in:

  - Monitoring the annunciation panels of the fire detection system.

  - Assisting the Floor Wardens and Fire Control Brigade in the performance of their duties.

  - Acting as a backup to the Floor Wardens and Fire Control Brigade in an after-hours emergency.

  - Providing traffic control in the vicinity of the building to allow fire department vehicles close-in access.

- The Security Manager will oversee all of the preceding programs in order to provide assurance to the Company's management that the threat of fire has been adequately addressed.

Actions

Evacuation procedures will be developed that describe the planned interaction among the Property Management staff, the Security Officers, the Floor Wardens, and the responding fire department officers. For example, the fire alarm announcement will be made by a Security Officer; the Fire Brigade will be dispatched; the Property Manager will assume management of the initial response; the Floor Wardens will shepherd the evacuation; and the senior fire department officer will assume control upon arrival.

Floor Wardens

A Floor Warden will have these overall responsibilities:

- Educate co-workers concerning individual responsibilities for fire prevention, reduction of safety hazards, how to report a fire, how to evacuate, and where to assemble following evacuation.

- Prevent, report, and correct fire and safety hazards through daily inspection of the floor.

- Exercise leadership during an evacuation by directing co-workers down stairwells and ensuring that no-one has been left behind.

- Provide first-responder medical assistance to persons who are in need of CPR or first aid.

- Know the locations of the fire stairwells and the pull stations on the floor.

- Know the floor diagram that shows the most direct routes to the fire stairwells, and ensure that the diagram is posted on the bulletin board in the coffee/copy rooms.

- Obtain volunteers on the floor who will direct employees away from the elevators and down the fire stairwells.

- Inform every new person on the floor concerning what to do in case of an emergency.

- Keep a list of the persons on the floor so that they can be accounted for immediately after an evacuation.

- Identify persons with medical conditions, such as asthma or pregnancy, who may need help during an evacuation. Arrange in advance with someone on the floor to provide the needed help. Inform Security of any handicapped persons.

- Be alert on the floor for fire hazards, e.g., overloaded electrical circuits, unattended cooking appliances, and materials blocking stairwell doors.

In responding during a fire emergency, a Floor Warden will immediately look throughout the entire floor for fire conditions, starting with the coffee/copy rooms, since these are the places where fire is most likely to occur.

If a search of the floor reveals fire conditions (i.e., visible flame or smoke), the Floor Warden will pull a pull station, report the fire by calling the Fire Department and the Fire Director, check the stairwells to ensure they are free of fire or smoke, and begin evacuation immediately. When the floor has been completely evacuated, the Floor Warden will notify the Fire Director.

Employees will be directed away from the elevators unless specifically told otherwise.

If a search of the floor does not reveal fire conditions, the Floor Warden will wait for the arrival of the Fire Brigade. The Fire Brigade will double-check the floor to validate that the initial search was thorough. When this has been done, an announcement of the findings will be made over the loudspeaker.

A Floor Warden does not have to wait for an evacuation announcement to be made to begin evacuation. If fire conditions are present on the floor, the Floor Warden will immediately begin instructing people to leave via the stairwells.

During an evacuation, the Floor Warden will make a final search of the floor to ensure that no one has been left behind. Rest rooms, conference rooms, and closed offices will be checked. The Floor Wardens will then assemble with their floor employees at pre-designated places in the adjoining parking garage.

Security Officers

Security officers will be on duty 24 hours per day throughout the building and at the Security Center. Annunciation devices in the Security Center will alert officers to report fire conditions and location. The response will be as follows:

- One or more officers will proceed without delay to the affected floor for the purpose of assisting/backing up the Floor Wardens.

- The findings of the on-scene officers will be reported immediately to the Security Center and, in turn, to the Fire Director at the Fire Command Center in the lobby.

- If an evacuation is ordered, the security officers will:

  - Assist the Floor Wardens in guiding people from the building.

  - Provide traffic control as may be needed to move fire fighting apparatus into close proximity to the building.

  - Serve as a communications link between Floor Wardens at the assembly area and the Fire Department.

If a fire alarm occurs during other than normal working hours the Security Officers will perform the functions of the Fire Brigade, i.e., determine the cause for the alarm and respond accordingly.

Individual Employees

The Floor Wardens will educate employees on an on-going basis to assure that everyone will know what to do in the event of an evacuation. Each employee will be expected to:

- Listen for and follow instructions given over the public address system or by Floor Wardens, building management staff, and Security Officers.

- Use the nearest stairwell for evacuation, unless otherwise directed.

- Not run and not smoke.

- Remain calm. Keep talking to a minimum.

- Obtain needed assistance by seeking the help of a fellow employee, a Floor Warden, a Security Officer, or a building management employee or by calling the Security Center.

- Once out of the building, proceed directly to the designated assembly area in the garage.

- Stand by for instructions.

Training and Drills

Floor Wardens and Security Officers will be trained in CPR, first aid, operation of ABC fire extinguishers, and operation of oxygen resuscitators.

Floor Wardens will receive refresher training at quarterly meetings and Security Officers will receive training in the post orders and special instructions that relate to fire safety at time of hire and periodically as part of regularly conducted refresher and advanced training.

Security Officers will engage in fire response drills and conduct tests of detection and annunciation equipment on a regular on-going basis. Such drills and tests will be conducted during other than normal working hours.

Fire drills for the benefit of Floor Wardens, Security Officers, the Fire Brigade, property management staff, and all occupants of the building will be conducted at a frequency of at least one every 6 months. The nature of the drills will be specified by the Fire Marshal's Office and sometimes monitored by that office in order to assure compliance with the fire code.

KIDNAP

This Plan outlines the actions to be taken in response to kidnap events. The overriding goal will be to help prevent harm to kidnapped Company employees and their families and to help effect their safe return.

Preparation and Responsibilities

The handling of kidnap events is assigned to the Crisis Management Committee (CMC), which is chaired by a member of the Company's Executive Committee. The CMC Chairperson will appoint to the CMC senior representatives of the following departments:

- Operations

- Security

- Human Resources

- Legal

- Public Affairs

Each of the CMC representatives will develop in their departments sets of operating procedures that support this Plan. For example, the Corporate Security Director will be prepared to inform and interact with law enforcement and the military, oversee installation of telecommunication equipment in the Emergency Operations Center (EOC), and acquire additional physical security and guards as needed to increase protection that may be needed.

The implementing procedures, when appended to this Plan, will provide assurance to the CMC Chairperson that the Company is prepared to respond to kidnap events quickly and effectively.

Implementation

Any report of a kidnapping will be immediately channeled to the CMC Chairperson. The Chairperson will inquire with the employee's business management to determine if in fact the employee or employee family member is missing. If confirmation is made, this Plan will be activated.

Plan activation includes:

- Convening of the CMC.

- Opening the EOC and readying the equipment and supplies that have been set aside for the execution of this Plan.

- Briefing the Executive Committee.

- Notifying all interested parties, e.g., next of kin, law enforcement, military and embassy representatives.

- Preparing media releases, if needed and as appropriate.

Considerations

Kidnapping is a crisis involving human life. While the release of the victim will always be paramount in every decision made, the release and the well-being of the victim cannot in every case be assured by yielding to the kidnappers on every point. Dealing with kidnappers is difficult for many reasons but none is more difficult than having to respond to demands that are often irrational and impossible to meet.

This Plan cannot anticipate every kidnap scenario, but experience in these affairs has shown the value of considering in advance these questions:

- What protective steps should be taken in the immediate aftermath of a kidnap? For example, move expatriate family members out of the country, suspend travel, suspend or reduce operations.

- Should the Company purchase insurance as a hedge against losses associated with kidnap-related extortion?

- Should the Company use the services of an outside consultant skilled in kidnap negotiations?

- Who in the Company will have the authority to pay an extortion demand? How will funds be obtained?

- What laws apply in countries where kidnapping is likely? What requirements exist to notify particular agencies of the host government, and what is the government's policy on paying extortion?

- Should the Company immediately concede to the kidnapper's demands?

- Besides killing the victim, what else can the kidnappers do to force acquiescence?

- Should the Company pre-determine a level of acquiescence? Should the Company resist kidnapper demands until the level of acquiescence is reached through negotiation or other means?

- Should the Company pretend to negotiate while at the same time prepare to mount a rescue attempt? What are the downside risks, e.g., death of the victim, legal liabilities, commercial sanctions, reputation damage, and lowered employee morale.

- Should the Company remove itself from negotiating by ceding control to others, such as law enforcement and the military?

Motive

The answers to the above questions, while never easily deduced, can be facilitated by knowing the motive of the kidnapper. For example, is the motive:

- Driven by greed, such as personal financial gain?

- Driven by an ideology or a religious or political conviction?

- Driven by revenge, such as to right a wrong?

- Driven by all or combinations of the above?

A careful analysis of motive can lead to judgments about the capabilities of the kidnappers (e.g., weaponry), their sophistication (e.g., intelligence-gathering ability), their dedication (e.g., willingness to die), and their leadership (e.g., the level at which a successful bargain can be struck).

Post-Incident Tasks

The lessons learned in dealing with a kidnap event must be passed on. At a minimum, the following two tasks will be completed:

- The CMC Chairperson will prepare an after-action report.

- The Corporate Security Director will modify this Plan based on the after-action report.

PHYSICAL SECURITY

The Perimeter

The Company's perimeter should serve as both the defining line of ownership and the starting point of protection. The Company's protected perimeter line must:

- Operate as a visible sign that discourages intrusion.

- Delay intruders.

- Assist control of entry and exit.

- Facilitate guard dog operations.

- Facilitate intruder detection systems.

The choice of fencing materials can conform to needs for privacy as well as security. For example, opaque fencing, screens, and walls can have the following additional benefits:

- Conceal site operations, particularly in urban areas.

- Prevent observation of guard and patrol movements.

- Reduce the effectiveness of attacks with rockets, small arms fire, and small bombs.

Ditches, moats, and protective vegetation can provide obstacles to hinder easy approach to perimeter fences, although care must be taken not to provide cover to intruders. These means are best used in support of clear zones inside perimeters.

Barrier Planning

When planning a perimeter barrier, account should be taken of the following:

- Walls are usually more expensive than fences, observation enclosures, and closed circuit television (CCTV). Opaque fences may provide a cheaper alternative.

- Fences and walls provide only limited delay against intruders, the least secure types can only delay a skilled intruder for a few seconds. A perimeter barrier intended to provide substantial protection against intruders should therefore combine a fence or wall with security lighting, an intruder detection system, CCTV, and security guard forces.

- The perimeter should be as short as possible and illuminated.

- The perimeter should run in straight lines between corner posts to facilitate surveillance.

- Drains or culverts giving access beneath the perimeter barrier should be protected.

- The ground on both sides of the perimeter barrier should be cleared to deny cover to an intruder.

- Emergency gates may be required to prove safe evacuation routes.

- A sterile zone protected by a double fence may be required for certain types of intruder detection sensors.

- A security guard force should support any perimeter security system.

Fence Standards

The perimeter should have a fence or wall that meets the requirements of local planning and licensing authorities while remaining an effective deterrent against intruders. As a guide, any fence less than 7 feet high is unlikely to do more than demarcate a boundary.

Generally the basic perimeter fence should have concrete fence posts with three strands of barbed wire at the top. The barbed wire should be at a 45-degree angle pointing upward and outward. The foot of all chain-link fences should be embedded in a concrete kerb in the ground that slants away on both sides from the fence to shed water and is buried deep enough to prevent burrowing.

Where local factors require an enhanced level of security, anti-intruder fencing is recommended to a height of 9.5 feet with razor or barbed wire at the top. The base of the fence should be embedded as described above.

Where the value of the protected site is particularly high and there is known risk (such as terrorist attack), consideration should be given to augmenting the selected fence with security lighting, CCTV, an intruder detection system, and a security guard force.

Types of Security Fences

The following fences are available for security use, listed in ascending order of their effectiveness against intrusion:

- Industrial security chain-link fence.

- Standard anti-intruder chain-link fence.

- Standard steel palisade fence, security pattern standard expanded metal (Expamet) security fence.

- High-security weld-mesh fence.

- High-security steel palisade fence.

- Powered fencing. This is similar to cattle fencing in that it will give an electric shock to anything touching it. This type of fencing is generally safe to use around hydrocarbon sites, but the manufacturer's advice should be sought on its exact deployment. Powered fencing sends an alarm when touched, thus making it a barrier with intruder detection. It is also good to use above walls in high-risk areas on domestic properties.

- Palisade fences are more expensive than chain-link fences but have better potential for upgrading to increase effectiveness against intruders and for the addition of fence-mounted intrusion detection sensors. Galvanized palisade fences have a much longer life than chain-link, Expamet, or weld-mesh fences. The high-security fences are significantly more effective against intruders than the other fences.

Fence Enhancements

The use of barbed wire, razor tape, and rotary spikes can increase the effectiveness of a security fence. Wire or tape concertina are standard forms of fence topping. Fence gaps or other weaknesses can be offset using wire or tape at ground level.

Outside observation of a site can be prevented by an opaque fence constructed of corrugated or profiled galvanized steel sheets bolted to a suitable frame, e.g., to the framework of a steel palisade fence. It should be remembered that these types of fences may need enhancing with CCTV to allow security personnel to observe the approaches to the site.

It may be necessary to employ natural vegetation to provide perimeter protection or to supplement existing fences. Acacia, blackthorn, blackberry, dog rose, hawthorn, and holly are considered effective barriers when mature but require regular maintenance.

Walls

If perimeter protection against rockets, small arms, and blast is required, specialist engineering advice should be sought. Perimeter walls required for other purposes should be constructed of reinforced concrete or solid brick and be not less than 10 feet in height overall. They should be fitted with a topping of barbed tape or spikes. Pre-cast concrete panel walls offer little resistance to forcible attack, but may be useful for certain urban sites.

Gates

Gates must be of an equivalent standard to the fence or wall of which they are a part. Hinges should be designed to resist removal of the gate. The bottom of the gate should have a ground clearance not exceeding 6 inches in the closed position.

The number of gates should be kept to a minimum consistent with operational and emergency requirements. Separate pedestrian gates adjacent to vehicle gates may be an advantage.

Unmanned gates should be kept locked and inspected regularly. Keys of emergency exit gates must be securely held but readily available. Manned gates should be supervised from a position with good communications to a security control room.

The use of remotely controlled sliding powered gates should be considered at vehicle entrances but must be supported by CCTV. Space needs to be provided for vehicles and pedestrians awaiting clearance for entry.

Security Lighting

Properly utilized security lighting is a highly cost-effective security measure; if incorrectly used, however, security lighting may actually assist the intruder. A good security lighting system should:

- Deter intrusion, or at least reduce an intruder's freedom of action.

- Assist in the detection of intruders either by direct vision or by CCTV.

- Help to conceal guards and patrols.

It is often impossible to achieve all these aims; one or more may have to be minimized to accommodate the others.

Lighting Requirements

The security lighting requirements should be specified by a lighting engineer. Ideally, lighting requirements will be identified as part of a security survey. The lighting scheme should take account of the following:

- Lighting should not illuminate guards or patrols. Where security patrols cannot be kept out of the zones of illumination, a judgment must be made between the advantages of the lighting and the reduction in patrol effectiveness.

- Lighting must be combined with surveillance. The deterrent effect of lighting depends on fear of detection and arrest. This requires surveillance by CCTV or guards on static and mobile patrols.

- Lighting must not cause nuisances or hazards. Adverse effects may be caused to adjacent roads, railways, airports, harbors, or neighboring buildings.

- Lighting must be cost effective and compatible with site conditions. It may not be economic to light very large areas. Account must be taken both of existing lighting outside the perimeter (the district brightness) and of the lighting installed within the site for operational or safety purposes.

Lighting Systems

The basic systems of security lighting that may be used either singly or in combination are: perimeter lighting, area lighting, and floodlighting. Other forms of lighting may also be required, such as gatehouse lighting and topping-up lighting.

Perimeter Lighting

Perimeter lighting is used to illuminate the fence itself and an area beyond it (i.e., the detection zone). When used with chain-link fencing, a narrow strip inside the fence is also illuminated. When double fences are used, the detection zone lies wholly or mainly between the two fences.

The objective is to reveal an intruder's approach and produce glare toward him, thus reducing visibility into the site. It may therefore be suitable for use with patrolling guards. However, it can be difficult to apply because it may create nuisance or hazard or because of a lack of sufficient open flat ground outside the perimeter.

Area Lighting

Area lighting is used to illuminate the area within the perimeter that an intruder must cross to attack the target. The aim is to produce even illumination without dense shadows.

Floodlighting

Floodlighting is used to cast a strong light on the walls of buildings so that intruders are visible either in silhouette or by the shadows they cast.

Gatehouse Lighting

Gatehouse lighting is used at the perimeter entrance and gatehouse in order to:

- Reveal approaching vehicles and pedestrians and allow guards to identify them, verify passes, and carry out vehicle searches.

- Conceal guards within the gatehouse while allowing them to see out.

Topping-Up Lighting

Topping-up lighting is used to eliminate dark areas not adequately lit by area or floodlighting. Such areas may be lit locally by small luminaires, e.g., bulkhead fittings, or from a distance by narrow angle floodlights.

Equipment and System Design

The detail design of the system and choice of equipment must be carried out by a qualified lighting engineer who must be briefed on the requirement. Account should be taken of the following points:

Controls

Automatic control of lights by photoelectric cell is often convenient, but manual override at a central control point may be required to switch off all, or selected parts, of the system. Switching on lights in response to a signal from an intruder alarm, although economical in running costs, is of doubtful value.

Wiring

Electrical supply cables to lights should be buried; where unavoidably exposed they should be armored or contained in steel conduit.

Electrical Supply

Whenever possible there should be a standby electricity supply with automatic switching in the event of power failure. If high-intensity discharge lamps are used it may be necessary to specify a "no-break" supply to avoid "re-strike" (re-lighting) delay.

Lamps

The choice of lamp (i.e., bulb or tube) is based on the task it must perform and on its capital and running costs, color rendering, life, and electrical characteristics. There are three broad groups of lamps used for security lighting:

- Incandescent

- Fluorescent

- High-intensity discharge (HID)

HID lamps have high efficacy (efficiency of lamp measured in lumens per watt) but do not re-strike immediately if the electricity supply is interrupted. The delay can be reduced by special igniters. Incandescent and fluorescent lamps are best used for topping-up and gatehouse lighting; fluorescent tubes can also be used for some forms of perimeter lighting when only low-intensity lighting is required.

Luminaires

Each type of luminaire (lamp fitting) is designed for a particular use, i.e., to concentrate or direct the light in a particular direction.

Luminaires should be resistant to damage. Types with large flat areas of glass should be avoided. Types made of modern plastics, such as polycarbonate, are very tough and will not easily fracture. Luminaires with cast metal bodies should be selected over types made of thin sheet metal.

Luminaires should be positioned to facilitate cleaning and lamp replacement. On a perimeter, they should not be accessible to a person outside the fence.

Maintenance

Proper provision must be made for regular inspection and maintenance. All faults must be reported immediately.

Technical Advice

Local electricity authorities will often be able to assist in the planning and installation of lighting

Intrusion Detection System (IDS)

Physical security will be augmented by an intruder detection system (IDS), an arrangement of electronic devices for detecting the entry or attempted entry of an intruder and sending an alarm. The main rationale of an IDS is the substitution of electronic surveillance for human surveillance, the result of which can reduce the need for security manpower.

An effective IDS will be professionally designed and installed and periodically serviced. Otherwise, the IDS may be vulnerable to circumvention, malfunctioning, and false alarms.

System Components

The basic components of an IDS are:

- Sensors that detect intrusion.

- Circuits that connect sensors to a control unit and the control unit to an alarm display panel.

- A control unit that monitors the sensors and receives signals from them.

- An alarm display panel that alerts response personnel to an intrusion through visual and audible alarms.

Sensors

Sensor selection is determined by a variety of factors that include the intrusion threat, the operating environment (e.g., indoors, outdoors, sub-sea, hostile climate, etc.), and power source constraints. Types of sensors are as follows:

- Volumetric and spatial sensors detect movement within a confined area, such as a room, and are referred to in terms of their scientific principles, e.g., ultrasonic (sound waves), microwave (interruption of a linear signal), and passive infrared (detection of body heat).

- Beam sensors operate on infrared and microwave principles.

- Contact sensors activate when an electric circuit is broken, i.e., by the separation of a magnet installed on a door or window.

- Vibration sensors can be attached to rigid structures. They include the inertia switch, which reacts to physical vibration; the geophone, which reacts to sound vibration; and the crystal vibration switch, which reacts when a piezoelectric crystal is compressed by physical vibration.

- Closed-circuit sensors activate when an electrical circuit is broken, e.g., by the cutting of a charged wire inside a wall or inside the mesh of a window screen.

- Pressure mat sensors activate when weight is applied, such as an intruder stepping on a pressurized mat concealed under a rug.

- Video motion detectors activate when movement is picked up by a video camera.

Standards

An IDS must:

- Conform to the environment in which it operates, e.g., the equipment must meet the demands of weather, topography, and other influencing factors.

- Resist and detect tampering.

- Be fail safe; i.e., signal an equipment failure.

- Have a backup electrical power source.

- Be linked to a designated response capability, such as a security guard force.

- Be planned and designed by an IDS-certified engineer, with input from a security professional.

Closed-Circuit Television (CCTV)

CCTV provides area surveillance, even remotely without cabling. Properly specified for, installed, and maintained, CCTV is a reliable and cost-effective adjunct to systems that detect intrusion, control access, and monitor assets that cannot be guarded or placed under lock and key. CCTV can be configured to detect movement automatically, record what it sees, and send a warning signal. A significant advantage of CCTV is the opportunity it presents to reduce manpower. CCTV, however, cannot operate without a human component to monitor the views and respond as needed.

CCTV can be applied in a wide variety of environments, both internal and external, e.g., in verifying right of access at gates and doors, monitoring vehicles in parking garages, monitoring traffic, scanning an area in which an intrusion sensor has activated, monitoring valuable assets in storage, and monitoring human activity at cashier stations.

Types

The simplest system is a camera cabled to a monitor. More complex systems have multiple digital cameras linked to a computer. The cameras pan and tilt; the lenses zoom in and out; wide-angle imaging is possible. Clear pictures with high resolution are possible in low light level conditions using white light and infrared light. The cameras operate remotely, are sensitive to movement in the field of view, track objects, scan slowly, are mounted in weather-resistant housings, and send their signals along fiber optic cabling.

Monitoring and recording equipment are also numerous and varied in the ways images are captured, displayed, and stored. Real time and time lapse video recorders can be used. A real time video recorder has the ability to record in slow time for up to 300 hours on a single reel. Time lapse recorders can be automatically switched to real time in response to a signal from an intruder detection system. The monitor and recorder automatically switch to the camera associated with the alarm signal.

A CCTV system should have uninterrupted power supply (UPS) protection, as well as protection from damage caused by electrical spikes and surges.

Selecting quality equipment and ensuring quality installation will reduce later breakdowns and costly maintenance.

Advantages

- Many locations can be watched simultaneously at one central location.

- Intrusion can be detected and reported early.

- Security manpower and related costs can be reduced.

- Errors related to human failure can be eliminated.

- Flexibility, e.g., cameras can be applied covertly to identify offenders or discourage potential offenders.

Disadvantages

- Cost. Complex systems are expensive.

- Design may absorb considerable time to get the system right.

- Maintenance may be an issue in extreme conditions, such as tropical heat, arctic cold, desert sandstorms.

- Routine system maintenance may be a problem, e.g., tapes stored, tapes destroyed, visuals not always clear.

Acquiring a CCTV System

- Be clear as to what you want.

- Conduct a risk analysis, i.e., determine what is to be protected from whom or what.

- Survey the location where the CCTV is to be installed. In particular, note day and night conditions. Keep in mind that camera performance is affected by heat, ice, high rainfall, condensation, dirt, dust, high winds, salt-laden atmosphere, snow, fog, heavy rain, and other environmental/weather conditions, all of which are probably manageable with special protection, such as sun shades, wipers, washers, heaters, and special enclosures.

- Evaluate the effect of existing light sources, e.g., street lights; car headlights; sunrise; sunset; or reflections of sun from water, snow, and windows. Evaluate also the unique environments of refineries, oil terminals, chemical works, platforms, etc.

- Document your preliminary work with plans, drawings, videos, and photos.

- Develop a concept of how the CCTV system will address the protective needs identified in the risk analysis.

- Discuss the concept with experts in the field, e.g., CCTV system designers. Prepare technical design recommendations and conduct a cost-benefit analysis.

- Decide whether CCTV is a cost-effective solution.

- Choose a supplier (or run a tender process).

- The selected supplier must factory-test the equipment before packaging, or at least test parts of it, e.g., the motion detector component.

- Require the supplier to prepare and honor a schedule in respect to packaging, freighting, installation, commissioning, and maintenance.

- Ensure installation is supervised by the supplier's in-house expert. An efficient system depends absolutely on being installed correctly. Factors that may need correction are lens angles; resolution; fields of view; stability of panning; programming and sensitivity of motion detection; cable placement; calibration of infrared, laser, or microwave features; annunciation volume of alarms; and linkages to adjunctive systems (such as intruder detection and access control).

- Test and commission the system.

- Identify and correct system "bugs" before making full payment.

Operating the System

- Train the operators of the system. It may be desirable to prepare a job description and a job classification for the system operator.

- Issue written operating procedures.

- Monitor system performance, both in terms of equipment and the operators.

- Revise procedures as needed, re-train the operators, and look for opportunities to make the job interesting.

Technical Advice

CCTV technology continues to evolve very rapidly. Two considerations should affect selection of sources for technical advice: Look for experts who are up-to-date on the technology and who understand your unique security needs. The expert source should also be attuned to the concept you have in mind.

Obtain at least three sources for comparisons. Costs and proffered designs can vary enormously even when all meet the same project requirements. As a rule, the manufacturers of quality systems offer high-quality advice. Identifying the manufacturers of quality systems is nearly as simple as thumbing through the Yellow Pages or consulting a security buyer's guide.

Locks

The effectiveness of locks lies in their use as supplements to other physical safeguards, such as intrusion detection and access control systems. Questions that arise on choice of locks for a sensitive area should be referred to a security professional knowledgeable in locks. In non-sensitive areas, the choice can be made after study of a reputable lock manufacturer's list.

Security locks should be resistant to both apparent and nonapparent attack (i.e., an attack that leaves no trace). Locks offered by reputable manufacturers will usually provide good protection, but their resistance to determined forcible attack is low. In some situations it may therefore be necessary to supplement a single lock with bolts or to use two locks.

Types of Locks

Key Card

This electric lock is commonly found in access control systems that use card readers or push button panels to send a signal to an electrically operated door strike. The card reader reads the code on a card key; if the code is accepted, the lock opens. A push button system opens the door when the correct code is entered on a push button keyboard. In some high-security environments, both systems will be combined, and in an ultra-high-security environment, a key-operated lock might be added.

Push Button

An electric push button lock requires the authorized individual to press a series of digits, usually four. Many push button systems disconnect and/or activate an alarm after a number of unsuccessful tries to gain entry. A key-operated lock can supplement a push button lock when increased security is desired.

Mortise Lock

This type of lock is held in a mortise, i.e., a rectangular opening in the edge of the door. Because a mortise tends to weaken the physical structure of the door, reinforcement with mild steel plates behind or on both sides of the lock may be required, especially on wooden doors. Mortise locks are suitable for use on steel doors designed to accept them and on reinforced wooden doors. The following types are available:

Rim Lock

Rim locks are mounted on the inner surface of a door too thin to accept a mortise. The lock and its bolt are protected by the full thickness of the door and frame, but the weakness of the fixings, particularly on a wooden door, makes it vulnerable to forcible attack. Most rim locks have spring-loaded bolts, but rim locks with deadbolts are available. Alternatively, mortise deadlocks may be fitted as rim locks by enclosing them in steel boxes welded to steel doors, or fixed to wooden doors with special mounting. They may be used on single-leaf doors when fitted with straight bolts, and on double-leaf doors when fitted with hook bolts.

Automatic Deadlock

These locks are designed to provide the convenience of a spring-loaded latch with the security of a deadlock. They are used on self-closing doors and on any door requiring deadlocking on closing. The following types are available for single and double-leaf doors.

Locking Bar

A locking bar is a device that permits the use of a padlock to secure a door. A locking bar selected for high-security purposes must be constructed of steel and have a knuckle and hinge pin welded to prevent the hinge pin from being removed. The unit should be affixed with bolts (not screws) that pass through the thickness of the door and be inaccessible to tampering when the door is in the locked position.

Three-Way-Bolt (Multibolt) System

A three-way-bolt system is operated by a handle to secure the door at top, center, and bottom. The bolt-work is then locked in position by a key-operated deadlock. It is designed for use on single-leaf and particularly on double-leaf doors in conjunction with additional single bolts.

Two-Bolt Lock

This lock combines a handle-operated spring-loaded latch with a key-operated deadlock in the same case.

Lock Keep (Striking Plate)

Lock keeps or striking plates should preferably be of box type. If a wooden door frame is used, it should be reinforced in the area of the keep by a mild steel flat, a mild steel angle, or a mild steel channel slotted to accept the thrown bolt.

Padlock

Two types of padlocks deserve attention. First is the combined padlock and lock bar, so-called because the padlock and lock bar are one unit. The lock and staple are covered and protected by a seamless steel casing. This feature provides greater security than a unit that has separate padlock and locking bar. This type of lock works well on double-leaf doors, and is suitable for single-leaf doors where space permits. The second type of security padlock is the padlock with separate lock bar. It is mentioned only because it provides poor protection against forcible attack, and for that reason should be avoided for use wherever possible. The rule of thumb when choosing among padlocks is to favor padlocks that are seamless and have closed shackles or raised shoulders.

Combination Lock

Three-wheel or four-wheel combination locks made by reputable manufacturers offer good protection against surreptitious attack and can be adapted to give good protection against forcible attack. Combination locks can overcome many of the problems of key security but are slow in operation and are therefore unsuitable for frequently used doors. They should not be exposed to the weather. Combination locks come in two forms: as a padlock and as a mortise or rim lock. The padlock is less secure than the mortise lock because the hasp and the full casing of the lock are exposed to physical attack. The backside of a padlock is often the focal point of attack because the combination in some padlocks can be determined from a visual examination of the lock's interior. A mortise lock presents resistance to physical attack because only the face of the lock is accessible.

Setting and Changing a Combination

Select a lock whose combination can be easily set and changed. One of the simpler methods, yet secure, is the use of a special key that is inserted into the lock to release the wheels from the old combination while a new combination is entered by dialing. The combination should be changed when:

- First placed into service.

- The existing combination is lost or compromised.

- The use and custody of the lock is transferred.

- Any person having knowledge of the combination leaves or no longer requires access to the area protected by the lock.

- One year has elapsed since the last time the combination was changed.

Also in respect to a combination lock:

- Choose a combination that cannot be easily guessed.

- Limit knowledge of the combination to as few persons as possible.

- Keep a record of the combination in a container that provides a level of security at least equal to the level of security of the container protected by the lock.

Keys

The security of a key lock system is seriously weakened when keys are issued to a great number of people or to anyone who has no legitimate need for a key.

The key cut, or bitting, should be of a type that permits changes to be made, e.g., when the key for the lock has been lost or compromised. Changing the bitting is accomplished by changing the pins, wafers, or levers of the lock or by replacing the lock's core.

Master Keying

From a strict security point of view, master keying is undesirable; from a practical point of view, however, master keying may be necessary. Master keying presents two security drawbacks. First is the danger that any one lock in the system would be compromised, thus providing access to all locks. Second is the loss of a master key. An answer might be to use nonmastered key sets for high-security areas and mastered key sets for low-security areas.

Guiding Principles in a Key System

- Security of keys is essential from the moment they arrive on site. Locks and keys should be stored securely and separately until fitted. Keys should not be issued until after locks have been fitted.

- The minimum number of keys should be in use for any lock.

- Master key systems are inherently insecure. If their use is unavoidable, extreme vigilance is required to safeguard the master key or keys.

- No unauthorized person should be allowed access to any key, either to examine or handle it, since a photograph or impression can be taken in a few seconds and a duplicate subsequently made.

- Keys, when issued, should be signed for.

- A record should be maintained showing the whereabouts of every key, including spares, together with a note of the number of the lock to which they belong.

- Working keys held for emergency use (such as those used by security officers and maintenance personnel) should be kept out of sight in a central control point. They should be checked at the end of each working day and locked away in a secure container fitted with a combination lock.

- Spare keys should be held in a separate container of equal security to that holding the working keys. They should be issued only in an emergency, e.g., when a working key is lost or mislaid, and only to persons with authorized access to the area they protect.

- Spare keys should be checked with the working keys at intervals not exceeding six months.

- Additional keys should only be cut on the authority of a responsible individual, such as the security manager or property manager. They must be recorded.

- The loss or suspected compromise of a key should be reported immediately and, after due investigation, a decision made as to whether or not the lock should be changed.

SECURITY AWARENESS

This Plan recognizes that the security of the Company rests squarely on the practices of employees. The Corporate Security Manager can design the finest protective program, and the Executive Committee can support the program by providing the finest equipment and security staff. The security program, however, will surely be less than effective if the employees fail to meet their individual security responsibilities. No matter how perfectly conceived and abundantly funded, the security program will be incapable of rising above poor security practices by employees.

This Plan seeks to achieve consistent at-work behaviors that are appropriate to countering the security risks that face the Company. The first-line approach to achievement is through an awareness program having three dimensions:

- Employees are made to understand their individual security responsibilities.

- Employees are taught how to carry out those responsibilities.

- Employees are engaged in the first two dimensions willingly.

The first two dimensions require the employee to gain knowledge. The third dimension is distinctly different and almost always difficult to attain because it calls for an attitudinal shift on the part of the employee. The Corporate Security Manager, who is the designated sponsor of this Plan, must recognize that in the absence of a positive security attitude any efforts at promoting security awareness will be wasted.

The Security Awareness Program

The security awareness program will:

- Be a sub-part of the Company's overall security program. It will be a formal entity administered by one or more persons with security duties and subject to the routine processes of the business, such as planning, budgeting, and evaluation.

- Be an on-going effort, not a one-time effort. Although the program may be initiated with great fanfare and periodically reinvigorated, it will be a continuously operating enterprise.

- Be a local affair that serves the unique needs of the business unit. Although security topics may be suggested from outside of the business unit, the program will be principally dedicated to raising the awareness of security issues pertinent to the goals of the local business.

- Exploit all available forums that influence employee behaviors.

- Address security messages to all levels of the business unit.

- Vary the message style and mode of delivery according to the audience.

Formulate the Message

When selecting a topic for inclusion in the awareness program, certain questions should be asked: Is the topic important and does it need to be presented? If the answer is yes, then ask: "Is the content of the topic doctrinally correct? Is it consistent with the Company's policies and practices?"

If a topic is long or complicated, break it down into comprehensible parts. Arrange the parts in a logical series with each part building on the other.

Package the topic imaginatively. Go outside the envelope of traditional methods. Be innovative. Emulate the techniques of professional idea marketers.

Present the Message

The avenues for raising security awareness can include:

- Making presentations at employee meetings.

- Bringing in outside experts to address topics of concern, e.g., having a bomb threat specialist teach mail room employees how to spot parcel bombs or having a crime prevention specialist show employees how to protect themselves against crime.

- Conducting tutorials that meet special needs, e.g., providing crime-avoidance briefings to the family members of newly posted expatriate employees.

- Placing awareness materials on static and electronic bulletin boards, on the security web-site of the Company's local intranet, on placards in public hallways, and on signage at high-risk locations, such as the Company's parking lot.

- Encouraging employees to hold their own security awareness meetings.

- Conducting an annual security fair at which security experts and law enforcement officers teach employees how to avoid crime, such as by installing home and automobile alarm systems and engaging in crime avoidance tactics.

Conclusion

A security program typically consists of a guard force, an access control system, an intrusion detection system, an assortment of related hardware and equipment, and a set of plans and procedures that bring all of the parts into harmony. Central to all of these program components are the Company employees. Simultaneously, they are the practitioners of routine security practices and the chief asset under protection. The overall security program can be effective only to the extent that employees live up to their security responsibilities. Awareness is the key.

SEVERE WEATHER

Scope

The purpose of this Plan is to ensure preparedness at the Company's home office for a severe weather emergency, such as a major tropical storm or hurricane. Identified persons and groups are assigned specific responsibilities, which include ensuring the safety of employees, preventing loss and damage to physical assets, and establishing communications for coordinating preparedness and response actions.

Severe Weather Committee

This Plan establishes a Severe Weather Committee comprised of representatives from:

- Administration.

- External Affairs.

- Human Resources.

- Information Technology.

- Legal.

- Safety.

- Security.

- Telecommunications.

- Property Management.

The Committee will meet as needed to review this Plan and determine if substantive revisions are required. Substantive revisions recommended by the Committee will be forwarded for approval/comments to the CEO.

Committee members will be familiar with this Plan and maintain the current version of the Plan at ready access. In addition, each committee member will develop for use in his or her group a set of procedures for implementing the provisions of this Plan. Such procedures will address these actions:

- Identify, obtain, and keep in readiness the equipment, supplies, and materials required for responding to severe weather emergencies.

- Identify perishable supplies and arrange for their procurement in a timely manner following the detection of an approaching major storm system.

- Establish trigger points for initiating response actions, such as shutting down computers, installing window shields, moving valuable equipment to interior space, and sending employees home.

- Establish communication methods for persons who are assigned response duties and employees within the department or functional area generally.

- Conduct training that will prepare response personnel to carry out the required procedures.

- Provide education/awareness briefings to inform employees concerning response procedures.

Implementation

Decision Making

The senior executive present will decide when to begin and when to conclude Plan execution.

Alert Levels

From the outset of an impending storm, the security officer supervisor will receive storm charts and other weather advisory data coming into the security control center. These advisory materials will reflect when the storm reaches any of the four levels of alert that are described below. The security supervisor will route these advisory materials to the senior executive present.

The four levels of alert are:

Phase I becomes effective when a major storm develops that has the potential to strike the building. The security supervisor will at this point begin to monitor storm charts provided by the severe weather consulting service. These charts project the potential impact of the storm, magnitude, and direction.

Phase II becomes effective when a major storm develops in or enters a 200-mile radius of the building. The security supervisor will at this time begin to forward copies of the storm charts to the senior executive present at a frequency of every two hours.

Phase III becomes effective when winds ahead of a severe storm are within forty-eight hours of the building. The security supervisor will at this time forward copies of the storm charts to the senior executive at a frequency of not less than every one hour. The senior executive may elect to initiate a shutdown, partially or fully.

Phase IV becomes effective when winds ahead of the storm are within twenty-four hours of the building. If this phase is reached, the senior executive will make a decision with respect to a shutdown.

Notifications

The decision of the senior executive to begin response procedures and/or shutdown operations will be cascaded through the organization.

Return to Work

The External Affairs representative will prepare and update, as needed, a voice tape message that provides guidance to employees about returning to work.

The telephone number for obtaining the recorded message will be disseminated to employees as part of the cascade process.

Responsibilities of Committee Members

This section identifies the primary responsibilities of the Severe Weather Committee members. This section does not identify all the details contained in the procedures maintained by each committee member.

Security

- Maintain this Plan. Update the Plan at least annually. Distribute the Plan to Severe Weather Committee members.

- Chair the Severe Weather Committee. Call meetings as required.

- Educate employees generally concerning this plan and how execution of the plan will affect them personally. At least once annually, in conjunction with the storm season, inform employees of steps they should take to protect their homes in advance of an approaching storm.

- Maintain liaison with local emergency response agencies.

Property Management

- Develop and maintain a cadre of security officers who are trained and certified in the administration of CPR, first aid, and first responder medical assistance.

- Maintain a means for outside telephone and/or radio communication with local emergency response agencies.

- Follow and evaluate major weather conditions from the time they are first reported. Prepare and make entries to a storm system tracking map.

- Identify and arrange for the provision of security officers and security equipment or supplies that are needed to support response procedures.

- Provide a security officer presence at the building during a shutdown.

Administration

- Maintain and/or acquire at time of need those supplies, such as batteries and drinking water, that may be needed during a severe weather emergency.

- Coordinate with the property management firm those response activities that are of mutual interest to the Company and to the property management firm.

- Provide movers to get valuable equipment into space that affords a higher degree of physical protection and for securing materials that could pose a risk of injury or damage if left exposed to high winds.

Human Resources

- Provide guidance and assistance in matters relating to personnel issues arising from a severe weather incident.

Information Technology

- Protect computer assets.

- Prepare computer equipment and computer users for a shutdown, if required.

- Provide backup of data that might be adversely affected by storm conditions.

- Inform users of disruptions to service that may occur as the result of storm conditions and/or a shutdown.

- Be prepared to implement disaster recovery procedures.

Telecommunications

- Provide a backup communications capability for use during a major storm.

- In coordination with External Affairs, provide a means for employees to access taped messages by telephone.

External Affairs

- Provide to Telecommunications taped messages that inform callers concerning the status of work activities, opening hours, and similar details.

- Provide press releases that might be required in the event of significant property damage or personal injury.

- Monitor local broadcasts to obtain information concerning the availability of medical treatment and relief centers.

Legal

- Provide advice on matters regarding liability, damage claims, regulatory compliance, documentation, or other related legal issues.

Safety

- Serve as a resource to the Security Manager and the Severe Weather Committee.

PROCEDURES

procedure *n*, a series of steps followed in a
regular definite order.

AIDS CONTACT

These Procedures are precautionary. They apply in situations when security officers may have been exposed to HIV, such as after administering CPR and first aid, transporting a bleeding person, securing a crime or accident scene where human body fluids are present, or when subduing a violent person. While there are no known cases of security officers becoming infected through performance of their duties, these Procedures are intended to inform security officers of the potential risks and to guide them when exposure has occurred.

Situations and Actions

Follow the guidance for these situations:

- **If bitten by another person**. Transmission through saliva is highly unlikely. Milk the wound to make it bleed, wash thoroughly, and seek medical attention.

- **If spat upon**. Transmission through saliva is highly unlikely. Wash thoroughly.

- **If in contact with urine/feces**. Virus is in very low concentrations in urine and not at all in feces. Transmission is highly unlikely. Wash thoroughly.

- **If cut or wounded**. Needle stick studies show low risk of infection. Use caution in handling sharp objects and searching in areas hidden from view, such as when searching a person taken into custody.

- **When rendering CPR/first aid**. Minimal risk associated with CPR. Use mask/airway, and avoid blood-to-blood contact by keeping open wounds covered and wearing gloves when in contact with bleeding wounds.

- **When moving a body**. Those who must come into contact with blood or other body fluids in connection with a dead victim should wear protective clothing, mask, and gloves.

- **If in contact with blood/body fluids**. Wear protective clothing, mask, and gloves if contact with blood or body fluids is considered likely. Afterwards, wash thoroughly with soap and hot water. Clean up blood spills with one part water to nine parts household bleach.

- **If in contact with dried blood**. Despite low risk of infection, caution dictates wearing gloves, a mask, and protective shoe coverings if exposure to dried blood is likely.

ANTI-EAVESDROPPING

The full nature and extent of electronic eavesdropping in the business sector may never be known. We only know that it occurs, and if we possess sensitive information we must take protective steps. One of those steps is the technical surveillance countermeasures (TSCM) inspection, i.e., an organized search for electronic eavesdropping equipment.

TSCM

A TSCM inspection should be carried out by a specialist trained in this area. The TSCM specialist, who may be an in-house employee or an outside consultant, uses the following equipment:

- Telephone analyzer or time domain reflectometer for analyzing telephone system equipment and wire.

- Spectrum analyzer for examining video signals.

- Nonlinear junction detector for finding hidden recorders and transmitters.

- Amplifiers of various types for finding and listening to audio signals.

The TSCM specialist will make a thorough physical search in addition to searches by electronic equipment. The physical search examines adjoining rooms, walls, ceilings, duct work, electrical outlets and switches, furniture, plants, and any other place where tiny microphones and tell-tale wiring can be hidden. The physical search is comprehensive and involves a combination of looking and touching.

In advance of an inspection, the TSCM specialist will need to know:

- The number and size of rooms or floors or buildings to be inspected.

- The location of rooms, floors, and buildings relative to each other.

- The numbers and types of phones to be inspected.

- The locations of distribution cables, telephone rooms, and switching equipment.

- The types of ceilings, e.g., removable or fixed, recessed or not recessed.

- The types of electronic communications equipment at the place to be inspected that might interfere with the inspection. Such equipment could include public address systems, computer networks, microwave links, and teleconferencing facilities.

When scheduling the services of a TSCM specialist, the discussion should not be made over a communication line that will be among those inspected. The telephone used in the conversation might be tapped, therefore compromising the effectiveness of the later inspection.

Eavesdropping Devices

The common types of eavesdropping devices are:

- **Contact microphone**. It is placed in contact with the back side of a wall. A form of contact microphone uses a suction cup that also serves as a vibrating diaphragm.

- **Spike microphone**. A spike-shaped device that penetrates a wall from the back side. The tip of the spike contains the microphone.

- **Pin-hole microphone**. Similar to the spike, it is a tube-shaped device that is inserted into a tiny drilled hole in the wall.

- **Stethoscope microphone**. The eavesdropper places the stethoscope against the back side of the wall and listens to the conversation on the other side.

- **Wall plug microphone**. A noncontact microphone that is placed inside a wall plug.

- **Directional microphone**. A highly sensitive microphone that is pointed at the place of conversation. It comes in three forms: parabolic (shaped like a satellite dish), shotgun (held and aimed like a shotgun), and machine gun (microphone tubes arranged in the shape of a Gatling gun).

- **Miniature, battery-powered microphone**. Tiny, yet very sensitive, these devices can be concealed in jewelry, pens, cigarette lighters, etc.

- **Drop-in microphone**. It is placed into the mouthpiece of a telephone and does not require a battery because it draws power from the telephone line.

Nearly every microphone will be connected in some fashion to a recording device. When it is possible to do so, as would be the case with a spike microphone, the microphone and recording device would be connected. Where the listener requires greater geographical separation between the microphone and the recording unit, an amplifier/transmitter is used.

ANTI-STALKING

Background

These recommendations have been drawn from the experiences of stalking victims. Not all will be appropriate in every case. They are intended to serve as a guide to any employee who is being stalked, that is, being followed, accosted, called on the telephone, or visited at home or work without invitation.

Guidance to the Victim

Whether the stalking occurs on or off the job, you should inform the Company by making a report to your immediate supervisor, or your immediate supervisor's manager, the Human Resources Manager, or the Security Manager. A record will be made of the report and of the actions that result from it.

In addition, you should take these steps:

- Ignore the stalking individual.

- Be clear and unambiguous that any prior relationship is over and that you do not desire a relationship.

- Do not give your reasons why.

- Do not let the stalker see your concern.

- Cut off all contact.

- Do not have someone else intervene for you.

- Have your answering machine message simply state your telephone number, and use a voice other than your own.

- Use caller ID to screen your calls.

- Obtain an unlisted phone number.

- Mark your house number so that police and rescue personnel can find you easily in a response situation.

- Get a dog.

- Do not allow strangers in your home.

- Keep your address and schedule secret.

- Inquire about laws concerning your situation.

- Notify authorities every time the stalker bothers you. Keep copies of the reports.

- Treat all threats as legitimate and call police every time the stalker shows up.

- Press charges every time you can. Ask that a condition of a bond forbid any and all contact with you.

- Ask the police to periodically drive past your home.

- Obtain a restraining order.

- If the police tell you they have no authority to arrest the stalker, do not ask them to intervene because an intervention without arrest sends a message that your best defense is useless.

- Go public.

- Have an attorney send a registered letter informing the stalker to stop.

- Record the stalking with a video camera.

- Keep a log of stalking activities.

- Ask witnesses to testify as to the stalking.

- Keep all written materials received from the stalker.

- Document all medical reports of physical abuse.

- Take photos of wounds, bruises, and acts of vandalism.

- Join a support group.

- Vary your routine.

- Limit time spent walking alone or along the same route.

- Notify neighbors and co-workers about the situation, give them a photo of the stalker, and ask them to notify you if he or she is seen.

- Get an unlisted phone number for day-to-day business. Use an answering machine.

- Have mail screened by someone you can trust.

- Have co-workers screen calls and visitors.

- Have a co-worker check with other co-workers to see if the stalker is calling them as well.

- Alert security personnel at work.

- Stay in public areas and travel with friends.

- Get a car telephone.

- Accompany your children to the bus or to school.

- Do not park in garages that require the keys to your car.

- Lock your car door when traveling and be aware of other cars.

- Rent a mailbox from a private service.

- Lock your outside fuse box, car, and garage. Trim hedges near windows.

- Put a lock on your car's gas tank.

- Install deadbolts at home. Change door keys.

- Install outside lighting. Consider installing motion detectors.

- If you move, make it difficult for anyone to learn your new address.

- Ask for a job change that will throw the stalker off track.

- Hire a private security guard.

- Have a contingency plan that includes quick access to important phone numbers, a packed suitcase, and "escape" money.

- Alert a responsible person to your situation and your plan.

- Take legal action, in addition to a restraining order.

ATTACK AVOIDANCE

These recommendations are intended to guide employees whose duties place them in situations that expose them to physical attack, such as mugging and robbery. These recommendations can also be valuable to employees in their personal lives.

Actions

Attack avoidance is largely up to the individual. The chances of being victimized can be reduced by following these simple rules:

- Walk near the curb to avoid passing close to dark doorways. Don't give an attacker the chance to pull you into an isolated area.

- Don't take shortcuts through alleys, backyards, empty buildings or parking lots. If you're in a dangerous neighborhood, or fear you're being followed, walk down the center of the street if possible.

- Familiarize yourself with the areas you walk through frequently. Make mental note of which stores, restaurants, or gas stations are open late at night. Plan to run to the nearest one if you're approached by a stranger.

- Walk on well-lighted, well-traveled streets, even if it makes your journey longer. Don't stray from the crowd in a public place.

- Behavior on the street is important. Walk briskly, in a businesslike manner. Appear confident, as though you know exactly where you're going. An attacker seeks out passive victims. If you walk slowly or appear distracted, you will be more vulnerable.

- Observe closely the people who approach you. Avoid being confronted. When you walk at night do so with a companion or a group of companions.

- After getting off a bus or subway, take a quick survey of the people around you. Make sure you're not followed. Be alert after leaving a place where you've just received money, such as at a bank or store where you've cashed a check. Don't be lured to unsafe places by strange sounds, even a cry for help. Just hurry away and alert the police. Always carry enough change for carfare and an emergency phone call.

- When you head for an elevator, be alert for strangers. Don't choose a stairway in lieu of an elevator if you feel threatened. Stairways are favored by attackers.

- If you doubt the intention of someone waiting for the elevator with you, don't hesitate to walk away.

- Inside an elevator, look for the location of the alarm button and stand near it. If attacked, hit the alarm button and as many floor buttons as you can so the door will open at the nearest floor.

- Attackers hit drivers, too. In congested areas, drive with your doors locked and your windows raised so no one can reach in, open the door, and climb in with you or pull you out. Be careful when stopped at red lights. If someone tries to break in, drive through the light and sound your horn. Also, check the back seat and floor before getting into your car.

- If someone confronts you with a weapon, don't escalate the danger. If it's apparent that only money or valuables are at stake, give them up. Try to keep calm. The robber is probably as nervous as you and may be easily excited, especially if drunk or drugged. Don't verbally abuse a street robber. It may lessen your chances of escaping injury.

- If attacked, don't fight back unless you're convinced you have to fight for your life. Follow your instinct in making this decision. By fighting back too soon, you may make your situation worse and turn a robbery into a fight for life.

- The decision to fight depends on your personality as well as your age, physical condition, the size of your opponent, and whether or not he or she is armed.

- If you're forced to fight, be determined to go all the way. Do anything to hurt the attacker. Strike the most vulnerable areas such as the groin, eyes, and throat. Bite, scratch, kick, and scream. Remember, there are no rules of etiquette in a street fight for your life. Law enforcement officers advise you not to rely on lethal weapons, such as a gun or a knife, to defend yourself. They're too easily taken away and used against you. Other defensive items, however, may help. A police-type whistle or compressed air siren is good to have. A hat pin, ballpoint pen, key ring in the fist, nail file, or umbrella can also hurt and scare away a potential mugger.

- Finally, and most important of all, if a mugger attacks, your best defense is to break away and run for safety.

AUTO THEFT PREVENTION

Driver Responsibility

These Procedures are intended to guide employees who are assigned company automobiles. Like any other valuable company asset, automobiles are to be cared for and protected at all times.

Actions

Auto theft can be greatly reduced with a few simple precautions:

- Keep the auto locked at all times, even if it's parked on company property. Two of every five stolen cars have keys in them, and four of five are unlocked.

- Park in lighted areas. Two-thirds of all car thefts happen at night. If it's daylight when you park, take a moment to consider how that parking space will look when the sun goes down.

- Park where passers-by may serve as a deterrent to thieves. If you have a choice, don't park at an intersection at the end of a line of parked cars. The car is thus vulnerable to towing by thieves. When parking at a curb, turn front wheels sharply toward the curb.

- If you have to leave the key with a parking lot attendant:

  - Leave just the ignition key.

  - Don't be specific about when you'll be back. A dishonest attendant may steal new parts from the car and replace them with old parts. Check your mileage before and after to see if the automobile had been used while in the custody of the attendant.

- Don't hide extra keys in the car.

- Don't keep anything valuable in the glove compartment.

- Don't tempt a car "window shopper" by leaving items in plain sight within the car. If you must carry valuables, lock them in the trunk. Items of value or that appear to be valuable are tempting targets.

- Avoid being seen putting items of value into the trunk.

- Carry the vehicle registration certificate on your person.

- Use the anti-theft device installed on the auto.

BACKGROUND CHECKING

These Procedures, which represent a collaborative effort of the Human Resources and Security Departments, are intended to guide those persons who on behalf of the Company conduct inquiries into the backgrounds of job applicants. In some cases, the inquiries will be conducted by in-house resources, such as Human Resources and Security staff, and in other cases by vendors that specialize in conducting background checks. In all cases, background checking will be conducted in full compliance with the provisions of the Fair Credit Reporting Act (FCRA), the Americans With Disabilities Act (ADA), and any and all other laws or regulations that now or may later apply.

Areas of Inquiry

Criminal, Civil, and Bankruptcy Records Check

These three different types of court records are available in county, state, and federal offices and courts.

- Criminal records are often the product of a case brought by the government against an individual or a corporation for behaviors considered as acts against society. This category is divided into severe crimes (felonies) and less severe crimes (misdemeanors).

- Civil cases include disputes between private citizens, corporations, governmental bodies, and other organizations. These records often concern employer-employee conflicts, property, personal rights, personal injuries, liability suits, contract disputes, landlord-tenant conflicts, evictions, divorces, and probate. Civil records will be examined only when they are relevant to a specific job function and supported by appropriate policies and procedures. The use of civil information without a reasonable business necessity is prohibited.

- Bankruptcy records are generated under procedures very different from civil and criminal records. Court records of bankruptcy may be found only at the federal level.

Credit Check

Standard credit reports are available from vendors specializing in that area. The individual's credit history should be obtained for the most recent 7 years.

Driving Record Check

Driving record information can be obtained from state motor vehicle bureaus. A check should cover the most recent 3 to 7 years. Some state bureaus report infractions involving drugs or alcohol. Each report typically contains physical description, license information, infractions, home address, and previous driver's license number.

Education Credentials Check

The check will determine dates of attendance at educational institutions, programs of study, and degrees awarded. Vocational training, certification, and professional licenses will also be checked.

Social Security Number (SSN) Check

The applicant's name, address, and date of birth will be checked against SSN records.

Work and Personal References Check

Work references provided by the applicant will be checked in respect to:

- Names of former employers.

- Dates of employment.

- Job titles.

- Job duties.

- Salary.

- Reasons for leaving.

- Eligibility for rehire.

- Productivity.

- Punctuality.

- Relationships with others.

- Strengths and weaknesses.

- Notices given.

Personal references provided by the applicant will be checked as to:

- How long the reference has known the individual and in what capacity.

- The individual's character in the opinion of the reference.

- The individual's employability in the opinion of the reference.

Workers' Compensation Claims Check

Workers' compensation reports on file with state governments will be checked to identify reports of injury, court-contested claims, medical awards, lost time claims, and compensable claims.

Inquiry Sources

The following sources are appropriate for making the inquiries described above.

- **Address Update Combined:** Provides an individual's most current address, social security number, and year of birth based on credit profiles.

- **Social Security Number Track Searches:** Provides names and addresses of all persons who used a specific social security number for credit purposes. Date of birth and spouse's name or initial are sometimes included.

- **Social Security Number Plus:** Checks all three major credit bureaus.

- **National Moving Index:** Updates an individual's address based on information contained in consumer credit profiles. Often reveals social security number and telephone number.

- **FAA Aircraft Ownership Search:** Displays a list of aircraft owned by an individual or a business, nationwide.

- **Surname Scan:** Matches names, addresses, and listed phone numbers of up to 200 individuals who share a common surname within a specified geographic region.

- **Infoscan:** Verifies occupant name and telephone number for a desired address while uncovering occupant estimate income and length of residence. Also provides similar information for neighbors and individuals with the same last name.

- **National Address Change Records:** Uncovers new addresses for individuals based on a three-year history of federal address changes, coupled with publisher information ad mailing records from independent sources.

- **People Tracker Summary:** Provides an individual's current and previous residential address.

- **National Publishers' Change of Address:** Provides new address information on individuals based on changes of address filed with various magazine and publishing companies.

- **Neighborhood Search Index:** Matches occupant name, phone number, and length of residence at a given address while providing similar information on up to 30 neighbors. In addition, a demographic profile of the neighborhood is included.

- **Telephone Reverse Directory:** Searches either a listed telephone number or address to confirm occupancy and match the telephone number with the address. Searches both business and residential listings.

- **Business Credit I: Market Identifier:** Provides company reported sales and growth figures along with a company profile that may identify principals, years in business, and primary and secondary SIC classification.

- **Business Credit II: Payment History:** Details important financial information about a company, including account types, established payment terms, payment history, and average balances. Also, bankruptcies, liens, and judgments are included.

- **Dun and Bradstreet Business Information Reports:** Provides a business's name, address, Dun and Bradstreet ID number, and SIC code as well as background information about the company and its officers. In addition, important financial information is included, such as banking references, payment histories, current assets, sales liabilities and profits, and public filings (i.e., lawsuits, judgments, liens, and bankruptcies).

- **Consumer Credit Report:** Provides address and employment information along with a listing of credit accounts, balances, credit inquiries, and payment history. A signed release form is needed.

- **Consumer Credit Employment Report:** A complete consumer credit report used for employment purposes as allowed under the federal Fair Credit Reporting Act. This report allows the employee/applicant to receive a free copy of his or her credit report.

- **On-Site Civil Court Searches (Docket Scan):** Searches federal, upper, or lower court in any state to provide a history of litigation, providing plaintiff name, defendant name, file date, and file number.

- **On-Site Criminal Court Searches (Docket Scan):** Searches any federal, felony, or misdemeanor criminal court by name to provide file date, case number, level of charges, and disposition. Also provides major metropolitan area felony searches and nationwide felony searches.

- **FAA Airman Directory:** Verifies the status of an individual's pilot license. Provides address, certificate number, and effective and expiration dates.

- **National Death Locator:** Provides a decedent's name, date of birth, state of last residence, social security number, and year and state of issuance according to Social Security Administration records. Additionally, the zip code of the death payment recipient is provided.

- **OSHA Inspections, Accidents, and Violations:** Provides the name, address, county, and number of employees at the site of an OSHA inspection. Also includes type of inspection, accidents, penalties, violations, failure to abate history, and much more.

- **IRS Enrolled Agents Search:** Matches the name and address of individual enrolled tax agents who are qualified to practice tax law and represent consumers at audits and IRS hearings through passing a comprehensive IRS exam. Additionally, the IRS branch and region that issued the certification are identified.

- **IRS Tax Practitioners and Preparers Search:** Includes the name, mailing address, and classification of individuals and businesses who either file electronic tax returns or who are on the IRS mailing list for receiving newsletters, tax law updates, and other regularly scheduled mailings for professional tax practitioners and preparers.

- **Watercraft:** The U.S. Coast Guard file contains information on merchant and recreational vessels weighing no less than 5 net tons (approximately 27 feet or more) that are owned by U.S. citizens or corporations. The source for this information is the U.S. Coast Guard's Marine Safety Information System (MSIS).

- **UCC Searches:** Verifies a security interest has been perfected at the state level. Includes important filing dates, file numbers, and debtor and secured party names.

- **State Board of Equalization:** Provides names of owners and addresses of businesses holding sales or use tax permits.

- **Department of Motor Vehicles: Driver Records:** Provides a history of an individual's driving performance and a description of departmental action taken as a result of tickets or accidents. A driver's license number match and physical description are also provided.

- **Department of Motor Vehicles: Vehicle Records:** Matches registered and legal owners of a vehicle by license plate number or vehicle identification number (VIN).

- **Department of Motor Vehicles: Alpha Name Index:** Provides a list of vehicles owned by an individual or business, including year, make, model, and type of vehicle. Most states also include vessels (boats).

- **Real Property Ownership and Transfer Searches:** Searches by owner name, property address, or mailing address to provide property description, parcel number, assessed value, transfer date, transfer amount, and property use description for each parcel of property owned.

- **Bankruptcies, Liens, and Judgments:** Lists bankruptcies; federal, state, and county tax liens; and judgments filed against an individual or a business.

- **Marriage Index:** Searches by bride or groom name to provide file date and file number of a marriage certificate. May also provide age of bride and groom at the time of filing.

- **Divorce Index:** Provides file date and file number of a divorce petition.

- **Death Record Index:** Confirms filing of a death certificate by providing file date, file number, and social security number of decedent.

- **Contractor License Index:** Matches contractor license number, date of issuance, surety bond information, current status, and contractor specialization.

- **Professional Licenses:** Verifies that an individual or business is licensed to perform specific professional services. Provides license number, date of issuance, status, and expiration dates as recorded by state authorities.

- **Federal District Court Bankruptcy Filings:** Searches by debtor name to provide open and close date, file number, and chapter of a bankruptcy petition. Additionally, in NY and PA, the names and social security numbers of all debtors as well as a list of docket entries is provided.

- **Federal District Court Civil Filings:** Provides open and close date, case title, and party names for civil cases.

- **Federal District Court Criminal Filings:** Searches by name to provide open and close date, file number, and case title for criminal cases.

- **Registered Voter Profiles:** Searches statewide voter registration files to provide the name and address of a registered voter. Most states also provide voter's date of birth, gender, registration date, and party affiliation.

- **Real Property Ownership and Transfer Searches:** Searches by property address, parcel number or owner name to provide property description, parcel number, assessed value, transfer date, transfer amount, and property use description.

- **Real property Refinance, Construction Loan and Seller Carry Back Searches:** Searches by buyer, seller, or lender name to provide buyer name and address, seller name, lender name, loan date, loan amount, and transaction type.

- **Supreme Court Civil Index:** Searches by plaintiff, defendant, attorney, or law firm name to provide file date, case number, case type, and disposition for each filing.

- **Court of Common Pleas Index:** Searches civil complaints and judgments to provide file date, case number, case type, attorney name, and plaintiff and defendant name(s) and address(es).

- **Superior Court Civil Index:** Provides plaintiff and defendant names, file date, and case number for civil lawsuits. Most jurisdictions also include nature of the case.

- **Superior Court Criminal Index:** Searches by name to provide file date, case number, and possible alias names and charges filed.

- **Superior Court Probate Index:** Provides file date, file number, case title, and type of probate filed.

- **Superior Court Divorce Index:** Searches divorce filings to provide name of petitioner and respondent, file date, file number, and court location.

- **Municipal Court Civil Index:** Provides plaintiff and defendant name(s), file date, and file number.

- **Municipal Court Criminal Index:** Matches a name against a history of criminal filings to provide file date, case number, court location, and additional related information.

- **Municipal Court Civil/Small Claims Index:** Provides plaintiff and defendant name(s), file date, and file number.

- **Fictitious Business/Assumed Name Index:** Provides business name, owner name, and address of business in addition to the filing date and file number.

- **Registered Voter Search:** Matches an individual name against voter registration files to provide date of filing, file number, party affiliation, and address.

- **Marriage Index: County Recorder:** Provides bride and groom name, file date, and file number based on county recorder information.

- **General Index:** Provides grantor/grantee information from county recorder files. This may include property transfers, fictitious name filings, liens, and finance statements.

- **Judgment Docket and Lien Book:** Includes civil judgments hospital liens, mechanics liens, building loans, sidewalk liens, and federal tax liens. Provides lien or judgment amount, filing date, file number, and date satisfied.

BANK SECURITY OFFICER

General

- Present yourself professionally but courteously at all times.

- Maintain a businesslike appearance:

    - Ensure that your uniform is clean, in good condition, and wrinkle free.

    - Maintain a well-groomed appearance consistent with the established standards.

    - Use good standing posture. Keep your hands out of your pockets.

    - Do not eat or smoke while on duty.

Bank Opening

- Turn off the alarm system.

- Keep the front door locked until the bank officially opens for business. Allow only authorized bank employees (check identification) entrance into the bank prior to opening.

- Check the closed-circuit television (CCTV) and change the tape if necessary.

- Move signs to proper locations.

Customer Contact

- Move about the main lobby. Project a pleasant yet professional appearance.

- Always look directly at people and address them as "Sir" or "Ma'am." Avoid using first names.

- Do not socialize with the customers, but respond to their questions politely.

- Always appear attentive and alert.

Deter and Contain

- Serve as a visible deterrent to unlawful activities, such as robbery or disorderly conduct, but do not intervene in any act that could cause harm to yourself or others.

- Notify the police when intervention is required.

Miscellaneous

- Escort bank employees, e.g., to the outside ATM and customers to their vehicles.

- Refer customer questions to the appropriate bank employee.

- Arrange restroom and coffee breaks with the appropriate bank supervisor.

Bank Closing

- Patrol the facility to ensure that no one remains behind.

- Check the rest rooms, storage areas, and stairwells for people, packages, or other unusual items.

- Turn on the alarm system.

- Make sure that you are the last one to leave the facility.

BOMB PROTECTION

Throughout the world terrorist groups and other extremists frequently resort to bombing attacks to promote their causes. Because they choose different targets and employ different methods, it is not possible to provide a generally applicable guide to assessing the threat of such attacks.

Precautionary measures, however, can and must be taken. These Procedures describe such measures.

Bomb Types and Preventive Measures

Bombs can be constructed in many different ways and are easily disguised. They may be placed in bags, cases, or everyday containers that can be easily hidden. Vehicles can carry large bombs without showing any outward signs.

There are essentially four kinds of bombs:

- High Explosive

- Vehicle

- Incendiary

- Postal

All can be initiated by the use of timing devices, command detonation, anti-disturbance (pull, push, trip) or pressure pad. Vehicle and postal bombs can be either high explosive or incendiary, and all can be hand carried.

High Explosive

These can kill or injure people by their blast or by causing flying debris, particularly glass. Bombs small enough to be hidden in a hand-carried bag may be powerful enough to cause serious damage to property. Bombs using high explosives are typically made with commercial or military explosives in blocks or sticks. Some will include an electric detonator, timer, or power source and will be contained in some way with the explosive material.

Three simple steps can be taken to protect against high-explosive bombs:

- Prevent them from being brought onto the property, e.g., by stringent access control procedures, inspection of packages, and the use of explosive-detecting devices.

- Reduce the chances of someone planting a bomb which cannot be detected, e.g., by eliminating hiding places; not allowing packages, parcels, and bags to be left unattended; and not allowing vehicles to park near the facility.

- Keep close surveillance over the site by guards, employees, and technical means, such as CCTV surveillance.

Vehicle Bombs

A vehicle containing high explosives can cause considerable damage and loss to life. Smaller bombs can be attached to the underside of vehicles either to kill the persons inside when they drive off or to smuggle a bomb into premises.

To protect against vehicle bombs:

- Control access to your parking lots and garages.

- Have people park their vehicles well away from buildings, when possible.

- Stop and search vehicles entering property.

- Keep close watch over the outside of the property.

- Have drivers check their cars before driving off.

Incendiary Bombs

The purpose of these bombs is to cause fire. They are normally small and difficult to detect and are often concealed inside or among other apparently innocent objects.

To protect against incendiary bombs:

- Inspect packages entering the premises.

- Look out for people who act suspiciously.

- Search the premises regularly.

Postal Bombs

Letter and parcel bombs are envelopes and packages designed to kill or injure people when they are opened. They may not come through the mail and can be delivered by hand. Any of the following are signs that the letter or package may be a bomb:

- Grease marks on the envelope or wrapping.

- A smell like marzipan or machine oil.

- Visible wires or foil, especially if the package is damaged.

- The package may feel heavy for its size.

- It may be heavier in some places than others and may appear overwrapped.

- The envelope may feel soft but the contents feel hard.

- The package may have been delivered by hand.

- There may be poor handwriting, spelling, or typing.

- It may have come from somewhere unexpected.

- There may be too many stamps on it.

If you have any reason to suspect that a letter or package may contain a bomb:

- Put it down gently and walk away from it.

- Ask everyone to leave the area.

- Sound the alarm.

- Do not put the letter or package into anything (including water).

- Do not put anything on top of it.

Protective Measures

Following are steps to protect people and property against bombs.

Make sure that the doors, gates, and windows of premises are well secured by key-operated locks and bolts. Good security lighting, CCTV coverage over perimeter boundaries, main entrance doors, and critical points within the site all help to deter attack.

Protect people from flying glass by having special thin polyester film fitted to the inside of the window and in some cases by hanging special net curtains. Glass can be replaced in some cases with laminated glass.

Make it difficult for unauthorized people to enter the property during business hours as well as when not operating by applying good access control procedures. If threat of attack is high, searches must be made of vehicles and those on foot entering the premises. Make sure people do not leave personal belongings unattended.

Educate employees to be alert for bombs and to report suspicious circumstances to authorities.

Telephone Warnings

Terrorists and others frequently (but not always) give warnings. So, unfortunately, do hoax callers. You may receive a warning that your premises are at risk. In such cases you will have to decide whether to evacuate.

Responding to warning calls often involves making difficult decisions. It is essential to get the maximum amount of useful information from the call. Switchboard operators most frequently have to deal with such calls but any member of staff who has a direct line might also receive a threatening call. The key rules are:

- Keep calm.

- Try to obtain as much information as possible.

- Keep the line open after the caller has hung up.

- Report the call upward as quickly as possible.

Searches

Bombs can be disguised in many ways. Search teams will look for an unidentified object that:

- Should not be there.

- Cannot be accounted for.

- Is out of place.

The rules for searching are:

- Do not touch or move the suspect object.

- Leave a distinctive marker near the object, if it is safe to do so.

- Move away from the object to the control point.

- Inform the search coordinator who will then consider evacuation options.

- Draw a sketch that depicts the location of the device.

- Make the finder immediately available for interview by authorities.

Hand-held communications are often the only appropriate way to carry out a search and evacuation plan. But where possible, the telephone is preferable. Once a suspect device is found, those using hand-held communications should move well away from the device and ensure others do as well.

Evacuation

The purpose of evacuation is to move people from an area where there might be a risk to a place of safety. This may be achieved by:

- Full evacuation.

- Partial evacuation (where large premises are involved and only a suspect letter bomb or small device is found).

- Internal movement to a sheltered area may be safer than to move people outside where a second bomb may have been placed.

In all cases the police or authorities should be immediately informed and advised what action is being taken. Depending on the assessment of the threat, the action choices are:

- Do nothing.

- Search, then evacuate if a suspicious object is found.

- Evacuate all except search teams and essential staff, then carry out a search and evacuate fully if a suspected device is found.

- Evacuate immediately without searching.

When the time of explosion has been disclosed in a threat call, searching must be finished and staff cleared at least twenty minutes before the deadline, whether any device has been found or not.

As in the case of search plans, evacuation plans and routes should also have been drawn up and both should be practiced every six months. As a general rule, if you are in a building move everyone to a meeting point at least 300 feet away from and out of sight of the place where the device has been found. The meeting point should not be a parking garage or other location where a secondary bomb may be concealed and awaiting detonation. If the suspicious object is larger than a suitcase or is a vehicle, the meeting place should be at least 1,500 feet away. In areas where there is likely to be increased danger, safer distances must be considered.

When evacuation is ordered:

- People should leave as quickly as possible using all available exits.

- Alternative routes should be available so that people can leave without passing close to the suspect device.

- Use the public address system to help in the evacuation process.

- Doors and windows should be left unlocked, especially in the vicinity of the device.

- Lights should be left on but plant and machinery shut down where practicable.

Sheltered areas within a building may sometimes be safer to evacuate to, but the areas should only be selected by a qualified structural engineer with expertise in the effects of explosive devices. The area must be able to accommodate the total number of people sent to it.

Returning to the Site

If the premises have been evacuated without searching and there has not been an explosion, do not allow anyone to re-enter before the site has been properly searched. Where a time has been given for an explosion, at least one hour must elapse before search procedures are initiated or re-commenced. When police or authorities have ordered the initial evacuation, they will declare the premises safe for re-entry. Civil engineers need to approve reoccupation in every case where structural damage has been caused.

BOMB THREATS

These Procedures apply to bomb threat incidents at the Company's home office and are based on requirements of the applicable fire code and law enforcement guidelines.

Receipt of the Threat

Guidance to employees who receive telephone bomb threats is provided in the Bomb Threat Checklist that appears at the end of these Procedures.

A bomb threat is rarely made in person and is sometimes transmitted in writing. A bomb threat made in writing should be handled carefully and touched by as few persons as possible and the envelope or any other accompanying materials should be retained and preserved. Observing these simple precautions can be extremely helpful to a post-incident investigation.

A probability exists that a bomb threat against the building will be made to another party, such as the police department or fire department. If this should occur, the initial notice would come from the police department by telephone or in person. This initial notification might be supplemented by a police patrol being sent to the building to stand by to render possible assistance.

Initial Response

Receptionists and certain secretaries will be trained to call the Security Control Center upon receipt of a bomb threat call. The objective is to begin implementation of these procedures as rapidly as possible.

When the Security Control Center receives, or is informed of a bomb threat, the following initial actions will be:

- Notify the Building Manager or Assistant Building Manager.

- Notify the Security Supervisor.

Evaluation

Evaluation of a bomb threat will be made by the Building Manager or Assistant Manager. Evaluation will be made on the basis of all facts available at the time. Many of the available facts will be obtained from the person who received the bomb threat. Evaluation is the process for judging the credibility of the threat. When a threat is judged to be false, the evaluator may elect to take no action. An example might be a bomb threat made by a child over the telephone. When a threat is judged to have possible credibility, one of three decisions will be made:

- To search without evacuation.

- To evacuate, partially or fully, and then search.

- To evacuate and not search.

When a threat is judged to have no credibility at all, the decision will be to take no action.

Evacuation Options

If a credible bomb threat is received and if the decision is not to evacuate, the Building Manager will make a public address announcement to the effect that:

- A bomb threat has been received.

- There is no reason to believe that anyone is in danger.

- The decision has been made not to evacuate.

- Any person in the building who wishes to leave may do so.

If the decision is to evacuate, the announcement will include brief instructions to employees to:

- Take with them any personal belongings (particularly purses, briefcases, and packages).

- Make a quick visual surveillance of their immediate work areas for the purpose of detecting suspicious objects.

- Report their suspicions to the security officer in the lobby as they exit the building.

The decision to evacuate will take into consideration the location of a suspect bomb relative to the fire stairwells. If a suspect bomb is believed to be in or near a stairwell, the evacuation announcement will direct evacuees away from the danger zone.

Total evacuation will not be an automatic response. Partial evacuation would be an appropriate response in those instances where the bomb threat caller mentions a specific location.

Communications

There have been very few recorded instances of explosive charges triggered by radio frequency energy. Generally, therefore, it is considered that use of hand-held radios to assist in search procedures is not a serious hazard. However, operate a hand-held radio beyond a radius of ten feet from the suspicious object. If in doubt, use the telephone as the primary means of communication.

Suspicious Object

If a suspicious object is found, the finder will call the Security Control Center without delay, ensuring first that the suspect device is not touched or moved by another searcher or an uninformed bystander. These actions will follow the discovery of a suspicious object:

- The Security Control Center will notify the Building Manager and the Security Supervisor. The Building Manager or the Security Supervisor will ask the police to take command of the situation with respect to handling of the suspect bomb.

- Depending on the circumstances, a partial or full evacuation will be immediately implemented.

- The Security Control Center will ensure that the fire department has been notified and that first aid supplies have been readied for possible use.

The police may ask for help when a device is found. This help might be to:

- Place calls to the bomb disposal unit or other elements within the police department.

- Open doors to dissipate a possible blast effect.

- Confer with knowledgeable employees to learn of other possible hiding places where a secondary device could be concealed.

- Question employees who may be able to account for the device being in fact an innocent object.

Floor Wardens

Floor Wardens will perform their functions with respect to evacuation. Assembly locations will be the same as those for fire emergencies.

Coordination

The Security Control Center will serve as the focal point of telephone communications during a bomb incident. At the earliest possible moment following the initiation of a bomb incident, the Building Manager and the Security Supervisor will proceed to the Security Control Center to coordinate management of the incident.

If the Security Control Center is within the danger zone posed by the bomb, all personnel in that area will evacuate to the assembly area. Before leaving the Security Control Center, the telephones will be placed on call forwarding to the office of the Building Manager. The Building Manager and the Security Supervisor will proceed to the Building Manager's office to coordinate management of the incident from that location.

Police Involvement

The initial notice to the police department of a bomb incident will result in a patrol unit being sent to the building. Depending on the nature of the threat, the police will decide what other notifications are appropriate with respect to the fire department, paramedics, and bomb disposal unit. The principal functions of the police will be to:

- Provide guidance to the Building Manager.

- Conduct certain limited searches of areas surrounding a suspect device.

- Dispose of suspect devices.

CANINE SECURITY

Dogs can be utilized to deter and apprehend intruders, protect people and property, and detect items, such as drugs and explosives.

Intruder Deterrence and Apprehension

The attributes of a dog are as follows:

- A dog can pick up human scent over a considerable distance.

- A dog possesses acute hearing, estimated at ten times that of humans, and an ability to detect movement at long range.

- A dog possesses a high-detection capability at night. Where a human will pass close to an intruder without awareness, a dog will react immediately.

- A dog can move faster than a human, thus being able to intercept before an intruder can reach the target or escape.

- A dog can be used to guard or hold an intruder at bay while the dog's handler summons help.

- A dog presents a low moving silhouette that is difficult for an intruder to neutralize.

A dog that is used to detect and deter intrusion will be trained to:

- Patrol quietly on the leash until it picks up human scent, then indicate the presence of an intruder to its handler.

- Chase when slipped from the leash and given the appropriate word of command.

- Stand guard over an intruder until the handler arrives.

- Apprehend a fleeing intruder by seizing him. The dog will be trained to increase teeth pressure if the intruder struggles.

- Defend the handler against an intruder's attack and will attack an intruder while under fire.

Protection of People and Property

A dog that is suitable for protecting people or property is often called an attack dog. This type of dog works on a lead and is trained to attack aggressively on command. An attack dog will seek to incapacitate an individual whose movements indicate aggression against the protected person or property.

Use of attack dogs is limited to areas that are fully enclosed by security fences, such as the domicile of a protected executive or a highly secure industrial facility. Attack dogs are not recommended for use at standard industrial installations.

Detection

A detection dog is specially trained to find prohibited materials, such as explosives or drugs. Because sniffer dogs are highly specialized and require constant training, the Company's preference is to acquire them on a contract basis. Because of the mental concentration involved, sniffer dogs cannot work long hours.

Cautionary Notes

Trained dogs are most effectively used in areas that have

- Few buildings within a fenced perimeter.

- Little or no human traffic.

The larger the area, the greater the saving on labor costs. Large open sites are therefore excellent venues for dog protection.

When necessary, dogs can be used inside fenced areas that are smaller and contain buildings. Where there is human traffic, however, the dogs' effectiveness is reduced by the interference of human scents and sounds. Further, a dog should never be released at will inside such an area. Even in areas where humans are not present, the use of unoccupied dogs running free is prohibited. If the area is sited in open ground, the better alternative is to patrol outside the perimeter.

Dogs can work a maximum of sixteen hours per day. A dog patrol should not exceed three consecutive hours including a rest period. The number of dogs to be used and the area to be covered will depend upon a variety of factors, e.g., prevailing wind direction, obstacles, and buildings. Other considerations include:

- Hydrocarbon products will seriously reduce the effectiveness of dogs to track intruders.

- Dogs must be properly cared for, correctly housed, and properly fed.

- Medical examinations of dogs must be made at frequent intervals.

- A contractor supplying dogs as part of a security service should be required to house dogs off site. Fresh dogs should be brought to the site with each change of shift.

- The contractor must supply written assurance of competence to handle dogs and that the dogs have been trained and are able to perform the required tasks.

- The dogs must have received all relevant inoculations.

- Dogs that are not at work should not be kept on Company premises between shifts or overnight.

- Employees must not be tempted or permitted to pet guard dogs.

- Local Company management must consider the potential reputation damage inherent in the use of guard dogs.

- Care must be taken to ensure compliance with any legislation pertaining to the use of guard dogs.

- The contractor must provide indemnity against harm or damage arising from the use of guard dogs.

CIVIL PROCESS ACCEPTANCE

Civil process means an order of the court, such as a summons to appear at a judicial proceeding or a subpoena to produce certain records. From time to time, persons hired by the court will appear at the lobby security desk wishing to serve civil process on the Company, a Company officer, or an employee.

Actions

The security officer will ask the process server to wait at the security desk until telephone contact is made with one of the following positions:

- Corporate Legal Counsel

- Corporate Security Director

- Property Manager

One of the above-identified individuals will meet with the process server and:

- Accept service on behalf of the Company or Company officer.

- In the case of an employee, ask the employee to meet the process server in the lobby to accept service.

If the civil process relates to employee personnel records or the garnishment of pay, the Human Resources Manager will be contacted to accept service.

Note

The serving of civil process is different than the performance of a warrant. A warrant is an order by a court to a law enforcement officer. When a law enforcement officer appears on Company premises with a warrant (e.g., an arrest warrant or a search warrant), the officer will be asked to meet with one of the above-identified individuals. If the officer refuses and insists on carrying out the warrant without delay or interference, the senior security officer on duty will instruct the security desk officer to inform the Corporate Legal Counsel and Security Director without delay. The senior security officer will accompany the law enforcement officer during the entire process and observe all that takes place. The senior security officer will take notes and prepare an incident report.

CLASSIFICATION OF SENSITIVE INFORMATION

Company policy requires protection of sensitive information consistent with the need to share such information within and outside of the Company. Sensitive information, in any form or medium, must be classified and consequently handled according to established procedures. These Procedures dictate the process of classification.

Three Classes

Sensitive information is grouped into three classes: SECRET, RESTRICTED, and PRIVATE.

SECRET information is defined as information that, if disclosed, would cause serious damage to the interests of the Company. It is information of such high value or sensitivity that it needs to be restricted to a small number of specifically identified individuals. Items that have any of the following characteristics are to be classified SECRET:

- The information relates to a current significant acquisition/divestment project.

- It could affect the price of Company shares.

- It has high political or legal sensitivity.

- It concerns a major reorganization or has a high impact on the workforce.

- The information would be prejudicial to the interests of the Company, or would cause embarrassment or difficulty for the Company or its employees.

RESTRICTED information is defined as information of significant value or sensitivity. Items which have any of the following characteristics are to be classified RESTRICTED:

- Contentious or sensitive items.

- A confidential agreement or contract.

- Other items where the potential loss through unauthorized disclosure is significant.

PRIVATE information is defined as information relating to employees. Examples include any data relating to:

- Salary, bonuses, wages, etc.

- Health and medical treatment.

- Performance.

- Disciplinary actions.

CLEANING CREW ACCESS CONTROL

The Company requires strict monitoring of cleaning crews. The Security Officer's responsibility in this regard is threefold:

- Ensure that members of the cleaning crew are on the access list before they are granted access.

- Monitor the crew during the cleaning.

- Account for all crew members when they leave the facility.

Actions

Greet the cleaners courteously and professionally.

Ask the cleaning crew supervisor to record the names of crew members in the Sign-In Log.

Compare the names against the Cleaning Crew Access List.

Escort the cleaning crew to the areas to be cleaned and remain with the crew during the cleaning.

Open office and conference room doors as needed, but restrict the number of such open doors to two at a time. Ensure that doors are locked when the cleaning is done.

If an office contains sensitive material in plain view (such as a document on top of a desk or a schematic pinned to the wall), call the Security Supervisor so that the material can be placed into protective custody. Sensitive material is any item marked SECRET, RESTRICTED, or CONFIDENTIAL. An Incident Report and an entry in the Daily Log Book are required.

While monitoring the cleaning crew, be alert to attempts at theft, tampering, examination of documents, and any other activity not directly related to cleaning.

Require that collected trash be taken to the dumpster after the cleaning has ended. Monitor the placement of trash into the dumpster. If an item appears to be other than trash, confiscate and hold the item for later examination by an appropriate Company employee.

Do not allow the cleaning crew to take trash, such as computer paper that may have a scrap value.

Ask the Cleaning Crew Supervisor to sign the log-out sheet. Verify that all crew members are accounted for as they leave.

CLEAR DESK

The Company requires that all classified and sensitive materials be adequately protected when unattended. This is best achieved by completely clearing working surfaces of all removable items, where practicable. Working surfaces include desks, credenzas, tops of cabinets, conference room tables and display boards, and walls.

Actions

The following actions should be carried out for any absences of more than a few minutes, unless other trusted employees will be in attendance or a specially secure environment has been provided:

- Classified materials must be securely locked away in appropriate containers. This includes any sensitive items that have not yet been assessed, plus any proprietary third party documents.

- Personal computers and terminals must be switched off and/or protected against unauthorized access, and diskettes/tapes should be securely locked away.

- Flip charts, posters, and wall displays containing classified or sensitive information should be removed, and black/white boards wiped clean.

Alternatively, during brief absences (e.g., lunchtimes), the room may be securely locked and any necessary steps taken to ensure that the information cannot be seen from outside (e.g., curtains closed).

Enforcement

Security officers who patrol the premises will be alert to offices, conference rooms, and working areas that contain classified or sensitive materials in plain view and unattended. When a violation is discovered, the Security Officer will:

- Either secure the area or move the materials in question to a secure location, such as the Security Center.

- Prepare a detailed Incident Report.

- Inform the Security Supervisor.

The Security Supervisor will release the materials to the offending employee's supervisor.

COMPUTER VIRUS PROTECTION

Computer viruses and other malicious software can spread very rapidly between personal computers. They can cause substantial damage to information and sometimes result in severe inconvenience. Use the following guidelines to reduce the risk of problems caused by computer viruses:

Actions

- Make sure that no diskettes are inserted before switching on a PC. This is one of the most common ways to become infected.

- Keep your anti-virus software up-to-date.

- Scan diskettes before they enter or leave your area, whenever possible.

- Back up important information regularly, so that it can be recovered if it becomes damaged by a virus.

- Use only software from a reliable source, and be suspicious of new software.

- Electronic mail messages may include attachments infected by a virus. If the anti-virus software finds a virus in an attachment, don't forward the message to others, even if it says it has been disinfected (because it only clears the temporary copy of the attachment on your PC, not the original stored within the message).

- Write-protect diskettes that you will only need to read information from, before insertion. With 3.5-inch diskettes, this involves sliding a plastic tab in the corner to expose the hole (often coincides with a closed padlock symbol).

- Use a password to protect your PC when unattended. If you receive a strong virus warning from someone external to the Company, call your Security contact so that it can be checked.

- If you suspect your computer may have been infected by a virus:

  - Don't panic.

  - Don't try to fix the problem yourself. You could make things worse. Unless your anti-virus software reports that it has successfully repaired an infected file, stop using your computer but leave it switched on, and call for help.

- Isolate any diskettes that have been used recently.

- Inform the people working around you that there may be a problem.

CONFERENCE SECURITY

These Procedures provide direction on protective measures at Company-sponsored conferences and meetings. The primary focus of protection is upon Company employees and other participants. The secondary focus is upon protection of the company's information and property.

The protective measures applied should reflect a careful assessment of the participants and the risks presented. A pre-conference survey is the appropriate modality for making an assessment. Factors to be considered include:

- The number of participants.

- The individual rankings of participants within the Company so that personal protections can be applied differentially, e.g., greater protection for the Chairman of the Board than for a line manager.

- The conference site and surrounding areas in terms of crime and safety risks.

Next to be considered are the degree of sensitivity of the information to be presented and the value of the equipment to be assembled. The assessment should match the protected assets (i.e., people, information, and property) against their respective vulnerabilities. Consider these examples:

- A senior executive who enjoys an evening jog may be exposed to crime risk to a greater degree than other participants.

- Sensitive information that is planned to be presented orally will be vulnerable to electronic eavesdropping, thereby requiring that eavesdropping countermeasures be applied.

- If expensive laptops are to be used at the conference, they will require special protection when not in use.

Security Coordinator

When security threats are foreseen for an upcoming conference, a Security Coordinator should be appointed early in the planning stage. This individual should:

- Be sufficiently senior to exercise authority.

- Have administrative and executive ability.

- Have a sound working knowledge of protective security.

The administration of a conference is usually directed by an executive secretary. In that role, he or she is called the Conference Organizer. The Security Coordinator is responsible to the Conference Organizer for the provision of security services. For smaller and/or less sensitive conferences in relatively secure locales, the Security Coordinator tasks can be handled by the Conference Organizer.

Conference Location

A high level of security can best be provided in a building which is free-standing in its own grounds with a well-defined perimeter. However, the choice of sites is likely to be limited and preferences should be given to holding the conference in a suitably equipped hotel or conference center where an in-house security professional is available to assist with the arrangements.

Planning

The following points should be considered in the planning of a conference:

- The participants, support staff, and presenters.

- The sensitivity levels of the information.

- The formats in which the information will be presented, e.g., oral presentations with and without microphones, handouts, flip charts, slides, and transparencies.

- The venues in which the information will be presented, e.g., auditorium, conference rooms, breakout rooms, hospitality suites, banquet halls, coffee bars, and restaurants.

- The equipment to be assembled, e.g., laptops, desktop computers, fax machines, printers, copiers, and telephones. Consider both the value of the equipment and the value of the data that will be processed.

In light of the above factors, the Security Coordinator will:

- Assess the threat, e.g., host government intelligence agency, industry competitor, terrorist group, protest group, and common criminals. Confer with local authorities.

- Assess security measures already in place at the conference site, e.g., in-house security officer force, control of vehicles and parking, control of access, alarm systems, and security containers for participants' papers/laptops.

- Assess the recent history of crime or disorder at or nearby the conference site, e.g., confer with the conference site's security manager, confer with local police, and confer with industry peers who have previously used the conference site.

- Determine the locations and availability of emergency response services, such as the in-house security service, police, fire, ambulance, and hospital.

- Coordinate with the company's press or public affairs office if demonstrations at the conference site are anticipated.

Access Control

The number of entrances to the conference venue should be kept to a minimum, without compromising emergency fire exits.

The Security Coordinator should decide which are to be secure areas, i.e., those parts of the conference building to which only participants and conference staff should have access. Strong consideration should be given either to issuing passes for access where this is practicable, or to having the Security Coordinator or other member of the conference team monitor access on the basis of personal recognition.

The Security Coordinator is required to control access to the conference room during the conference and after hours. In this regard, he or she should obtain and hold keys, guard papers and briefcases left in the room during short breaks, supervise maintenance and cleaning staff, and respond to any emergency.

Security of Information

When highly sensitive information is to be discussed, a physical and technical search of the conference room should be made before the conference begins and at the beginning of each day. Once such a search has been completed, the room should be kept sterile, i.e., locked or monitored physically until the conference begins. All telephones should be disconnected and preferably removed from the room.

Document security is the responsibility of each individual participant. However, the Security Coordinator is responsible for ensuring that no documents have been left behind at the end of the day.

All typing, collation, and reproduction of sensitive documents should be done in the administration area.

The appropriate type of shredding machine should be available for disposal of classified waste.

Security containers should be provided in the administration area so that sensitive documents, laptops, and other valuables can be stored overnight. The Security Coordinator should hold the keys and ensure that combinations are reset to the maker's number at the conclusion of the conference.

Security Guidance to Participants

Brief written instructions should be provided to the participants at the outset of the conference. Points for inclusion could be:

- Name of the Security Coordinator, location, and telephone numbers.

- Details of access control, and passes if used, with procedures for the reception of visitors.

- Document security rules, availability of storage space for papers and laptops, and disposal of classified waste.

- Room security and arrangements for handling door keys.

- Reference to notices for action to be taken in case of danger, such as fire and bomb threat.

- Advice on local conditions, likely demonstrations, and crime areas to be avoided.

- Advice on transport for participants in the event of a situation requiring quick departure.

- A reminder that security is everyone's responsibility.

Please see Advice to Conference Participants which appears at the conclusion of these Procedures.

Travel

All major conferences should have the facility of immediate transport, such as a hotel car, a 24-hour taxi service, a taxi rank outside the premises, or a dedicated car and driver. It is always useful to have backup transport to ensure that participants will not be delayed.

Communications

Effective communications are essential between the various bodies involved in ensuring the security of the conference. Mobiles or dedicated common-link radios should be provided.

Post-Conference

After the conference, a meeting should be held to discuss the effectiveness of security at the conference. A record of the security measures applied, together with any lessons learned, should be placed on file for use as a guide for later conferences.

Advice to Conference Participants

To ensure the protection of yourself, your valuables, and the Company's sensitive information, please take the following precautions.

- Protect sensitive information in accord with the Company's Security of Information Policy. A copy of the policy is available at the Company's administrative office located near the main conference room.

- Utilize the hotel-provided safe deposit boxes for your personal valuables. Sensitive materials are to be stored at the administrative office.

- Leave at the administrative office any hard copy sensitive materials that need to be destroyed.

- Your conversations outside of the conference room and other meeting rooms should not include sensitive information.

- Report the loss of a room key immediately.

- When you check out, ensure that you have not left behind sensitive materials.

- Keep your room locked while you are in it, and identify visitors before opening the door.

- Familiarize yourself with the fire evacuation routes that pertain to your room, the conference and meeting rooms, dining room, and other facilities at the hotel.

- Medical, fire, and police emergency services can be summoned by calling the hotel operator.

- For security-related assistance, contact the conference security coordinator in person or call him or her through the hotel operator.

DRIVING SAFEGUARDS

These Procedures are intended to guide employees who drive automobiles in the course of their duties.

Protecting Against Hijacking

- Drive with your windows closed and your doors locked do not open them if you are approached by someone while stopped.

- If your car is bumped from behind by another vehicle, evaluate the situation before getting out of your car. The bump may be a prelude to a hijacking, robbery, or assault.

- If you are attacked, drive away if it is possible to do so. If driving away is not an option, switch on your hazard lights and press your horn to call for help or attract attention that may frighten away the attacker(s). If you have a cellular phone, use it to call for help.

- Request identification from police and traffic officers at unusual roadblocks before opening your window or door.

- Avoid driving alone at night or stopping in deserted areas.

- Front gates and driveways are high-risk areas. Before turning into a driveway, look for anyone who might be lurking to attack, when you get out of the vehicle.

- Report unfamiliar, occupied cars parked in your neighborhood for long periods.

- Protecting your life is your first priority. If while in your car you fall under the control of a criminal, you may be able to avoid being assaulted by cooperating. However, resist to the greatest degree possible any demand that you drive or accompany the criminal to another location. The criminal's intent may be to transport you there in order to murder or assault you or hold you for ransom.

- If the criminal makes clear an intent to steal your vehicle, cooperate fully. Mentally accept the loss of the vehicle and its material content.

- Consider that a criminal who approaches you in your vehicle is likely to be dangerously nervous and/or under the influence of a drug. Therefore, make no hasty movements, react as calmly as possible, display your agreement to give up your car. Keep your hands in sight. If you have passengers, tell them to cooperate.

- If you have to get out of your vehicle, do so slowly and calmly. Leave the car keys in the ignition. If wearing a seat belt, make sure you are in full view of the criminal before seeking to undo the belt, and state loudly what you are about to do.

- Avoid eye contact with the criminal. He or she may think you are storing details for later use in providing suspect identification details to the police.

- Do not talk unless the criminal demands it. Do not reveal your anger. Do nothing to antagonize.

- Walk away quietly from the vehicle, facing the criminal but with eyes averted.

- If your vehicle is equipped with a kill switch that can be operated remotely, wait until the criminal has departed before you activate the switch.

- Develop a set of personal habits designed to keep from becoming a victim. For example:

  - Watch out for suspicious people before you leave or approach your car.

  - Make sure that no one is hiding in your car before you get in.

  - Drive with locked doors and ensure that windows are either fully or very nearly closed.

  - Avoid using the same roads routinely and avoid isolated roads.

  - Keep your car keys and house keys separate.

  - Do not pick up hitchhikers.

  - Be extra vigilant when sitting in a stationary vehicle.

  - Always lock your car when parked.

  - Always carry an identity document with you.

  - Never leave firearms in your car.

  - Always wear a seat belt.

  - Never let the gasoline tank get below quarter full.

Protecting Yourself While Driving

- Make sure that someone knows the time you left, the route taken, and your expected time of arrival.

- Keep a map in your car, mark the high crime areas, and use the safest travel routes. Drive on well lit, open, and busy streets. The chances are low of being victimized on streets where people can easily see each other's movements.

- If you are a woman driving without an adult companion, keep your purse out of sight. Park in attended lots or other areas that are well lit or close to people who can provide assistance if you are accosted. Take a good look around before you unlock the door to get out. When returning, look for people who may be following you or waiting near your parked car.

- If someone is following your car or threatening you, don't be afraid to make a scene. Blow your horn in short blasts, and turn the headlights on and off. Drive to a police station, a fire station, a hospital, or any all-night business where people are present. Don't feel embarrassed by calling attention to yourself. This is the best way to frighten off someone who intends to do you harm.

- Never agree to give a stranger a ride.

- If you have a flat tire in an area you regard unsafe, drive slowly until you find a safe place to stop.

- When approaching a traffic light, observe the situation carefully before stopping. If the scene looks suspicious, treat the traffic light as a yield sign, especially at night. In some high-risk countries it is customary not to stop at red traffic lights at night for security reasons.

- When stopping behind another vehicle leave enough room to enable you to pull out and around. This technique will keep you from being trapped by front and rear vehicles.

- Remain fully aware of the situation around you at all times. Be aware of the vehicles around you, especially motorcycles, and be prepared to avoid driving into risky situations.

Parking Tips

- Never leave the key in the ignition when leaving your car, even if it is only a minute or two.

- Always park your vehicle in a well-lit secure area, especially if you are visiting a restaurant, shopping center, or sporting facility.

- Reverse into parking spaces so that you can leave quickly if required.

- Activate your steering lock when parked.

- Place all valuables out of sight. If possible, remove your car radio and carry it with you. Lock it in the trunk if this can be done.

- Never leave children or pets locked in a parked car it could mean never seeing them again.

- Do not make things easier for the thief by leaving the vehicle's documents in your glove compartment.

- If parking your car in a high-risk area, do not transfer your valuables to the trunk in open view. You might be under observation by an opportunistic thief.

- Make sure that all doors are locked and that windows and sun roof are completely closed before leaving your vehicle.

- Have your keys ready to open the door when returning to your vehicle.

- When parking your vehicle in a parking garage, always take the ticket with you.

In the Event of an Accident

In some countries, if you encounter someone in the street who is apparently hurt, you should not stop to help the victim but drive straight to the nearest police station and report the incident. Hostile mobs can gather very quickly and drivers should be alert to any such situations developing.

If you are at all unfamiliar with the local conditions and laws concerning traffic accidents, it is better to employ a local driver who can act as an intermediary in the event of an incident.

When Car Trouble Strikes

If your car breaks down in an area where you cannot safely get help, pull off the road far enough that you won't be hit by a passing car but close enough that you can still be easily seen from the roadway. Turn on your emergency flashers, raise the hood, and tie a white towel or handkerchief to your radio aerial or door. Better still, be prepared by keeping in your car a light-reflecting sign that says "Send Help" or a similar message. The next step is to wait until help arrives. Eventually a passing motorist will call the police.

If a motorist stops, roll down your window just far enough to ask for help. Don't get out of the car or unlock the doors. Under no circumstances should you accept a ride with the motorist. Really helpful people will understand your caution and will gladly arrange to send help to you.

By the same token, if it is someone else who needs highway assistance, there is no need for you to stop on the roadway. Simply get to a phone and call the police.

Common Auto Theft

It is a sad truth that the car thief's best friend is the car owner. This is because many of the cars stolen each year are left unlocked, frequently with a key in the ignition. Like most crimes, auto theft is a crime of opportunity. The best way to prevent your car from being stolen is to reduce the criminal's opportunity. There is very little you can do about the criminal's desire to steal, but you can do a great deal to keep that desire from being acted upon.

An owner of an older car might be careless, believing the car is not a particularly attractive target. It may be true that professional car thieves will seek to steal new, expensive cars, but the majority of car thefts are committed by amateurs who are looking for opportunities to "joy ride" or to get from one place to another at someone else's expense. The amateur thief operates not from choice but from chance.

The professional car thief will have little difficulty in opening a locked car, but will avoid cars that have special security features. Extra protection can be provided by a security alarm, special switches that disconnect the ignition or carburetor, and deterrents such as warning decals and identification numbers etched in the glass. Also available are electronic anti-theft devices that notify the owner and/or the police when the vehicle has been turned on. Supplemental devices include global positioning systems that allow the vehicle's movement to be tracked, a mechanism that shuts down the engine, and doors that lock, trapping the thief inside.

CB radios, portable tape decks, and other valuable items visible from outside the car are tempting targets. If your car is to be unattended in a public location for any period of time, such items should be put away or stored in the trunk. The components of your car are also vulnerable to strip thieves who are skilled at dismantling a car without even moving it. All they need is time and relative privacy. You can counter this risk by parking your car in safe locations.

DURESS ALARM

Background

Duress alarms are in place at a variety of locations on Company premises, e.g., the receptionist's desk on the executive floor, the credit union teller's station in the lobby, and the operator's desk at the computer center.

Also positioned at these locations are CCTV cameras that automatically go into the record mode when the duress button has been pressed.

The duress alarm button at each location has been positioned to minimize accidental activation.

Alarm Activation

Upon receipt of a duress alarm, the console operator will look at the CCTV monitor to learn the nature of the emergency. If the emergency is of a nonviolent nature, such as an injury or sudden illness, the console operator will:

- Use the base station radio to dispatch the roving patrol to the incident location and provide details as to the nature of the emergency.

- Call 911 to ask for an ambulance, if appropriate.

If the emergency is of a violent nature, such as a robbery in progress at the credit union, the response will be to take no action that could cause an escalation of violence. The console operator will:

- Call 911 to ask for police assistance.

- NOT dispatch the roving patrol.

- Continue to watch the CCTV monitor and respond appropriately ,e.g., relay further details to the police, such as descriptions of the offender, the offender's vehicle, direction of travel from the scene, or make a request for an ambulance if injuries occurred.

An activation of a duress alarm will in every case require a Daily Log entry and an Incident Report.

Preparedness

The Security Supervisor will at a frequency of once every 6 months provide one-on-one tutorials to the employees who work at duress-alarmed locations. The training will cover the circumstances when alarms are to be activated and the actions the employee should take in situations where activation is appropriate. Duress alarm drills will also be conducted.

ELECTRONIC INFORMATION SECURITY

Electronic information and associated storage, processing, and networking systems are assets of high vulnerability which require active management. The growth and general use of electronic systems capable of accessing large quantities of information make EIS a significant responsibility for all employees. These Procedures have been written to help all personnel develop and maintain a cost-effective security environment for safeguarding Company electronic information, hardware, and software assets.

Application

EIS Standards reflect prudent business practices which are accepted as minimum baseline controls within the Company. They are applied in a manner commensurate with the value of the asset being protected.

EIS Standards will be adhered to by all users of Company Electronic Information and Electronic System Assets world wide. This includes, but is not limited to, Company and subsidiary employees, contractors, agents, and trading partners. Comparable standards will be in place within our controlled affiliated companies.

Definitions

For the purposes of these Procedures, the Electronic System Assets of the Company include but are not limited to all computers, workstations and terminals, all telecommunications systems, networks and their servers, and all peripherals and supporting facilities and equipment which are owned, leased, rented, on loan, being tested, or temporarily left on our premises by a third party.

Furthermore, for the purposes of these Standards, the Electronic Information Assets of the Company include all information stored, processed, or transmitted in an electronic form through Electronic System Assets. This will include, but is not limited to data, text, graphic, image, video, and voice/audio information.

Electronic information processing capabilities are associated with all aspects of our business. As the hardware, software, electronic information and network connections move into the business and staff functions, the responsibility for protecting and managing those assets moves with it.

Specific Responsibilities

Corporate EIS Manager
- Maintain high-level expertise in electronic information systems technology and serve as an information resource for function EIS Coordinators.

- Assist in educating senior line management on EIS responsibilities and alternatives.

- Maintain liaison with Auditing and the Corporate Security Director's office.

- Prepare an annual report that summarizes the status of security implementation in the Company and provides recommendations for improvement.

- Chair the Corporate EIS Policy Committee.

EIS Policy Committee

- Act as a collective resource to assist in resolving electronic information security issues.

- Update EIS Standards to remain current with business needs and available technology.

Business and Staff Management

- Protecting their electronic assets based on the guidance in this document. If the Business or Staff Function management determines there is sufficient justification requiring a variance to any specific action, the situation and reasoning behind the decision should be documented.

- Developing and executing written security practices and procedures deemed necessary for local control. These practices and procedures will be based upon EIS Standards and must provide for security levels at least equal to those found within these Standards. These practices and procedures will be available for audit.

- Designating an individual with appropriate skills to coordinate electronic information security activities within the business or staff function. This person will be known as an EIS Coordinator.

EIS Coordinator

- Be the focal point for all EIS subjects within the business or staff function.

- Take a leadership role in providing guidance for global security issues (e.g., network security, encryption, security Standards).

- Establish expertise in EIS matters.

- Help line management promote the value and awareness of EIS Standards. Take a leadership role in the preparation of local electronic security practices and procedures.

- Develop communications channels to elevate general employee awareness of EIS Standards and local practices and procedures within the business or staff function.

- Work with line management to promptly resolve EIS concerns. An example may be resolving recommendations reported by Auditing.

- Coordinate business security issues with all security-related organizations impacting the business function, such as Auditing, Legal, Facilities Management, Records Retention, Internal Control, and Management Information Systems.

- Develop and implement an activity/incident reporting mechanism that will facilitate the timely distribution of Corporate EIS information throughout business units and speed the flow of local information to the Corporate EIS group for possible Corporate-wide distribution.

- Help to develop appropriate metrics to gauge the business unit's improvement in EIS Standards implementation.

- Identify and report needed changes to EIS Standards.

- Participate in EIS Coordinator meetings and activities.

The major objective of electronic information security is to apply cost-effective controls commensurate with the asset at risk, in order to ensure the integrity, confidentiality, and availability of information. To achieve this objective, Standards will be established to govern access to electronic information. The effectiveness of access Standards depends on the correct identification of specific individuals who are the owners, custodians and users of electronic information. As with any Company asset, and to the extent permitted by law, Company management reserves the right to inspect its assets.

Where appropriate, the asset's integrity and security may be delegated to a custodian. The owner and custodian of electronic information and associated processing, storage, and transmission facilities will be uniquely identified and documented. All owners, custodians, and users of Company electronic information will abide by the Standards and responsibilities

The term "owner" is a convention used within these Standards to identify an individual who has management responsibility for acquiring and controlling the use and disposition of an electronic information resource. The term "owner" does not mean that the person actually has any property rights to the asset. For control purposes, ownership may reside with a workgroup leader.

Owner

- Assess the business value of the electronic information.

- Perform a yearly risk assessment and classification for loss of the electronic information and associated applications.

- Determine appropriate electronic information retention assessment.

- Evaluate the cost-effectiveness of security controls.

- Authorize access to and assign custodianship for the electronic information.

- Specify controls for use and communicate the control requirements to users and custodian.

- Document and gain line management approval for justification when business reasons override the use of Standards control.

A custodian is the individual who maintains operational custody of the electronic information, application software, and/or system hardware assets, as needed and specified by the owner.

Custodian

- Implement the controls specified by the owner of electronic information.

- Provide physical and procedural safeguards for the storage, transfer, backup and disaster recovery of electronic information.

- Manage and enforce physical and electronic access control Standards.

- Assist users in understanding and using available controls.

- Add and delete users in a timely fashion when instructed by owner.

Any person who reads, enters, updates, sends, or prints electronic information using a computerized system is a user of that information. Users must have an informational "need-to-know" and be must authorized by the owner of the information.

User

- Use the electronic information prudently for the business purposes specified by its owner and in accordance with Company policy and practice.

- Comply with all controls established by its owner and custodian.

- Prevent unauthorized disclosure compliant with the information's classification.

Exposure Classification

The cost of security measures should not exceed the loss they are designed to prevent. Determination of this cost-benefit relationship will be done in association with the following Exposure Classification Standards.

All electronic information will be classified following the designations of "Confidential—Special Control," "Confidential," "For Internal Use Only," or "Public." Furthermore, labeling will be such that users of information classified as "Confidential-Special Control," "Confidential," and "Public" will be able to implement appropriate handling and storage procedures. Documents not showing any designation will be treated as "For Internal Use Only."

Confidential—Special Control

Information of the highest sensitivity that, if revealed, could cause irreparable harm to the Company, its image, or financial stability. Access to such information will be strictly limited and controlled at all times. Examples include earnings reports, sales forecasts, selected research and process information, and business strategies and tactics.

Confidential

Information of high sensitivity because of its timeliness, possible financial impact, or personnel-related content. Such information should be revealed only on a need-to-know basis. Examples include business objectives, planned advertising programs, technical information, and personnel matters such as proposed organizational changes or individual employee benefit plans.

For Internal Use Only

Information that has not been classified "Confidential-Special Control," "Confidential," or "Public." Information not showing any designation will fall under this classification. Examples include Company telephone directories and technical information for use by sales representatives.

Information that willfully has been selected and properly approved or that has been mandated by law, for dissemination to all employees or the public at large (e.g., material safety data sheets or product advertising). Such selection must not be in conflict with other existing information classification policy or guidelines.

Whenever practical, electronic information should be classified when being defined (e.g., during the system development process) or when being created or acquired.

Information recorded in several formats (e.g., source document, electronic record, report) should have the same information classification regardless of storage or output media.

Electronic information should be examined at the file, document, or element level to determine the impact on the Company if the information were disclosed or altered by unauthorized means. General areas of exposure are:

- Information that gives the Company a leading edge over its competitors (e.g., marketing strategies, manufacturing process information, financial information, names and addresses of customers, traders' positions, and most computer programs written for the Company's business).

- Information that provides access control (e.g., passwords, encryption keys).

- Information protected by current or possible future privacy legislation (e.g., credit or health information, customer account information).

- Information that is of unusual interest to employees, such as salary or performance information.

Applications dealing with "Confidential-Special Control" and "Confidential" should be written to inform the user of its information classification both on screen and on hard-copy output.

Management of Electronic Information

Within our information management programs, the term "Record" encompasses all information in any physical form, including written documents, printed matter, microforms, computer information, and reproductions of any kind, created or procured for business purposes relating to the Company, its subsidiaries and affiliates, domestic and foreign. Proper adherence to record/information management, when dealing with electronic information, is necessary to maintain uniform business practice.

Electronic Information Retention

All personnel will be individually responsible for the management of Company information. Such management will include retention and/or destruction of electronic information in compliance with corporate information asset management program requirements.

The following apply:

- Backup media containing Electronic Mail records will be retained for no longer than 90 days. At the end of its retention period, the media will be erased before being made available for reuse.

- All electronic information has an owner.

- It is the responsibility of the owner of an electronic document to properly label that information in accordance with Corporate Records Management guidelines.

- Destruction and/or retention of electronic information in abidance with Record Management guidelines is the responsibility of the owner.

Electronic Information Access Control

Electronic information, computational assets, and associated telecommunications networks will be adequately protected against unauthorized access, modification, disclosure, or destruction. Intelligent use of access controls prevents inadvertent employee error and negligence and reduces the possibility of computer crime.

Each access to Company-owned electronic information will pass through a security control function that provides individual accountability and auditability, whether the access is direct, by dedicated line or dial-in circuit. Each user will be uniquely and authentically identified to the networks, computer systems or electronic information assets being accessed. This does not, however, apply to the reading of electronic information classified as "Public."

Read access to Company-owned "Public" electronic information will not require individual accountability in those instances where controls to limit access to any and all other electronic information, hardware, or network assets have been demonstrated.

User access activity records, commensurate with the value of the information being accessed, will be produced. At a minimum, such records will include all hardware access attempts, and upon user authorization, the user's identity as well as the date and time of use.

Anomaly and exception reports should be monitored periodically at a rate commensurate with the value of the asset at risk. These activity records will be stored securely.

The following guidance will apply:

- Ideally, an individual's user ID will be the same on all Company systems.

- User IDs and system node names are generally "For Internal Use Only" and should be appropriately handled. While it is recognized that this information is sometimes shared with specific trading and research partners, it is inappropriate to include user IDs and/or system node names on business cards.

- User IDs dormant or not utilized for a period in excess of 6 months should be deactivated or removed from a system.

- A procedure should be in place to ensure that the user's access to a system is removed from the system when an employee is terminated or transfers to a position where access to the system is no longer required. In high-risk situations, the removal should be immediate.

- Some access control systems allow users to be restricted by time-of-day and day-of-week. This type of control should be used judiciously so as not to impede legitimate emergency access.

Password Control

Passwords are confidential. It is the responsibility of the user to prevent their disclosure. A user's password may only be divulged, when necessary, to appropriate security personnel. Although discouraged, where justified by business needs, a user's password may be shared with another user for purposes of effective electronic mail usage; however, the user continues to bear responsibility for the use of the account. Passwords will have a minimum length of six characters and will contain at least one alpha and one numeric character if the access control facility permits. Every password will be changed at least once every three months. Privileged accounts should change passwords every month or more frequently.

In addition:

- Passwords will not be incorporated, directly or indirectly, in pre-coded computer access routines (script files).

- Passwords will be entered in a nondisplayed field.

- Passwords will not be printed on hard-copy output.

- Passwords stored in a computer or transmitted using telecommunications services will be encrypted wherever technologically possible.

- When permitted by the technology in use, privileged accounts should use passwords of 8 or more characters.

- Should it be felt or known that a password has been divulged or otherwise discovered, the user shall immediately change the password.

- User-chosen passwords should not be easily guessed.

- Obvious words and personal information (names, dates, etc.) should be avoided.

- System software should force users to change their passwords. When possible, the user should be prevented from choosing a password that had previously been used within the past 12 months or is known to be commonly used.

- Passwords not selected by the users should be distributed in "Confidential" envelopes.

System Access Control

System software will disable a user's account for a minimum of one day following five consecutive unsuccessful access attempts. The account may be enabled at any time following confirmation that the user was the person causing the unsuccessful access attempts.

These rules apply:

- Where technologically possible, at log-in time, the system software should display the last time the user logged on successfully and unsuccessfully. When checked by the user at log-in, it will assist in determining if there has been an attempt to compromise the user's account.

- System software to "secure" unattended terminals and/or workstations will be employed wherever technologically possible.

- If the available software is inadequate in controlling access to the electronic information within the computer, access to the entire computer system will be restricted to those with authority to access all the electronic information within the computer.

In mainframe-based production environments, and wherever else possible, particular care should be exercised to ensure that no one person has total control. System operators, for instance, should not have unlimited access to "Super-Passwords." Such passwords are only needed in an emergency and will be carefully controlled. Strict monitoring and documentation of the use of privileged passwords are mandatory.

Test and Development Environments

A "test/development environment" will be kept, either physically or logically (ideally both), separate from a production environment.

No developmental changes to a production system wlll be initiated unless it has been requested by the owner, authorized by management, and fully documented.

The implementing guidance is:

- Use of product information in testing/development should only occur to resolve emergencies. Such access should be documented. Acceptance tests are considered production work and, therefore, will be run by production personnel.

- Copies of production electronic information should not be used for normal testing unless such use is authorized by the information's owner. Test electronic information should not be traceable to a real individual or real corporation. Company Confidential electronic information should not be used for testing purposes.

- A naming standard should be in effect to distinguish between test/development jobs and production jobs and between test electronic information sets and production electronic information sets.

- Update access to production program libraries must be restricted to specifically authorized individuals.

Office and Laboratory Automation

When individual workstations or personal computers store "Confidential-Special Control" or "Confidential" electronic information on nonremovable storage, appropriate physical and software security controls will be applied to protect such information and prevent unauthorized access.

- The use of software "hard-disk locks" is recommended for all workstations or personal computers.

- The use of anti-viral software scanning and detection procedures is recommended for all workstations or personal computers.

- The use of automatic "screen blanking" and keyboard locking software is recommended for all workstations or personal computers.

- In vulnerable situations, encryption is recommended for "Confidential-Special Control" or "Confidential" stored information. This provides a degree of protection not dependent on physical security.

Nonemployee Access Control

Each request for direct access to Company-owned networks, computer systems, software, and data by nonemployees should be carefully evaluated. Related exposures and risks for the Company will be weighted against business advantages and benefits.

Whenever possible, third party Value Added Network (VAN) services should be preferentially evaluated for use before direct connection requests are made to Company Computational, Network, and Information assets. This is particularly true in the area of electronic and voice mail. Third party services often offer us increased security, broader communication options, and lower costs.

If access is granted, it must be limited to a certain application or task within a confined environment. This means that nonemployee users will have no method of access to system commands, Company-owned information, or network facilities to which they have not specifically been granted access.

Contractors, customers, or other nonemployees of the Company (e.g., consultants, research collaborators, sponsored customers, and vendors) will sign a contract establishing the intended relationship between the nonemployee and the Company prior to accessing or reviewing any Company information, or using any of the Company's processing, storage, or networking facilities. The contract should specify the requirements and conditions for electronic information access and specific computer usage. Confidentiality and nondisclosure agreements also will be signed.

The Company employee responsible for the activities of the nonemployee users will be defined for EIS purposes as the "sponsor."

The sponsor or the sponsoring organization will assess and document the risks associated with granting access and will limit access on a "need-to-know, need-to-use" basis. The risk assessment will include:

- Evaluation of nonemployees and their employers to determine potential exposures based on competitive considerations. Questions should be asked; e.g., has the nonemployee been properly screened? Does the employing firm perform services for competitors?

- Determination of the technological, emotional, environmental, and monetary impact of the disclosure of the authorized Company proprietary information.

The sponsor or the sponsoring organization will ensure that nonemployees understand the Company's security standards and procedures applicable to them.

All nonemployee access authorization documentation will be retained by the sponsor and will be available for audit review.

Hardware and Software Usage and Ownership

The hardware facilities and associated operating systems to process, store, transmit, display, and print electronic information are valuable corporate assets. The unauthorized use of these assets represents a violation of policy subjecting the employee to disciplinary action.

Use of Company Computers and Networks

All computer, network, office automation, laboratory automation, and process control equipment leased or owned by the Company and all computing and communications services billed to the Company will be used only for the purpose of conducting Company business. Specific management authorization is required for any other intended uses.

Software Ownership

All computer software developed within the scope of Company employment is property of the Company. All software developed by third parties must be specifically assigned to the Company in writing in order for the Company to have title to it. All programs for which the Company has title will include a copyright statement to be displayed in an obvious location upon inspection or execution of the program code.

Programs and program documentation owned by the Company should be copyrighted with a display of those rights clearly visible.

Changes to applications will be reviewed by the application owner for appropriate copyright and patent actions (including infringement studies).

Contracts for programming and consulting work by outside personnel will clearly spell out the ownership, the current and future use of the software, and the contained technology.

Programs written by employees in the performance of their job belong to the Company and may not be distributed to outsiders unless permitted in writing by an authorized supervisor.

Use of Software

Only licensed or otherwise authorized software will be used on Company hardware. Software license agreements provided by vendors clearly define the limits of use. Employees are strictly forbidden to copy or use such software in a manner contrary to the provision of the license agreement. Violation of the license agreement is prohibited.

- Keep original software, manuals, and license agreements as they constitute generally accepted proof-of-purchase.

- Products purchased/leased/borrowed to run on a specific processing hardware, or at a particular site, may not be copied and run on additional processors until/unless an agreement is obtained in writing from the vendor that provides such usage.

- Personal computer software products may not be copied except as provided by the vendor's license or contract agreement (i.e., a backup copy for protection).

- Special care should be taken in multi-user LAN environments to ensure that an adequate number of licenses have been obtained to support the user population.

Electronic Information Security Incidents

All actual and attempted computer security incidents (e.g., computer viruses, computer fraud, hacker symptoms, system or account abuse) will be immediately investigated by local line management with findings forwarded to the EIS Coordinator. If the incident warrants, the Helpline management will assemble a working investigation team unique to the problem at hand and will communicate with Regional and Corporate EIS, Auditing, and the Director of Security, as necessary.

The team will have the authority and responsibility to:

- Contain the security incident.

- Document the sequence of events.

- Document symptoms.

- Determine the extent of the exposure (business and technical).

- Build a recovery/action plan based upon the facts.

- Determine how to avoid similar future security incident.

- Communicate findings to senior management, Corporate EIS, and the Director of Security whenever appropriate, for action and future reference.

Networks and Telecommunications

Networked hardware systems are more vulnerable to unauthorized usage than stand-alone computational devices. Owners of computers and networks that are interconnected to other Company networks will operate them in a manner that will preserve the security and integrity of stored electronic information and other system assets on all Company networks. The Company's information and system assets are best protected by ensuring that all network entry points have an adequate and common level of security protection to prevent unauthorized access.

Remote Network Access

Networks will employ protective measures to prevent unauthorized access. Any remote dial-in data access to Company-owned facilities will be authenticated by a system that meets the criteria for protected access point, or will require token-based authentication. (A protected access point is one that requires each user to pass through a security control function that provides individual accountability and auditability whether the access is direct, by dedicated line, or by dial-in circuit.)

Dial-in port telephone numbers and system node names are considered "For Internal Use Only." Individuals are accountable for keeping access methods to Company information confidential.

Network hardware devices such as multiplexers, and cluster controllers should not be configured for dial-in since there is no way to detect when someone dials in.

The company employee responsible for the activities of the nonemployee users will be defined for EIS purposes as the "sponsor."

- The sponsor or the sponsoring organization will assess and document the risks associated with granting access and will limit access on a "need-to-know, need-to-use" basis. The risk assessment will include:

- Evaluation of nonemployees and/or their firm to determine potential exposures based on competitive considerations. For example, is the firm a competitor and who are the firm's clients, present and future?

- Determination of the technological, emotional, environmental, and monetary impact of the disclosure of the authorized Company proprietary information.

- Ability to limit access to authorized applications.

- The sponsor or the sponsoring organization will ensure that nonemployees understand the Company's security standards and procedures applicable to them.

- All nonemployee access authorization documentation will be retained by the sponsor and will be available for audit review.

- All default login IDs and passwords should be removed from PBX maintenance ports. Passwords will be changed every 3 months or following personnel changes. (EIS password requirements must be followed.)

- Be aware that PBXs typically have multiple remote maintenance ports.

- Dial-in access to dial-out ports is prohibited unless an access control facility that uniquely identifies and authorizes the user is in use.

- Direct inward station access (DISA) should be removed from all systems.

- Network management and configuration devices accessed through dial-in console ports will be carefully monitored and controlled.

- Hardware and software vendors dialing in for maintenance and diagnostics should be carefully monitored and controlled. Passwords should be assigned only for the duration of the task and changed afterwards. Vendor activity should be logged and reviewed after each maintenance session.

- Appropriate techniques and products for dial-in access control include random password generators or "tokens" combined with PINs or passwords and biometric devices.

- The business or staff function network and telecommunications groups should maintain an up-to-date inventory of their participating network nodes, interconnections, and network access controls. This applies to both LANs and WANs. This information will be useful to their installation of uniform and appropriate access control technologies.

Warning of Penalties for Unauthorized Use

Prior to network or computer log-on, an EIS-approved warning banner stating the penalties for unauthorized asset usage will be displayed clearly.

The following also apply:

- The warning banner should be presented before a sign-on occurs.

- The system should not be identified as belonging to the Company before a successful sign-on.

- Node names are considered "For Internal Use Only" and will not be displayed prior to successful sign-on.

- HELP information should be limited to that necessary to facilitate those authorized for system sign-on.

- No HELP information following a failed sign-on attempt will be provided.

Connection to Non-Company-Owned Networks

Physical interconnections between Company-owned and non-Company networks will be established only with the knowledge and authorization of the Corporate Networking organization.

The use of network management/monitoring software and hardware will be limited to those individuals specifically authorized by business or staff function information systems management, and only upon demonstrated "need-to-know."

Voice-Based Electronic Information Systems

Voice-based electronic information systems containing Company electronic information will employ the same level of information access control described within these Standards. Telephone answering machines without access controls should only be used to store or forward "Public" or non-Company-owned information.

Electronic Information Encryption

Encryption will be used to protect "Confidential-Special Control" electronic information when transmitted over a network or telecommunications service. Passwords, identification codes, and dial-in terminal identifiers should be encrypted during transmission and in storage.

Manufacturing and Facilities Process Control Equipment

Process control systems are at the heart of many of our manufacturing operations. As such, they monitor, adjust, and document the yields and quality of our products. Access control to such systems is vital to our products, the safety of our people, and the Company's overall future.

Site Controls

Site management will establish and document security procedures for managing physical and remote access to all process control equipment to ensure continuity and integrity of operations and protection of proprietary electronic information, consistent with the need to operate the system in an effective manner. Whenever technologically possible, process control equipment and systems will comply with all of the EIS Standards governing access and usage of electronic information and systems found herein.

Process Control Function Categorization

The categories are:

- Sensors/analyzers/microprocessor-based sensors

- Sensor bus

- Programmable logic controllers and distributed control systems

- Networks (broadband, baseband, process control)

- Supervisory control system, lab automation system

- Higher-level optimization (modeling)

- Interaction with technical data base

Each process control system will have an owner.

- Electronic access to process monitoring and control system components via directly connected terminals and operators' consoles will be regulated through physical access security controls.

These system components will remain on-line to properly carry out their monitoring/control function.

- The system owner will establish and document procedures that will allow limited remote electronic access to Category 1-3 components (recognizing the access requirement for maintenance and the limited security capability currently available in these components).

- Site management will establish and document procedures to ensure that any access to Category 4-7 components passes through a security facility that provides accountability and auditability.

- Computer systems management, local or remote, will provide and maintain reliable tools to control electronic access to information, applications, and operating system software.

Contingency Planning and Disaster Recovery

Electronic information processing, whether on a mainframe, minicomputer, file server, or personal computer, has become vital and indispensable to the Company's operations. There is a heavy reliance on computers, networks, applications, and data to provide up-to-date and accurate information. Therefore, provisions must be made to establish an environment to ensure the continuance of business operations in the event of a disaster to the electronic information facility used to provide these critical functions.

Owners and custodians, jointly responsible for computer-based electronic information processing or network systems within their area of control, will provide a written assessment of EIS Standards compliance that includes:

- Areas of vulnerability.

- Controls and safeguards needed.

- Potential loss exposure.

All electronic information processing applications will be classified as CRITICAL or NOT CRITICAL. Applications designated as CRITICAL require special attention in contingency and disaster recovery planning. Applications not specifically designated as CRITICAL will be considered NOT CRITICAL.

Critical applications are those whose disruption would result in significant damage to the owner's area of responsibility or the business as a whole. Specific disruption time frames can be agreed to and documented by the owner and custodian of the application to denote different levels of criticality and the contingency planning necessary for them.

Disaster Recovery Plan

It is the joint responsibility of owners and custodians of computing and networking facilities to develop and test regularly, when appropriate, an effective electronic information system disaster recovery plan that complements a business or staff function's overall business resumption plan. Specifically, an electronic information system disaster recovery plan is a written description of the actions to be taken, the resources required, and the procedures to be followed before, during, and after the disruptive event.

Development of a disaster recovery plan must be appropriate for the system and information being considered.

Users of individual workstations (PCs) should regularly make backup copies of the business information stored on the hard disks of these computers. The frequency of backup should be governed by the business importance of the information, but at a minimum should occur monthly. These backups should be stored in a secure, remote location. It is important that this electronic information and its copies be disposed of in compliance with corporate records retention guidelines.

Disaster recovery plans for larger systems usually include, but are not limited to, the following:

- Identification of Critical Applications. Development of a methodology to identify current and future critical applications.

- Risk Assessment. A determination of the general nature and range of events in order that adequate disaster recovery plans can be developed. The cost involved should be appropriate in comparison to the expected loss.

- Disaster Prevention. Installation of equipment, procedures, and controls that will assist in preventing or minimizing a disaster. These disaster prevention procedures may include, but are not limited to, fire prevention/detection/ extinguishing equipment; uninterrupted power supplies (UPS); water detection and removal equipment; water damage prevention; heating, ventilating, and air conditioning needs; and physical security.

- Emergency Procedures. Development of procedures and assemblage of the facility's engineering design drawings to enable an immediate planned response to emergency situations to minimize the impact upon the safety of personnel and to curtail loss or damage to the Company's assets.

- Restoration of Facilities. Development of procedures to ensure timely assessment of damage to the primary site and the repair or reconstruction of the site to facilitate an orderly resumption of operations.

- Contingency Procedures and Backup Operations.

Development of manual or automated procedures for the continuation of operations while the primary facility is disabled. Items that should be considered when preparing contingency procedures usually include, but are not limited to:

- Off-Site Storage of Electronic Information: procedures for the retention, rotation, and retrieval of electronic information and files. Media stored outside of the Corporation's jurisdiction will be transported and maintained in a secure fashion to ensure the integrity of the electronic information.

- Manual Work Procedures: Procedures and necessary materials (forms, ledgers, etc.) for manual implementation of any operation critical to a business to enable its continuance during the disaster recovery period. Such procedures and practices should ideally include the ability to easily merge information back to the critical electronic business application upon its recovery.

- Critical Resource Planning: The identification of and procedures to obtain critical resources necessary for recovery, i.e., hardware, software, telecommunications, space, files, personnel, transportation and accommodations, utilities, and attendant financial considerations.

- Backup Electronic Processing: The identification of alternative processing sites and the development of procedures for backup operations when the primary processing site is inoperable.

- Testing and Maintenance: Must be performed on a regular basis (no less frequently than every 12 months) to ensure currency of the plan and maintain the validity of testing strategies.

Physical Security

Physical protection of electronic information systems and networks is a critical component of any electronic information security program in order to safeguard against unauthorized access, theft, and malicious destruction, as well as to reduce the risk of fire, water, and other environmental hazards.

Protection of Electronic Information Processing Systems

All computer, network, office automation, laboratory automation, and process control equipment will be physically secured and protected from loss. Preparation of documented physical security plans appropriate for the size, complexity, and cost of the equipment, as well as the criticality and sensitivity of the electronic information, will be a line management responsibility.

The cost/benefit relationship of the protection program should be applied against the criticality of the system. Example controls may include:

- Low criticality

  - Access to computing equipment will be within a lockable facility.

- Medium criticality

  - Access to computing equipment will be within a lockable facility.

  - The entry into the computing/networking area will be recorded.

- The physical construction of the area will deter forced entry attempts.

- An assessment will be conducted to determine if the system or electronic information must have special protection from fire and flood exposure.

- High criticality

  - The system will be located within a locked and guard-attended facility.

  - The entry into the processing area should be through a man trap or turnstile.

  - The entry and exit to and from the area will be recorded.

  - The physical construction of the processing area must resist the spread of fire or flood and deter forced entry attempts.

  - The area will be electronically monitored at a remote location with electronic systems that are configured to detect fire, water, and unauthorized access.

  - The equipment and electronic information must be protected from fire and flood exposure using the most effective systems available.

Securing Equipment and Software

Appropriate physical security and accounting controls will be employed for all "Theft Sensitive" electronic information communication and processing software, equipment, and peripheral components, in order to safeguard against unauthorized removal and/or tampering thereof.

The recommended practices are:

- Any capitalized electronic component is defined as "Theft Sensitive."

- All "Theft Sensitive" components and all licensed software will be inventoried and the inventory will be kept up-to-date.

- A physical audit of theft sensitive property will be taken each year. Exception reporting will be presented to management for review in accordance with corporate theft reporting guidelines.

- Spot audits by local management should be conducted each quarter. Exception reporting will be presented to management for review in accordance with corporate theft reporting guidelines.

- Terminals, personal computers, printers, and other control and peripheral items not located within secure facilities should be physically secured and permanently identified as Company property.

- All support equipment that has a direct electronic information-processing role will be located in areas or closets that are secured with restricted use locks.

- Support equipment associated with a highly critical class of processing system will be located in areas or closets that are electronically monitored at a remote location to detect fire conditions and unauthorized access.

- Any removal of equipment or electronic media from the premises will be approved by authorized personnel.

Compliance with Laws and Regulations

Physical security controls will be in compliance with existing fire and safety regulations, local laws, insurance requirements, and international communications and power regulations.

ELECTRONIC MAIL PROTECTION

The Company's electronic mail system (Email) has security features that provide a reasonable level of protection to internal messages moving among and between employees. External messaging, however, requires additional care. External Email systems are much less secure because many systems store and transmit messages in an easily readable form, thus subjecting the messages to interception or unintended reading by unauthorized individuals.

Actions

- Use care when selecting Email recipients from directories. It is sometimes easy to send messages to the wrong person.

- Do not include external recipients on internal distribution lists. This will help avoid accidental sending of messages to external addressees when distribution is intended for internal addressees.

- Only send Email externally if the contents would cause no problems if made public.

- Carefully construct messages intended for third parties; avoid language that is overly familiar; and use a style consistent with that of a formal letter.

- When appropriate, add to external messages a disclaimer: "This message contains an individual's views, which are not necessarily those of the Company."

- Do not auto-forward your Company Email mailbox to an external Email service.

- Do not send classified information through external Email without encryption. Do not indicate the classification in the message title.

- Be suspicious of Email attachments that contain software or documents with macros. If in doubt, avoid activating them until they have been checked for viruses.

- Do not send or forward chain letters.

EMERGENCY CALLS

Emergency response personnel are able to respond quickly and effectively to the extent that the call for assistance is delivered quickly and effectively. It is therefore of critical importance that the caller communicate concisely and distinctly.

Guidelines

- When making an emergency call to an emergency response agency (such as the police, the fire department, or ambulance service) it is important to:

    - Have your facts together and your thinking organized logically.

    - Speak slowly, clearly, and calmly.

    - Provide all of the essential information and do not hang up until you are sure your message has been understood.

- Expect the response agency to ask you to:

    - Identify yourself.

    - Identify the company and location.

    - Provide details on pertinent circumstances, such as gunfire and injuries.

- Report a factual account. Keep your opinions to yourself.

- If a responding agency is to come to the facility, explain where they can be met.

- After hanging up, keep at least one line open in case the agency needs to call back.

EMPLOYEE ACCESS CONTROL

Entry to Company premises and to restricted areas within the premises requires each employee at points of entry to place the Company-issued identification card before a card-scanning reader. The security officer's responsibility in this regard is to watch for unauthorized entry, e.g., tailgating, and the use by one employee of another employee's identification card.

Actions

On a random basis, ask employees to display to you their identification cards so that you can verify they are using their own cards.

Randomly watch employees present identification cards to the card-scanning readers.

Allow only one employee through the entrance at a time. Watch for employees who attempt to gain entry on another employee's card.

If an employee does not have an identification card, deny access to the employee until you receive access authorization. Keep in mind that a consistent approach to access control is essential.

When questioned by an employee concerning access control procedures, politely state that company policy requires presentation of the Company-issued identification as a condition of entry. As appropriate, advise the employee that access authorization is not granted by the Security Department but by supervisors and managers whose names appear on the list of approving access officials.

Incidents involving actual or attempted breaches of the access control system must be reported on the Incident Report and entered in the Daily Log Book. Incidents in this case include expressions of dissatisfaction by employees. In all incidents, the Security Supervisor must be briefed as soon as possible.

Persons who appear to be strangers, lost, confused, or unaccountably nervous should be approached and asked their business; for example, "May I help you?" or "Are you lost?" or "Do you have an identification card?" If the answer reveals that the individual is not authorized to be on the premises, explain in a firm but polite manner that the individual is on private property and must leave. If the individual refuses, contact the Security Supervisor. If the individual is unruly or disruptive, call the police.

Problems with the card-scanning system should be reported immediately to the access control system repair vendor.

EXECUTIVE PROTECTION

These Procedures apply to event-based executive protection, such as when the protected person travels abroad or attends a public function where high risk is present. These Procedures do not relate to the day-in and day-out protection program afforded certain senior executives. The users of these Procedures are intended to be those employees who work directly for the protected person and those employees charged with providing the protection at the travel destination or the event location.

Actions by the Protected Person's Staff

Prior to the trip or event:

- Book travel and hotel accommodations in the name of the Company's local representative rather than the name of the protected person. Communications about the visit should be treated as confidential for as long as possible prior to the arrival date.

- Develop a working plan that includes all details of the proposed travel or event. Identify travel and lodging arrangements, including any side trips or social diversions, such as sightseeing and shopping. Identify any anticipated problems, such as unfriendly news reports, or potential demonstrations for or against the protected person.

- Send the working plan to the Company's security professional at the travel destination or event location. Photographs and personal particulars should be included where justified by the risks.

- Make clear to the security professional and to the management of the host agency that responsibility for security during the visit rests with them. Ask for confirmation and for details of their intentions to provide security. If the protected person wishes it, or the host agency finds difficulty in meeting the security responsibility, the Corporate Director of Security will provide full-time bodyguard protection.

Actions by the Host Agency

- Involve the local police in the planning of the visit; obtain their advice on security threats and a recommendation on the level of protection required; and invite their participation in the protection program.

- Consult with other relevant agencies, such as an embassy or consulate. Obtain intelligence estimates on possible security threats.

- Avoid advance publicity.

- Schedule local ground transportation as tightly as possible. Local ground travel should be in a Company vehicle operated by an experienced, vetted, and CPR-trained driver having knowledge of the roadways and of available emergency medical treatment facilities. The vehicle should be equipped with a telephone. A backup vehicle should always be available, if only in case of breakdowns, and can be used to escort the protected person's vehicle. An experienced local employee equipped with communications should travel in the escort vehicle to help resolve any incidents that may develop. A primary and an alternate route should be selected, and these routes should be tested in advance.

- Confer with the security professionals at hotels to be used. Evaluate the security normally afforded protected persons and, where necessary, augment to ensure an adequate level of protection.

- Ensure that the protected person is met and escorted throughout the visit and that he or she is provided with a contact telephone number to use in case of a change in schedule.

- Hire bodyguards only in exceptional circumstances. Hiring should be through a reputable security company recommended by the police. The police must be informed of any decision to engage armed bodyguards.

- Hire an anti-eavesdropping specialist if information security will be an issue at any discussion venues.

- Inform the protected person's staff of the planned security measures. Ask for feedback. If the protected person cannot be satisfied that the security measures are adequate, consideration should be given to canceling the visit or attendance at the event.

FIRE RESPONSES BY SECURITY OFFICERS

Alarm Response

The building fire alarm system indicates the floor and general location of the cause of a fire alarm and notifies the Fire Department automatically via an off-site monitoring facility. The system control and indicator panels are in the Fire Command Center adjacent to the Security Control Center. In an emergency, the Fire Command Center operates under the control of building management. The person in charge of fire response is the Property Manager and is called the Fire Safety Director (FSD). The FSD is responsible for all communication with the city fire department officers and all instructions for evacuation. The Property Manager will be notified immediately, at all times, of any fire alarms.

Security Officer Duties

At night or when the building is unoccupied:

- Maintain constant radio contact with the Fire Safety Director.

- Follow the Fire Safety Director's instructions exactly, and be prepared to:

  - Locate cause for alarm.

  - Describe cause for alarm.

  - Evacuate if required.

  - Supervise the recommended route and evacuation of any others present in the building.

In daytime, when the building is occupied:

- The Fire Safety Director will communicate only with fire wardens who have already been appointed on each floor.

- Security Officers will locate the affected floor or floors and report to the fire warden there.

- Security Officers will assist the fire warden as directed.

- In the event of evacuation:

  - A Security Officer will remain on any floor from which evacuation is not required.

  - If all floors are evacuated, the Security Officer will report to the Fire Safety Director and assist as needed.

During a fire emergency, all movement by Security Officers from floor to floor (up and down) shall be via the fire stairs.

Once a day the Security Supervisor will make sure all fire extinguishers are in their proper places and that they are completely charged. Entries will be made in the Log Book and Daily Guard Report of any discrepancies.

Fire Alarm Test

The following Procedures are to be observed when testing fire alarms that have fire alarm pull stations:

- Floor-by-floor tests will be conducted between 11:00 p.m. and 6:30 a.m. on the first Wednesday of the month.

- The Security Supervisor will be responsible for conducting this test and officers on the swing shift will assist him. He will note that a particular alarm station has been pulled/reset and that the appropriate intercom announcement was made. The Security Officers on the test floors will note any malfunctions of the alarm intercom system. The Security Supervisor will also provide a key to reset the pull station alarms.

- The test will begin by pulling an alarm on the selected floor. All card readers should change to the green light (open) position, and all reader-equipped doors on the floor should open. Check each door to ensure it can be opened by hand. Also, readers on the floor above and below should activate. The intercom system will be used to announce the beginning of the test. The system will also be used when each pull station is pulled to announce that a test is being conducted.

- When all reader-equipped doors have been checked, the Security Supervisor in the Fire Command Center will reset the Fire Alarm. The pull station is manually reset by using the pull station key. The card readers are checked to ensure that a normal ("enabled") condition (no green or red light indicated when the door is shut and no key card is inserted) has been restored.

These Procedures will be repeated on each floor. Only one pull station per floor will be tested (with the location noted). A different pull station will be tested each month until all stations on a given floor have been checked (after which time the cycle will be repeated). An Incident Report will be written to note any malfunctions that occur during the test.

FLAG ETIQUETTE

The flag is an object of reverence. People often given close attention to the manner in which security officers treat the flag. Any handling of the flag, whether lowering, raising, or carrying, requires care and respect. For example, the flag must not touch the ground. The following guidelines apply:

- A two-person team should be used to raise and lower the flag, particularly for large flags.

- The senior person on the team should handle the halyard while the junior person holds the folded flag. After the halyard has been connected to the flag, it is raised slowly. The junior person should help the flag to unfold as it is raised and to keep the flag from touching the ground.

- When the flag is out of arm's length, the junior person should step back about 10 feet and render a hand salute until the flag reaches the top of the pole.

- The flag should be flown at full staff from sunrise to sunset. At the onset of inclement weather that could damage the flag or the pole, it should be brought down and put away.

- On days of national mourning, the flag is flown at half-staff. The flag is raised to full-staff and then lowered to half-staff. The bottom of the flag should touch at about the halfway point on the pole.

- When the flag is flown with other flags on U.S. soil, it is flown to the right. The order after that will depend on the applicable protocol.

- When the flag is lowered at the end of the day, the junior person renders a hand salute as the flag is brought down slowly by the senior person. When the flag reaches head height, the junior person drops the salute, steps forward, and grasps the bottom end of the flag.

- The senior person stops the flag's descent and takes hold of the top end of the flag. After the senior person has disconnected the halyard, he and the junior person each takes hold of the end corners of the flag. They will fold the flag lengthwise and then once again lengthwise.

- Starting at the striped end, the junior person makes successive diagonal folds, ending with the last fold displaying white stars on blue. A properly folded flag will show no red and white stripes.

- The junior person will release the flag, tie the halyard to the pole, and take up a marching position to the left of the senior person. The senior person will give the march order and carry the flag to its designated storage location.

HANDLING CLASSIFIED INFORMATION

The Company's sensitive information is organized into three classes: SECRET, RESTRICTED, and PRIVATE. These Procedures dictate the manner in which such information is to be handled.

SECRET Information

- The originator should make clear his or her intentions for initial and onward distribution.

- A register of all recipients must be maintained by the originator.

- The top of every page must be boldly marked and each copy serially numbered, e.g., No. 2 of 6 copies.

- Copies must be controlled by a distribution list.

- A document should reflect the date or event after which it should be re-classified or made unclassified. These examples illustrate:

  - "SECRET until after release of fourth quarter productivity results, then RESTRICTED for the following six months."

  - "Review classification following the Omega Acquisition Project."

- In unguarded buildings, store in a steel safe with combination lock.

- In guarded buildings, store in a safe or metal filing cabinet with combination lock.

- Protect combination codes and change as required, e.g., transfer of a person having knowledge of the code.

- Photocopying must be carried out or supervised by either the originator, a trusted nominee, or a trusted service organization that has signed a nondisclosure agreement.

- Destroy by burning or shredding. If shredding, use a cross-cut shredder that produces particles no greater than 2 mm by 15 mm. If the necessary equipment is not available, use a standard shredder, and then place the shredded remains in a locked waste container.

- Where a site uses a trusted third party for disposal of classified waste, a nondisclosure agreement must be signed and a certificate of destruction received in respect of each destroyed batch.

- When sending via the postal service or internal mail, use double envelopes with the inner envelope marked SECRET. Show the sender's address, and seal in a way that highlights any attempt at tampering. The outer envelope must not be marked with the classification and must be thick enough to hide the contents. An acknowledgment slip must be enclosed, which must be signed by the recipient and returned to the sender.

- Telephones must not be used to discuss SECRET information unless equipped with an encryption feature. Voice messaging and answering machines must not be used.

- The word SECRET must not appear in the names of any electronic documents, files, or directories. However, the electronic documents themselves must be boldly marked at the top.

- SECRET information must not be stored on servers unless strong security protections are in place, such as encryption. File servers must have passwords and be sited in a secure area, e.g., a computer room having controlled access.

- SECRET information must not be stored on personal computer (PC) hard disks unless a strong security mechanism is in place, such as disk encryption. PCs must be attended by an authorized individual or locked using an effective access control mechanism, e.g., a passworded screensaver.

- Files and documents containing SECRET information must not be electronically transmitted unless strong security mechanisms, such as encryption, are in place.

- The viewing screens of PCs containing SECRET information must be situated to avoid unauthorized viewing.

- Diskettes and tapes must have labels marked SECRET. Each copy must be serially and copy numbered. Copies must be controlled by a distribution list, and when not encrypted must be treated as SECRET paper.

- When destroying information on diskettes and tapes, one of the following must be carried out:

  - All SECRET files erased, then fully overwritten by either re-formatting or by using special software, e.g., Norton utilities.

  - Physical destruction, either manually or using a special shredder.

  - Magnetic destruction using special degaussing equipment.

- Computer printers must be attended by a trusted individual while printing. Printers must be connected to a restricted network.

- Readable printer ribbons must be removed after use and stored as SECRET paper, until destruction.

- SECRET information must not be published on the Company Intranet unless a specially protected facility has been implemented.

- Electronic mail must not be used unless messages can be encrypted. Where used, the message title must not include the word SECRET.

- Fax should not be used unless special equipment is available with encryption facilities. Fax machines must be attended by a trusted nominee or locked in a secure cabinet.

- Telex/EDI/video conferencing must not be used, unless encryption is provided.

- Presentation transparencies, e.g., 35 mm overheads, must be clearly marked and the classification displayed when projected for viewing. When no longer needed, they must be physically destroyed, e.g., incinerated. Other aspects of handling are the same as for paper documents.

- Audio tape, e.g., Dictaphone tapes, should be kept in containers the outside of which must be marked. The tapes should contain an audible message stating the classification. These items must be physically destroyed, e.g., incinerated. Other aspects of handling are the same as for paper documents.

- The SECRET classification must be clearly stated when such information is transferred face-to-face. Also:

  - Rooms should be periodically checked for telectronic eavesdropping devices. When very sensitive subjects are being discussed, detection equipment should ideally be switched on.

  - In hotel rooms, background noise should be introduced, e.g., TV, radio.

  - Phones in meeting rooms should ideally be disconnected.

  - Phones with an auto-answer facility should have this facility turned off.

- SECRET material carried during business travel must be kept in the traveler's personal possession or placed in a Company office safe. SECRET material must never be read or discussed when on public transport or in transit areas where it could be overlooked or overheard. Briefcases, even when locked, must not be left unattended. SECRET information must not be stored on portable computers or similar devices unless a suitable access control and encryption mechanism are in place.

- SECRET material must not be left unattended in a car.

RESTRICTED Information

- The originator should make clear his or her intentions for initial and onward distribution.

- Distribution should be consistent with the originator's intention.

- The top of every page must be boldly marked.

- Copies must be controlled by a distribution list.

- A document should reflect the date or event after which it should be re-classified or made unclassified. These examples illustrate:

  - "RESTRICTED indefinitely."

  - "Review classification following the Borealis Project."

- In unguarded buildings, store in a safe or metal filing cabinet.

- In guarded buildings or where an alarm system is in operation, store in a safe or metal filing cabinet with combination lock.

- Protect combination codes and change as required, e.g., transfer of a person having knowledge of the code.

- Photocopying must be carried out or supervised by either the originator, a trusted nominee, or a trusted service organization that has signed a nondisclosure agreement.

- Destroy by burning or shredding. Where a site uses a trusted third party for disposal of classified waste, a nondisclosure agreement must be signed, and a certificate of destruction received in respect of each destroyed batch.

- When sending via the postal service or internal mail, use double envelopes with the inner envelope marked RESTRICTED. Show the sender's address, and seal in a way that highlights any attempt at open or tampering, e.g., sender's signature across the opening, then covered with clear tape. The outer envelope must not be marked with the classification and must be thick enough to hide the contents. An acknowledgment slip must be enclosed, which must be signed by the recipient and returned to the sender.

- Telephones may be used with discretion.

- The word RESTRICTED must not appear in the names of any electronic documents, files, or directories. However, the electronic documents themselves must be boldly marked at the top.

- File servers containing RESTRICTED information must be sited in a secure area, e.g., a computer room having controlled access.

- RESTRICTED information stored on personal computer (PC) hard disks must be protected by a password or similar mechanism. PCs must be attended by an authorized individual or locked using an effective access control mechanism, e.g., a passworded screensaver.

- Documents that contain RESTRICTED information must not be electronically transmitted unless a strong security mechanism, such as encryption, is in place.

- The viewing screens of PCs containing RESTRICTED information must be situated to avoid unauthorized viewing.

- Diskettes and tapes must have labels marked RESTRICTED.

- Destroy information on diskettes and tapes by:

    - Overwriting or reformatting.

    - Physical destruction, either manually or using a special shredder.

- Computer printers must be attended by a trusted individual while printing. Printers must be connected to a restricted network.

- Readable printer ribbons must be removed after use and stored as RESTRICTED paper, until destruction.

- RESTRICTED information must not be published on the Company Intranet unless a specially protected facility has been implemented.

- In electronic mail, the message title must not include the word RESTRICTED.

- Fax should be used at the originator's discretion.

- Telex/EDI/video is at the originator's discretion.

- Presentation transparencies, e.g., 35 mm overheads, must be clearly marked and the classification displayed when projected for viewing. When no longer needed, they must be physically destroyed, e.g., incinerated. Other aspects of handling are the same as for paper documents.

- Audio tape, e.g., Dictaphone tapes, should be kept in containers the outside of which must be marked. The tapes should contain an audible message stating the classification. These items must be physically destroyed, e.g., incinerated. Other aspects of handling are the same as for paper documents.

- The RESTRICTED nature of the information must be clearly articulated when it is transferred face-to-face.

- RESTRICTED material carried during business travel must be kept in the traveler's personal possession or placed in a Company office safe. RESTRICTED material must never be read or discussed when on public transport or in transit areas. Briefcases, even when locked, must not be left unattended. RESTRICTED information must not be stored on portable computers or similar devices unless a suitable access control and encryption mechanism are in place.

- RESTRICTED material must not be left unattended in a car.

PRIVATE Information

- Documents in any form or medium are to be boldly marked at the top first page.

- Outer envelopes are to be boldly marked and sealed.

- Correspondence marked PRIVATE is to be opened only by the addressee.

- The titles of electronic documents and files must not be marked.

HAZARDS IDENTIFICATION

An important function performed by the security officer force is the identification of hazards. Identification is carried out as a deliberate and formal process and on an ad hoc basis, e.g., while officers perform their routine patrol duties.

Hazard Classification

The Hazard Classification System is a method of rating the degree of risk associated with an identified substandard act or condition in order to control and eliminate the hazard. Rating is done in conjunction with other inspections. Rating also allows for prioritizing corrective actions. An A, B, or C classification will be applied to all substandard acts and conditions.

- CLASS A is a condition or practice likely to cause permanent disability, loss of life or body part, and/or excessive loss of structure equipment or material. Class A hazards will be corrected by the end of the day discovered, unless the responsible supervisor dictates otherwise.

- CLASS B is a condition or practice likely to cause serious injuries or illnesses, resulting in temporary disability, or property damage that is disruptive but less severe than Class A. Class B hazards will be corrected within 15 days, unless the responsible supervisor dictates otherwise.

- CLASS C is a condition or practice likely to cause minor injury or illness or non-disruptive property damage. Class C hazards will be corrected in 45 days.

All hazards when noted will be followed by an immediate action intended to ensure they do not cause an injury, illness, or damage before corrective action is completed.

Hazard Identification

The identification of hazards requires a conscious effort. The effort is assisted when it is organized. Use a checklist and take particular note of the following:

- Floor Surfaces

  - Look for blockages in aisles, hallways, stairwells.

  - Look for tripping hazards.

  - Look for loose paper on floors.

- Look for slippery floors.

- Look for torn carpets and rugs.

- Halls and Ramps

  - Look for poor lighting.

  - Look for blockages, such as equipment and supplies awaiting movement.

  - Look for doors and drawers that people are likely to bump into.

  - Look for places where people are likely to collide, e.g., a sharp corner.

  - Look for the Fire Exit signs. Are they lit? Are they visible? Do they directly lead to fire exits?

  - Look for worn or defective nonslip surfaces.

  - Look for handrails in need of repair.

- Stairwells

  - Look for poor lighting.

  - Look for blockages, e.g., ladders and tools left by maintenance personnel.

  - Check to see if guardrails are in good condition.

  - Check door-locking mechanisms for proper operation.

  - Check to make sure doors open and close freely.

- Fire Extinguishers

  - Check for proper level.

  - Check the inspection tag date.

  - Check condition of storage box.

- Coffee Bars

- Look for coffee makers, hot plates, and the like that have been left on.

- Shredders

  - Check forward and reverse feed to ensure shredder is working safely.

HOME BURGLARY PREVENTION

These Procedures are provided as a guide to employees so that they may protect themselves from crime while at home.

Actions

These simple steps can discourage a would-be burglar.

- Make trade-off arrangements with neighbors. They watch your house you watch theirs. A face in a window next door can scare away a burglar as easily as a patrol car.

- One of the best deterrents to burglary is a barking dog. Dogs are usually effective because of their natural instinct to protect their territories.

- Lock your doors whether you're home or away. About one-fourth of all burglarized residences are entered through unlocked doors.

- A long absence from home deserves special precautions. Tell a trusted neighbor how long you'll be gone and ask police to keep an eye on your house. Have a friend collect mail, newspapers, and other deliveries that advertise the house is empty. Hire someone to keep the lawn mowed and snow shoveled. If a neighbor has a second car, ask him or her to leave it parked in your driveway. Purchase simple timing devices that turn lights and radio on and off. Never leave a note on the front door saying you're away and how long you expect to be gone, even if you're just leaving for the day.

- If there's a death in the family, a wedding, or any other event that may be publicized in the newspaper, leave a housesitter when gone. Burglars read newspaper notices to learn when a house is likely to be empty.

- In one common scam, a purse thief calls the owner at home pretending to be a police officer. He says the purse has been recovered and to come and get it. While the victim goes to the police station, the house is burglarized, entered with a key found in the purse.

- If keys are lost or stolen, change the locks and exclude from the new set of keys identification of any sort. Leave an emergency key with a neighbor, not under the doormat, in a flower pot, or on the sill above the door. When you leave keys with a valet attendant, take the house keys off the ring.

- Light the house at night, inside and out. It only costs about 4¢ to burn a hundred-watt bulb for 10 hours. Alter the inside lights and timers so the same lights aren't lit every night. And don't light your home in such a way that your valuables are on display in picture windows or easily seen from the street.

- Plant prickly bushes at each of your first-floor windows and keep them well trimmed so a burglar can't use them as a hiding place.

- Don't let strangers inside the house unless you're convinced they're legitimate. Check credentials and call the place of business. Look up the number in the phone book. Don't accept a phone number from the caller.

- Burglars often pose as salespeople, insurance investigators, pollsters, or workers to gain access to the house and case it for a future burglary. Report to police anyone who rings your bell and asks vague questions or questions about your whereabouts. If you buy something from a salesperson, don't leave the door open while you get the money.

- Because most chain locks can be broken with a strong shove or kick, it's safer to invest in a wide-angle peephole that lets you scrutinize callers without opening the door. Equip doors with sturdy dead-bolt-type locks. Many newer suburban homes and inexpensive apartments are now equipped with hollow-core doors that can easily be kicked out or broken apart with a heavy tool. Replace hollow doors with solid-wood doors or attach to them a thick plywood or metal facing.

- If the doors have external hinges and pins, move them to the inside so a burglar can't simply take the hinges off and walk in. Also, you may want to keep a wedge-shaped rubber door stopper handy to slow down a burglar who is trying to force the door open while you are inside.

- For window security, install locks that prevent opening of windows from the outside. A thief can always break a window, of course, but studies show that most burglars are reluctant to risk detection from the sound of breaking glass.

- Probably the most vulnerable openings to the home are glass sliding doors. You can double secure sliding glass doors by dropping a broomstick into the lower track or by installing pins in the top of the door frame. Then, even if the door lock is defeated, the burglar can't slide the door open.

HOTEL GUEST SECURITY

These Procedures are intended to guide employees at places of lodging while in travel status on behalf of the Company.

In Advance

- Select a hotel recommended by the Company's travel agency. The hotel is likely to be one of a chain of preferred hotels that provide a consistent and uniform level of security.

- If travel is to a high-threat country, consider making reservations using the Company's street address (without identifying the Company by name) and using your personal credit card. The less known about your travel itinerary and who you represent, the safer you are likely to be.

- If arriving in mid-afternoon or late at night, ensure that reservations are guaranteed.

- Obtain information about hotel parking arrangements before renting an automobile.

- Be aware that credit card information may be compromised by dishonest employees of the hotel, rental car company, and restaurants. Always audit monthly credit card statements to ensure that unauthorized use has not been made of your account.

Arrival at the Hotel

The most vulnerable part of your journey may be the trip from the airport to the hotel.

- Disembark as close to the hotel entrance as possible and in a lighted area. Remain alert to who and what is going on around you. Before exiting the vehicle, ensure there are no suspicious persons or activities.

- Do not linger or wander unnecessarily in the parking lot, indoor garage, or the public space around the hotel.

- Parking garages are difficult to secure. Avoid dimly lit garages that are not patrolled and do not have security telephones or intercoms.

- Watch for distractions that may be staged to set up a theft.

- Stay with your luggage until it is brought into the lobby.

- Laptop computers are particularly attractive items to thieves try to conceal them inside other bags or take particular care of them.

- Use the bell hop. Luggage in the care, custody, and control of the hotel causes the hotel to be liable for your property. Keep claim checks.

- Due to hotel liability limits, personal travel documents, laptop computers, valuables, and sensitive documents should be hand carried and personally protected.

- Car valets should receive only the ignition key.

- If you are required to use hotel car parking identity stickers in your car, make sure that they do not indicate your room number or name.

- Women travelers should consider requesting an escort to their vehicles.

Check In

- In some countries, a passport may be held by the hotel for review by the police or other authorities. If so, retrieve it at the earliest possible time.

- Position luggage against your leg during registration, but place a briefcase or purse on the desk or counter in front of you.

- Request a room between the second and seventh floors. Most fire departments do not have the capability to rescue people above the seventh floor.

- Avoid rooms on lower levels and rooms with sliding glass doors and easy window access. Exercise a higher level of security if assigned a ground level room.

- Request rooms that are away from the elevator and stairwells. This is to avoid being caught by surprise by persons exiting the elevator with you or hiding in the stairwell.

- Accept the bell hop's assistance upon check-in. Allow the bell hop to open the room's door, turn the lights on, and check the room to ensure that it is vacant and ready for your stay.

- Inquire how guests are notified if there is an emergency.

- Check on the whereabouts of the hotel's security office.

In the Room

- Check that your door lock works.

- Locate exits and stairways as soon as you check in be sure the doors open.

- Find the nearest house telephone in case of an emergency.

- Note how hotel staff are uniformed and identified. Verify hotel employees with the front desk before permitting entry to your room.

- While in the room, keep the door closed and engage the deadbolt and privacy latch or chain. A limited number of hotel emergency keys can override the deadbolt locks.

- Personal belongings are not necessarily safe in a locked hotel room. It is better to use the hotel's safe deposit boxes, but even these may not always be secure. For high value items or classified papers, it may be better to use the safe facilities of the office being visited.

- Stay only at hotels that have smoke detectors and sprinklers.

- Be alert to suspicious sounds outside the room door and windows.

- Put the "Do Not Disturb" sign on the door to give the impression that the room is occupied while you are out.

- Do not tell anyone in the hotel of your departure or return times.

- Call the maid when you are ready for the room to be cleaned.

- Consider leaving the light or TV on when you are out of the room.

- Carry the room key with you instead of leaving it at the front desk.

- Do not accept packages or open the door to workers without verification from the front desk.

- If the hotel has a fire alarm system, find the nearest alarm. Read the fire instructions. Find out where the fire exits are and how to get to them.

- Ensure that your room windows open and that you know how the latches work.

- Check the windows in the bedroom to see whether they can be opened and, if so, how they can be secured from the inside.

- If the room has more than one door, ensure that secondary doors are locked.

- Check whether there is a balcony, fire escape, or ledge outside the window that could be used to gain access. A simple booby trap, such as a lamp or table placed close to the window or door, might give warning of an attempted intrusion.

- If you receive a hang-up call, it may be someone testing to see if the room is occupied.

- Remember that hotel telephones are in no way secure. In some countries they are tapped by government security agencies.

- As a businessperson, you may be the target of commercial information gatherers. Do not leave any Company papers or diskettes in your hotel room. Do not engage in business conversations in the hotel lobby where you can be heard, as they are often frequented by competitors seeking inside information. If you have to leave your laptop computer in your room, lock it away, and if possible remove the hard drive and secure it separately.

- Be particularly careful about responding to unexpected callers at the door. Remember that even when there is a peep hole, it can be masked by one person acting as a decoy to conceal another. Always check first by opening the door on the chain. If you are unsure about the caller, tell the individual to go to reception and leave a message there. Call reception yourself and alert them of the caller and explain your concern.

- It is noted that few hotels cater to female business travelers and rarely consider their security. Females are vulnerable to robberies and sexual attack. There have been instances when females have been given rooms on the ground floor adjacent to car parks. If you have any concerns for your safety or security when reaching your room, insist on being relocated.

- When you retire at night ensure that your room is secure and know exactly where to find room keys so that if it is necessary to leave the room in an emergency, the key is at hand. If there is no door chain fitted, place a chair against the door so that if the door is opened the chair will fall, making a noise and acting as an impediment to entry. Make a practice of carrying a pen-light torch when traveling. Keep it by your beside where it can be found at once.

- Make sure you know where the telephone is and how it works so that if woken in the night you can use it.

- If you determine that an item in your room is missing, conduct a thorough search before reporting it to hotel security. The incident should also be reported to the local police and to the Company's security department. The hotel should provide you with a letter verifying that you reported property missing. The letter may be later required for insurance purposes.

- Prior to traveling it is recommended that you photocopy all credit cards, passports, and air tickets to facilitate reporting loss and replacement. Secure the originals of your passport and visa in the hotel safe during times they are not needed.

- Request that housekeeping make up your room while you are at breakfast rather than leaving a "Please Service This Room" sign on the door knob. The sign is a signal that your room is empty.

Fire Precautions

- Orient yourself to the hotel during check-in. Take note of fire exits, fire escape routes, and fire equipment available for guest use. For example, count the number of doors from your room to the nearest fire exit. In a smoke-filled hallway, you may have to feel your way, door by door, to the exit. Plan in your mind a primary and an alternate escape route from your room and for other places in the hotel, such as the restaurant and lounge. If you develop a plan of escape in advance, you will be less likely to panic and more likely to survive.

- Check the smoke detector in your room by pushing the test button. If it does not work, have it fixed or demand to be moved to another room.

- Keep the room key and a flashlight on the bedside table so that you may locate the key quickly if you have to leave quickly.

- If you see fire or notice the indications of fire, call the front desk, and then leave.

- If the fire alarm sounds, follow evacuation instructions given by hotel staff and/or announced over the public address system.

- If you awake to find smoke in your room, grab your key and crawl to the door on your hands and knees. Fresher air will be nearer the floor.

- If your exit path is clear, crawl into the hallway. Stay close to the wall to avoid being trampled.

- As you make your way to the fire exit, stay on the same side as the exit door.

- When you reach the exit, walk down the stairs to the first floor. If you encounter heavy smoke in the stairwell, turn around and go to the roof exit.

- If all exits are blocked, or there is heavy smoke in the hallway, you will be better off staying in your room.

- If fire conditions are not in your room but appear to be nearby, place your palm on the interior side of your room door and then on the door knob. If either feels hot, do not open the door.

- If it is safe to exit from your room, head for the stairs, not the elevator. Take your room key with you.

- If the corridor is full of smoke, crawl to the stairwell door and again check before opening the door to see if it is hot. The fire could be in the stairwell.

- If you cannot leave your room, or if the stairwells are unsafe to enter, return to your room. Notify the front desk that you are in your room awaiting rescue.

- Open a window for fresh air. Do not break the window as you may need to close it if smoke starts to enter from outside.

- Fill the tub and sink with water. Soak towels and blankets and use them to block vents and openings around doors to keep the smoke and fumes out. As much as possible, keep the towels and blanket wet.

- A wet towel swung around the room will help clear the room of smoke.

- Cover your mouth and nose with a wet cloth.

- Stay low, but remain alert to any signs of rescue from the street or the halls. Let the firefighters know where you are by waving a towel or sheet out of the window.

HOTEL SECURITY OFFICER

A hotel security officer's main responsibilities include detecting safety hazards, deterring objectionable and unlawful behavior, and keeping the hotel's management informed of security-related incidents through timely and accurate reports.

Guidance

- Present yourself professionally and courteously at all times.

- Maintain a businesslike appearance.

- Ensure that your uniform is clean, in good condition, and wrinkle free.

- Maintain a well-groomed appearance.

- Use good standing and sitting posture. Keep your hands out of your pockets. Do not slouch or tip back in your chair.

- Do not eat or smoke while on duty.

- Do not socialize, and respond to questions and requests politely.

- Always look directly at people and address them as "Sir" or "Ma'am." Do not call people by their first names.

- Listen attentively to requests from hotel staff and customers and offer assistance within the limits of your post orders.

- Patrol the designated areas, e.g., the main lobby, the lounges and restaurants, the swimming pool, the drive-up areas, and the parking lots.

- By your presence and demeanor, operate as a deterrent to rowdy behavior, vandalism, unauthorized use of the facilities, and entry onto the premises by unwelcome individuals, such as uninvited salespersons, vagrants, and prostitutes.

- Be courteous when talking to people. If rules are being violated, politely intervene. If the offending individuals refuse to cooperate, notify the hotel management.

Special Areas

- In the parking areas, look for headlights left on, car doors open, and loiterers. Report your observations to the front desk and ask for guidance.

- Check stairwells for obstacles that would impede a safe evacuation in the event of fire. Look also for loiterers.

INFORMATION PROTECTION AT THE OFFICE

Simple Safeguards

The following easily-applied safeguards can provide a reasonably strong degree of protection to sensitive information:

- Lock away all classified or sensitive documents, computer diskettes, and other information-storing media when not in use.

- Never place sensitive information on the Internet or the Company's Intranet.

- Don't leave keys lying around or hide them in unsecured places, such as unlocked drawers or under plant pots. Keep them with you or in a key safe.

- Dispose of sensitive material by shredding, burning, or leaving in a securely locked special purpose container. Don't simply throw sensitive material in the waste basket.

- Switch off, disconnect (log off), or lock personal computers and terminals when unattended (e.g., by using a secure screensaver).

- Choose computer passwords that are difficult to guess (e.g., not Christian names); change them regularly; don't write them down in obvious places (e.g., desk calendar or diary); and never disclose them to anyone.

- Think twice before using fax, electronic mail, or telephones (especially mobile and hotel phones) for communicating sensitive information.

- Make sure that you can't be overheard when discussing sensitive items, especially when outside the Company's offices.

- Take special care of portable PCs. If they contain sensitive information, treat them with them same care that is required for sensitive documents.

- If in doubt, ask for guidance from a security representative or an information technology coordinator.

INTERNET PROTECTION

The Internet is a massive collection of computers around the world, all of which are linked together, and accessible from anywhere. The Internet is often called the Information Superhighway. Significant benefits accrue from having access to this vast information resource, but with access comes risk.

Actions

- Use a connection to the Internet that has been established by the Company. Do not connect a Company computer to the Internet in any other manner.

- Do not download software from any Internet source not known as reliable. The risk of infection from malicious software is too high. Malicious software containing computer viruses is scattered widely and is often disguised as useful or entertaining software.

- If you acquire software from a reliable Internet source, make sure you have the skills to check it, including carrying out a scan for known viruses.

- Comply with licensing and export restrictions on shareware obtained through the Internet.

- Avoid Internet browsing that can trigger software to be executed automatically. So-called cookies are small files that can be created on your PC by Web sites that are visited.

- Don't change the security settings on your PC or within your Web browser. Observe all warnings made by the security features of your equipment.

- Use different passwords for Internet services than you use for internal computer systems. Passwords can sometimes be captured by unauthorized individuals.

- Choose passwords that can't be guessed.

- Be on the lookout for electronic mail attachments that include software or document/spreadsheet macros. Don't activate them if in doubt, until they have been checked for viruses.

- Email messages that are sent externally require extra care. For example:

  - Don't include external recipients within internal distribution lists, to avoid accidental disclosure of messages.

  - Don't include embarrassing information in Email.

- Don't auto-forward your Company Email mailbox to an external Email service.

- Don't send sensitive information externally by Email unless secure encryption is used.

- Don't send or forward chain letters. Delete them immediately without reading the contents.

- Transfer large files only as absolutely necessary. Large files impact the Internet and the company's internal networks. Use discretion to avoid inconvenience to others.

- Do not browse inappropriate Web sites, such as those that contain pornography. Do not import inappropriate material. The Company's Internet connections are for company business only. Violators are subject to disciplinary action, including termination. Note also that transmission of some Internet material may be illegal and therefore prosecutable.

INTRANET PROTECTION

The Company's Intranet gives easy access to a large amount of information worldwide. Employees and selected third party partners who have access to the Company network can navigate the Intranet using standard browser software. This presents opportunities for information sharing and increased business efficiency. But Intranet access is also accompanied by risk of loss or compromise of sensitive information. The following simple guidelines apply.

Actions

- Information that is classified SECRET must not be placed on the Intranet.

- Information that is classified RESTRICTED may be placed on the Intranet but only with access restrictions.

- Information that is classified PRIVATE (i.e., personal employee information) should not be placed on the Intranet.

- Other information, although not classified but of a sensitive nature, should not be placed on the Intranet.

- Information displayed on the Intranet should be accompanied by a notice identifying who is allowed viewing privileges.

- Third party partners must be informed of their Intranet viewing and publishing responsibilities.

Knowledge Sharing

The need for security of knowledge varies throughout the Company. In some areas, sharing knowledge within a business partnership is an important means of working together effectively and profitably. In other areas, knowledge contains a technical or commercial edge, which must not fall into the hands of competitors.

The Intranet is not restricted to Company staff. It is common in partnership arrangements to make maximum use of the knowledge-sharing capabilities of the Intranet. This means that some non-Company employees have open access to the Company's Intranet.

The responsibility for security lies with the publisher. Authors, owners, and custodians of information are responsible for determining the degree of sensitivity and clearly articulating the intended readership. Security should not be an excuse for keeping knowledge from those who can put it to good use. Neither is it excusable to violate security rules by allowing unauthorized access to sensitive information. The correct approach is to publish the knowledge, but make it secure.

LOST AND FOUND

- When accepting a found item, list and describe it in the Lost and Found Log and make an entry in the Daily Activity Report.

- Do not assume the value of the item when you describe it in the Lost and Found Log. For instance, write:

  - "Yellow metal" rather than "gold necklace."

  - "Clear stone" rather than "diamond ring."

- Place the item in a plain envelope and seal it. Write a brief description of the item on the outside of the envelope. For example, "Man's watch."

- Place the envelope in the secure container (a safe or lockable file cabinet) set aside for found items.

- Inform the incoming relief that a found item has been received and logged in. Follow the standard receipting procedure when going off duty.

- When returning a found item to the owner:

  - Require the owner to specifically describe the item.

  - Examine picture identification of the owner and record that information in the Lost and Found Log and Daily Activity Report.

  - Require the owner to indicate receipt of the item by signing the Lost and Found Log.

  - Prepare an Incident Report if necessary, such as when the owner refuses to sign for the item or when you have reason to believe the person claiming to be the owner is making a false claim.

MEDICAL EMERGENCIES

Security officers are often the first responders to medical emergencies at work. These Procedures provide guidance to security officers when an employee is injured or becomes seriously ill.

When You Receive a Report

- When receiving a report of an ill or injured person:

    - Obtain the exact location and the name of the person making the report.

    - Dispatch a security officer to the scene immediately to assist as needed. The responding officer should take the First Responder Kit. Minor injuries may be bandaged, and the ill or injured person should be made as comfortable as possible. The officer should call for a stretcher if it is needed.

- If an ambulance is needed or requested, immediately call 911. Give your name and location to the 911 operator. Note the time the ambulance was called and the time of arrival.

- If someone other than a security officer has called for an ambulance, try to obtain the name of the person who made the call and the time the ambulance was summoned.

- When paramedics arrive, escort them to the ill or injured person. Arrange for another security officer to hold the elevator in case a quick evacuation is needed. The on-scene security officer should standby to assist in any way.

When You Witness an Accident or Illness Situation

- When you witness an accident or illness, evaluate the situation as quickly as possible using all available information. Ask yourself:

    - Is the situation serious?

    - What kind of accident or illness is it?

    - Is the person coherent?

    - Is the person intoxicated?

- Is the person complaining of chest pains?

- If the person is coherent and apparently back to normal, let the person decide what to do. You may want to:

  - Advise rest for a short period.

  - Offer to help obtain transportation if needed, such as call a friend or a taxi cab.

  - Offer to call the person's personal physician.

- If the person is seriously hurt or too sick to assume personal responsibility, call for medical assistance, such as the company doctor, nurse, and paramedics.

- When making the call for medical assistance, do not hang up until you have:

  - Reported the situation fully.

  - Given the location of the ill or injured person.

  - Explained which entrance to use upon arrival.

  - Ensured that the medical assistance will be dispatched without delay.

- Arrange to have someone meet the medical responders at the entrance and escort them to the patient.

- Calmly reassure the ill or injured person that help is on the way.

- Help make the person as comfortable as possible without moving the individual.

- Do not perform any first aid or CPR unless you are certified.

Post-Incident Actions

- After treatment has been rendered and the situation stabilized, obtain all details, e.g., name of the person treated; names of witnesses; the nature of the illness or injury; and how, where, when, and why it occurred.

- Take into custody any items that may have contributed to the incident, such as a work tool.

- Notify all interested parties, e.g., the Security Supervisor, and the managers of Human Resources, Safety, Security, and Property Management.

- Prepare an Incident Report and make an entry in the Daily Log Book.

OFFICE BUILDING EVACUATION

The individual responsible for directing the evacuation of the Company's head office building will be a responsible supervisor or manager in the Property Management Office. This designated individual will be called the Fire Safety Director (FSD). The FSD will:

- Develop a fire safety plan in coordination with the local fire department.

- Establish a Floor Warden Program that ensures that each floor of the building will have two or more individuals (called Floor Wardens) ready to oversee evacuation of the building in a major emergency such as fire, explosion, or natural disaster.

- Conduct fire drills at a frequency of not less than once every three months.

- Provide initial training to Floor Wardens. The initial training will have three parts:

  - Office Building Evacuation Procedures

  - Basic First Aid

  - CPR

- Provide refresher training to Floor Wardens. The refresher training will refresh the initial training and include also instruction on related matters, such as lessons learned from fire drills and from the actual experiences of other companies.

Preparing for an Emergency

Floor Wardens will prepare for emergencies as follows:

- Know the locations of the fire stairwells, the pull stations, and the emergency assistance refuge area on their floors.

- Meet with other Floor Wardens on their floors to establish a clear understanding of what each person is to do, including backup assignments in case a Floor Warden is absent during an emergency.

- Tell all new people on their floors what to do in case of an emergency. At a minimum, each employee should know:

- The location of pull stations on the floor, and, if fire is present, how to activate a pull station, call 911, and notify a Floor Warden.

- The most direct route from his or her desk to the nearest stairwell.

- That when the fire alarm sounds to move to the nearest stairwell and form an orderly line.

- To move down the stairwell if the evacuation order is given and to move quietly and quickly, without running.

- To proceed to the assembly area designated for their floor.

- Keep a list of the persons on their floors in order to account for every employee immediately after an evacuation.

- Identify handicapped persons and others with temporary medical conditions, such as a broken leg or pregnancy, who may need help during an evacuation. Arrange in advance with another employee to provide the needed help. Send the names of mobility-impaired employees to the FSD.

- On a daily basis, be alert for fire hazards and take immediate corrective actions. Hazards include overloaded electrical circuits, unattended cooking appliances, and materials that block the evacuation routes.

Responding to an Emergency

When the fire alarm sounds on a floor, two actions should begin simultaneously:

- At least one Floor Warden will immediately begin looking throughout the entire floor for fire conditions. Special attention will be given to coffee and copy rooms since these are the places where fire is most likely to occur.

- Floor wardens will begin telling employees to assemble in the hallways close to the stairwells in order to facilitate evacuation if evacuation is ordered.

Within a minute after the alarm has gone off, a PA system announcement will be made by the FSD or by the senior security officer present. The announcement will be to the effect that an inquiry is in progress to determine the nature of the alarm. The inquiry will be conducted by maintenance personnel during normal duty hours and by security officers during other than normal duty hours.

If the search of the floor:

- Reveals the presence of fire (i.e., visible flame, visible smoke or a strong burning odor), the person noting the conditions will call 911 to notify the Fire Department. The next call will be to the FSD.

In order to notify everyone, the next step will be to pull the lever on the nearest pull station and begin evacuation immediately. As the last employee goes down the stairwell on the floor, a Floor Warden will so notify the Security Control Center.

- Does not reveal the presence of fire, the FSD will be informed. The FSD will order a double-check by the first arriving fire department personnel. After the fire department has given the all clear, the emergency will be declared over, and the FSD will report such via a PA announcement.

When fire is present, Floor Wardens will instruct employees to evacuate, even when an evacuation announcement has not yet been made on the PA system. A Floor Warden has the authority to order an evacuation for any reason when there is a risk of danger to people.

The emergency assistance refuge area on each floor is the staging area for mobility-impaired persons who need assistance in going down the stairwell. The mobility impaired are persons in wheelchairs, in leg casts or on crutches, and persons whose movement down the stairwell might impede a safe, orderly evacuation. Each such person should be accompanied at the emergency refuge area by a nonhandicapped person who by prior arrangement of the Floor Warden has agreed to assist the handicapped person down the stairwell. When the stairwell is clear, the Floor Warden will give the instruction to evacuate the handicapped.

The last person to leave the floor in an evacuation is a Floor Warden. The last act of the departing Floor Warden is to ensure that no one has been left behind. This means checking rest rooms, storage rooms, conference rooms, and closed offices.

Floor Wardens will proceed to the pre-designated assembly areas for their floors. They will hold in the air the Floor Warden Clipboard as a signal to gather their floor's employees. The Floor Wardens will account for the employees on their lists. If a Floor Warden has reason to believe an employee remains in the building, a report of this fact will be made to the FSD immediately.

Responding to Other Evacuation Emergencies

Blackout

If electrical service is lost and is not expected to be restored momentarily, instructions may be given by telephone communication or by portable PA horns to evacuate employees through the stairwells. The same evacuation procedures apply except that:

- Floor Wardens should check elevator lobbies to determine if an elevator is stuck and, if so, to notify the FSD.

- Employees who have window offices may be allowed to remain.

- Floor Wardens should tell employees to take their purses and other personal valuables with them as they leave.

- Floor Wardens should use their flashlights to help employees get to the stairwells. Battery-powered emergency lights in the stairwells will provide illumination to the ground level exits.

Bomb Threat

If evacuation is ordered as the result of a bomb threat, the same Procedures apply except that Floor Wardens should tell employees to:

- Take with them any packages, briefcases, purses, or similar objects that might be construed to be an explosive device.

- Not touch any suspicious object and to report any such object to Security, ensuring first that no one else touches the object.

OFFICE INSPECTIONS

The Company requires after-hours inspections of offices to ensure compliance with information security rules.

Actions

The inspections are to be performed by security officers in the early evening. On weekday nights, they will be performed prior to office cleaning by janitorial staff.

The Security Supervisor will instruct the security officers in how to make an inspection.

The Security Supervisor will devise an inspection form for noting violations. Completed forms will be kept on file at the Security Center. Once per week the Security Supervisor will forward to the Security Manager a summary report of violations.

The Security Manager will communicate the details of the violations to the responsible supervisors and managers. The supervisors and managers will report back to the Security Manager the actions they have taken to prevent recurrence.

When an inspection reveals that sensitive material (i.e., material containing Company information classified as Confidential, Restricted, or Secret) has been left out, the security officer will confiscate the material, place it into the locked security container in the Security Center, and prepare an Incident Report (which is in addition to the inspection form). The Incident Report will be hand-delivered to the Security Manager at the opening of the next business day.

Elements of the Inspection

The security officer's inspection will address these questions:

- Has the key to the office door been left in the lock?

- Has the door key been hidden near the door?

- Has the office door been left unlocked?

- Have sensitive materials (both documents and visual depictions) been left out, such as on the desk, in a bookcase, or on the wall? (Note: Examples of sensitive materials include business plans, strategy papers, economic evaluations, staff appraisals, and salary data.)

- Is the desk and/or credenza unlocked?

- Is the file cabinet locked?

- Have keys been hidden in a desk calendar or inside a pencil holder?

- If a desk, credenza, or file cabinet is found open or can be opened because a key is accessible, does the container have in it any sensitive materials?

- Has the desk computer been left on? If so, can the contents be accessed, e.g., by reason of the password protection not being invoked?

- If the desk computer is a laptop model, is it locked to a docking station or to a fixed object?

- Is the computer user's password written down where it can be found?

OFFICE SECURITY

These Procedures apply to all employees at all Company locations. Supervisors and managers are charged with conducting periodic unannounced inspections to assure compliance. In addition, the Security Manager will conduct an annual audit that includes an assessment of compliance.

Required Actions

- Do not leave your office door unlocked at night or on weekends. Even at Company facilities protected at the entrances by security officers or electronic access controls, it is essential to keep internal office doors closed and locked when not in use.

- Do not leave work papers on your desk, especially at night or on weekends, and remove from the walls any classified maps, drawings, or schematics that are not in use.

- Keep filing cabinets and closets locked when they are not being regularly accessed.

- Be alert for unescorted strangers in your work area, and challenge their right to be there. If the answer given is unsatisfactory, notify a supervisor or a security officer.

- Don't reveal to unidentified telephone callers or visitors the comings and goings of company officials or of visits and meetings.

- Unless instructed otherwise, don't give out home telephone numbers, addresses, or personal information concerning fellow employees and company officials. If a caller expresses an important need to talk with an employee who is not in the office, call the employee and pass on the caller's number or obtain permission to give the caller the employee's contact number.

- Follow the prescribed procedures for marking, transmitting, and storing classified documents.

- Do not leave sensitive information displayed on unattended word processing equipment, and password your system and/or sensitive documents. When not in use, remove sensitive documents from the system and password them onto diskettes. Place the diskettes in a locked desk or cabinet.

- Don't leave your purse or other valuables unattended and where they can be seen. Do not leave your wallet in a coat on a hanger or over the back of a chair. If you are going to be absent from your work station for an extended time, put away items such as radios and hand calculators.

- Be alert to persons loitering outside the company's premises. Be especially wary in parking lots and garages. Avoid walking unaccompanied in isolated or unlit areas, and in stairwells. If you are approached by a suspicious person, walk to the nearest populated area and continue moving toward help if a stranger accosts you.

- Notify your supervisor or a security officer if an unexplained package is found in or delivered to the office. Grease stains, peculiar odor, foreign postage, and a hand-lettered address are indicators of a possible package bomb.

OFFICE SECURITY MANAGEMENT

The Company's most common working environment is the office. In some cases, the office will be a single suite; in other cases it will be a floor of offices in a building, an entire building, or a complex of buildings. By these Procedures, office security means the security that occurs within the office and in the environs immediately surrounding the office.

Responsibilities

In every case where the Company's employees are officed, the Corporate Security Manager (CSM) is charged with oversight of security. Oversight includes:

- Developing security policy as it pertains to office operations.

- Developing or participating in the development of security-related contingency plans, such as the Bomb Threat Plan and Disaster Recovery Plan.

- Advising office management in matters related to the acquisition and use of contract security services and security equipment, such as access control and intrusion detection systems.

- Advising construction management of security standards to be incorporated in the construction or retrofitting of office facilities.

- Conducting periodic security audits of office facilities.

The person who directly manages day-to-day office security will be a property management professional. In some cases, such as when the building is owned by the Company, the property manager will be a Company employee; in other cases, such as when the Company leases office space, the property manager will be employed by the building's owner or a contractor to the building's owner. The security-related functions of the property manager include:

- Acquiring and managing security officer services; providing an infrastructure for the services, such as space and equipment for a security center and standard operating procedures; and supporting the services with secretarial help, office supplies, etc.

- Managing fire detection and suppression systems.

- Performing a central role in the development and execution of security-related plans, such as the Bomb Threat Plan, Disaster Recovery Plan, and Severe Weather Plan.

Where an office building is occupied by several tenants, a security committee can be formed to agree and coordinate common security-related tasks. Multiple-tenancy can present special risks and will therefore demand special safeguards. For example, a tenant who keeps large sums of cash on hand will expose other tenants to the risk of violence associated with robbery. The challenge to managing office security is to establish and maintain a delicate balance between protecting assets and allowing safe and efficient office operations. The challenge is elevated when the balance must also include demands from fire, health, and safety advisers.

Security Risks

The risks are many and vary widely. They include:

- Theft and other crimes committed by opportunists who walk in off the street.

- Theft by persons with legitimate access to offices.

- Telephone threats, such as bomb and kidnap threats and extortion demands.

- Burglary.

- Theft, misuse of, and damage to information, including computer-stored information.

- Malicious damage.

- Civil disorder, demonstrations, and unwelcome occupation of offices.

- Terrorist attack.

- Workplace violence.

Factors Affecting Risk

Risks are elevated when an office:

- Is in a capital or major city where criminal activities and political protests occur with greater than average frequency.

- Has a high concentration of senior executives and expatriates.

- Contains a relatively large number of personnel and other high-value assets.

- Contains sensitive information that must be shielded from, e.g., an unfriendly host government, organized crime, competitors, activists, and the media.

Risk Analysis

Risk analysis is the process through which threats and vulnerabilities are to be identified. The tool of risk analysis is the security audit. The vulnerabilities identified through risk analysis are then addressed by offsetting safeguards.

The selection of an office site should be preceded by a careful examination of many factors, such as whether or not the site will be shared by other tenants, crime in the surrounding areas, the response times of emergency support services (e.g., fire, police, and ambulance), traffic congestion, public transport, parking, and demographics. A demographic assessment can include considering the office site location versus the home locations of employees. A security risk is presented when, e.g., a majority of employees would have to travel through a high-crime area in order to get to work. A demographic assessment can also consider risks not currently present but likely to evolve. An example might be the slow migration toward the office site of a high-crime population or of likely future changes to the surrounding roadways.

External Protection

- The building perimeter, including parking garages and lots, should be patrolled by security officers.

- Consideration should be given to using external CCTV with recording facilities that cover the accessible points. If appropriate, CCTV can be augmented with intrusion detection sensors.

- Depending on the criminal threats, strengthened doors and door frames and the provision of bars, grilles, security glass, or internally fixed security blinds to lower windows and the installation of electronic alarms may be necessary.

- The building should be well lit at night, and consideration should be given to fitting passive infrared (PIR) sensors at vulnerable points, especially entrances.

- Where there has been experience or threat of bombs being placed in the locality, anti-shatter protection should be provided to vulnerable windows up to the first five floors in suburban areas and up to ten floors in cities with tower blocks.

- Where there is a significant threat of personal weapons being carried into the office, a metal detector and a safe custody facility for such weapons should be installed.

Control of Vehicles and Parking

- Parking within the perimeter of office premises should be by permit only and entrance to parking space under or adjacent to the office should be controlled. An automatic or manually operated barrier may be required.

- Parking or loading bays under a building should be closed outside working hours with a steel roller or sliding shutter.

- Access from the parking garage to the office building should be controlled.

Access Control

- Entrances should be kept to a minimum.

- CCTV coverage should be considered for entrance/reception areas in main office buildings.

- All other doors giving access to the building should be identified and left locked (provided that the doors are fitted with emergency release devices on the inside).

- An access control system should be installed. Visitors should be issued passes and escorted to and from reception and within the building by a member of staff, to whom the pass should be handed as the visitor leaves. Passes should be worn visibly at all times to deter/detect unauthorized entrants.

- Additional access controls should be installed to restricted areas such as computer suites or areas where classified information is readily accessible.

- If the building is shared with other occupants, unauthorized access via elevators and fire escapes should be prevented.

Reception

- Siting: The desk should be sited with an uninterrupted view of the access doors, and between the access doors and the elevator, stairs or other access to the building so that everyone entering the building has to pass the desk.

- Display Board: A display board listing the occupiers of the building, with respective room numbers, should be placed beyond the reception desk so that a fraudulent caller cannot use the information.

- Duress Button: The receptionist should be provided with a concealed push button by which to summon assistance. Such an alarm should not sound in the reception area, but signal in an office that is continually occupied during office hours. The procedure for responding to such alarm calls must be known by all the occupants of that office. A visual (light) warning may be considered when security officers are present in the reception area.

- Door Release: An electric remote-control lock release (operated by the receptionist) may be desirable for doors and turnstiles leading into the building, thus enabling entry into the premises to be more securely controlled.

- Receptionist Protection: Where violent crime is prevalent, it may be necessary to provide the receptionist with protection (particularly where remote control locks are used to isolate the reception desk from the rest of the building). In this case, shatterproof or bulletproof glass, steel sheeting below desk level, and a substantial lock on the enclosed area may be needed to provide the receptionist with a protected environment.

- Signage: The whereabouts of the reception desk should be clearly indicated by a reception sign.

- Receptionist Duties: The receptionist should be thoroughly trained in the procedures for granting access to visitors. As a general rule, visitors are required to present identification, be logged in, obtain a visitor's pass, be escorted while in the building, and surrender the pass when exiting. The receptionist should also be trained in how to receive bomb threat calls, and how to respond in emergency situations, such as fire, serious injury, medical illness, protest demonstrations, and civil disorder.

Security Officer Duties

- Prevent unauthorized access to the premises.

- Monitor the security systems, such as intrusion detection alarms and CCTV.

- Carry out searches of employees, vehicles, or premises, if required.

- Carry out fire and safety checks and after-hours checks on the security of classified or valuable items.

- Respond to emergencies.

Management should decide, in the light of the threat and the operational needs of the office, whether officers should be employed to supervise the building after normal working hours or whether reliance should be put instead on physical protection measures and electronic sensing equipment.

If contract employees are employed, management should be satisfied with the contractor's standards of recruitment and training and of the supervisors employed by the contract firm. Contracts should be reviewed at regular intervals, preferably annually.

All security employees should be guided by and familiar with a set of written standard operating procedures.

Keys

- Arrangements should exist for the controlled issue of keys (master key system and key register) and for their safe custody outside working hours. Such keys should be accessible at any time should an emergency arise.

Security of Information

- Employees should be reminded periodically of their responsibility to safeguard sensitive information. All sensitive materials must be secured after hours. Where a project is being developed and classified material is required to be displayed on walls, the offices concerned should become a restricted area with limited access.

- Management is responsible for ensuring that suitable security containers are available to employees for storage of sensitive materials. Where there is a substantial quantity of classified material, it should be stored in a separate room with limited access. Backup tapes, disks, and the like should be secured in off-site storage.

- The use of key boxes is recommended for office areas in which several employees may require access to a number of keys.

- Mail should not be left in unattended in-trays, in public access areas (e.g., pigeon holes), or in mail trolleys over night.

- To avoid sight of classified faxes outside normal office hours, a fax box or a time switch should be fitted or the memory facility used.

- When classified papers are being copied, a responsible member of the department should supervise the operation to ensure that no additional copies are made and that all spoiled copies are shredded.

- Destruction of unwanted classified material should be made by the provision of shredders in a central facility or to individual users. Cross-cut shredders should be used for highly sensitive material. An alternative or supplemental method is to provide secure waste boxes at convenient locations, being sure that full bags of sensitive waste are sealed with security tags and stored securely for collection by a disposal contractor. Material that cannot be shredded, e.g., disks, tapes, and transparencies, should be placed into a separate container and secured until destroyed by a bonded disposal contractor.

- To ensure compliance with information security rules, management should carry out spot checks on a random basis.

Computer Security

- The location of computer centers should not be highlighted by notice boards or other signage. Signs at the entry points should clearly state that only authorized persons may enter, but reference to the area being a computer center should be left out.

- Consideration should be given to fitting anti-theft devices to desktop machines to prevent theft. Laptops should be secured by keys in their docking stations or in secured drawers/cabinets for safekeeping.

Suspect Letters and Packages

- The procedures for receiving and distributing mail should be studied and arrangements made to enable suspect items to be identified and dealt with safely. Incoming goods should be checked against delivery notes, and unsolicited goods and suspect parcels and mail should be treated with caution.

- Where local conditions and experience suggest that a threat exists of letter or package bombs being addressed to the office, radiographic (i.e., X-ray/fluoroscope) equipment should be purchased and operators trained.

Chief Executive's Suite of Offices/Boardroom

- Access to the chief executive's office should be controlled, such as by a combination of electronic access control and a receptionist/secretary. In high threat environments, there should be an escape route from or a safe haven within the CE's office. If a safe haven is installed, it should be equipped with a duress alarm and emergency communications.

Bomb Threat Planning

Each office should have a written contingency plan for bomb threats, covering:

- Written instructions for telephone operators on how to deal with a bomb threat call.

- Liaison with local police, fire department, and ambulance services.

- Search procedures.

- Evacuation procedures and safe areas.

- Training of response persons, testing, and practice drills.

Loss Prevention

- Equipment such as computers, printers, and fax machines should bear a tag or etched mark that corresponds to an inventory system.

- Inventories should be maintained for IT equipment, office furniture, art objects, and antiques. The cost, book value, and replacement and/or insurance value should be noted, and physical counts made on an annual basis.

- Access should be tightly controlled to areas containing high-value assets such as cash, stocks, bonds, check stock, and very sensitive information.

Personnel Issues

Background screening, worked out in advance with the human resources office, should be carried out prior to employment. The nature of the screening will vary according to the security risks present and the laws of the jurisdiction.

New employees, including contractors, should be briefed on their personal security obligations when first joining the company. New employees should receive copies of any currently applicable security policies and procedures, such as those that relate to the protection of sensitive information and the use of computer equipment.

Where the office is in a high-risk community, employees should be briefed initially and periodically as needed concerning security-related risks outside of the office, such as those associated with travel to and from work, robbery on the street, burglary at home, etc. Advice should also be provided when employees are scheduled to travel to high-risk areas.

When an employee leaves, measures should be in place to retrieve company property, such as identity card, files, PC, cellular phone, car, credit cards, and money advances.

Cashier Office

- The office should be a secure area.

- External windows should be fitted with high-security locks and alarm sensors. They should also be blocked, e.g., by external grilles.

- A metal door and frame with sturdy lock and bolts should be installed. The door should be kept locked from the inside when occupied.

- Bullet-resistant glass should be fitted to an internal window/counter.

- The safe or cash container should be fixed to the floor/wall.

- An internally operated audible alarm for use when the office is occupied should be fitted.

- An alarm to the door and a PIR intruder detector with alarm inside the office to be activated outside normal working hours should be fitted.

- Written procedures for banking and cash handling should be followed. The procedures should address the steps to be taken during a robbery. In the interest of protecting life, it is highly recommended that cashier office employees not resist, that the robber's demands be met, and that no attempt be made to capture the robber on the premises.

- Secure containers, and when necessary an escort, should be used to convey monies and/or checks to the bank.

- Cash, drafts, checks, etc. should be adequately protected.

- CCTV cameras should monitor the teller's area. A concealed button or pedal device should be installed for signaling a robbery in progress. The CCTV system should automatically go into a record mode when the alarm is activated.

Photocopying/Telephone System/Stationery

- All reasonable steps should be taken to guard against improper use of the photocopying machines, telephone system, and stationery supplies.

Cleaning Staff

- Cleaning of offices is generally carried out by a contractor outside normal working hours. It is therefore necessary to establish the reliability of the contractor; ensure the contractor carries out vetting procedures that assure a service free of the potential for crime and violence; monitor the work carried out; and conduct random security checks, such as searching the cleaning staff and the trash trucks as they exit.

- Offices containing classified material that cannot be locked away should be cleaned during working hours or cleaned in the presence of a security officer.

Disaster Recovery/Business Continuity

- The business unit's plan to recover from a disaster and return to normal business operations will include many security-related tasks. In every case where a task is to be performed, there must be a corresponding written instruction. A severe weather plan, for example, may require security officers in the aftermath of a hurricane to direct traffic. That task, along with any others that might apply, would be described in detail in a set of written instructions.

Following is a checklist for evaluating office security.

A Checklist for Assessing Office Security

Policy

- Does the office have a copy of the security policy?

- Has the security policy been communicated to all employees and contractors in writing with a supporting letter or note from management?

- Is a copy available or posted on notice boards throughout the building?

- Is the policy emphasized during new employee orientation?

- Is it supported by periodic written communications or posters?

Responsibility

- Is security responsibility clearly defined in the property manager's job description? Are responsibilities and tasks clearly set out in writing?

- Has the property manager received formal security training?

- Does the property manager have regular meetings with local management and the Corporate Director of Security to discuss security, and are the meetings recorded?

- Does the property manager keep and comply with all currently applicable security policies and procedures, such as those that apply to information security, personal protection, travel security, and business ethics?

Threat Assessment

- Has a threat assessment of the office location been carried out and main risks identified?

- Has an assessment been conducted during the last two years?

- Has there been liaison with the local authorities to validate the assessment?

- Has there been liaison with other companies in the area in respect of the assessment?

- In the case of a shared building, is there a committee to discuss actions in respect of the assessment?

Security Audit

- Was a full audit conducted to assess the need for security measures, systems, and devices when the offices were first occupied?

- Has this been reviewed on an annual basis?

- Are all security-related incidents noted and reviewed at regular intervals?

- Is there an up-to-date plan/drawing of the office building, and are all security features marked on it, e.g., alarmed exits, fire hoses, fire extinguishers, and first aid kits?

Perimeter

- Is the perimeter of the building checked on a daily basis (both during the day and at night)?

- Are trees and shrubs that are close to the building regularly trimmed?

- Have drain pipes been protected with anti-climb paint or anti-intrusion collars?

- If the roof of the building provides access to or from other buildings outside the company's premises, have measures been taken to secure access at this level?

- Are sensitive materials screened from public view?

- Is a tour of inspection at night carried out to ensure that external lighting is adequate?

- Have all exterior windows been treated with anti-shatter film?

- Is the responsibility for checking that all windows are closed allocated to an individual?

Access Control

- Are all employees issued an identity badge?

- Does the badge carry a photo?

- Has the company name been omitted?

- Are employees required to wear their passes?

- Does the facility have a time and attendance access control system?

- Are reports of access and egress maintained and regularly reviewed?

- Are all entrances equipped with electronic readers?

- Are measures in place to check the entry privileges of persons entering the building?

- Are measures in place to ensure that:

  - The security department is informed immediately of all employees leaving the company?

  - Terminating employees hand in their identification cards, credit cards, key cards, mechanical keys, and Company-owned property?

- Are there controls to prevent unauthorized use of entrances and exits?

- Is there a notice directing all visitors/temporary contractors to report to a reception point?

- Are all visitors received and dispatched at a reception point?

- Does the visitors register reflect date, time, name, firm, and person to see?

- Have employees been requested to inform reception on the day of expected visit, with name, firm, and time?

- Is the member of staff phoned to be told of visitor's arrival?

- Is the visitor provided with a visitor pass?

- Are visitors required to wear their passes?

- Does the member of the staff come to collect the visitor at the reception area?

- Does the member of the staff escort the visitor back to reception at end of visit?

- Are there procedures in place to account for visitors who have not booked out or handed back their passes?

- Are long-term contractors issued passes that differ from employee passes?

- Are short-term contractors or temporary employees issued passes that automatically expire at the end of the agreed work period?

- Is there an effective control for issue and collection of passes to contractors?

- Are contractors required to wear their passes?

- Have additional controls been installed for the following restricted areas?

  - Computer suites.

  - Cash desks.

  - Storage areas for classified information.

  - Storage areas for valuable goods.

  - Senior management offices.

  - Special project areas.

Loading Dock

- Are there adequate access control measures at the loading dock?

- Are messengers and couriers dealt with at a separate entrance or window and prevented from accessing the building?

Parking

- Is there a designated employee, visitor, or contractor parking area on company property?

- Is vehicle access to these areas controlled, e.g., by electronic means or by officers checking passes?

- Are vehicles required to display stickers?

- Is a list of owners and registration numbers of all vehicles parked on company property maintained?

- Are parking areas adequately secured?

- Is parking controlled, e.g., by electronic means or by officers checking permits or passes?

- Is there a control on visitor use of parking facilities?

- Are all entrances, parking areas to offices controlled, e.g., by swipe cards or digital pads?

Alarms

- Has the installation of an alarm system been considered?

- If considered necessary, has it been installed?

- Is it a local alarm or is it linked to a central station?

- Does it cover the whole of the premises?

- What forms of intrusion detection are employed at the site?

  - Passive infrared detectors?

  - Door and window contacts?

  - Roof and floor beams?

- Are all exits alarmed?

- Is the control unit in a secure location?

- Has somebody been allocated with the task of switching the alarm off and on?

- Have the police been supplied with names and addresses of key holders in the event of an alarm being activated?

CCTV

- Has the installation of CCTV been considered?

- If CCTV is installed:

  - Does it fully cover the perimeter?

  - Does it cover vulnerable points?

  - Are the monitoring procedures adequate?

  - Are the pictures recorded?

  - Is a motion detection system installed to activate cameras?

  - Is there an adequate response procedure for a security incident?

  - Is there a procedure that deals with camera failure or picture loss?

- Is there an adequate maintenance program?

- Is an inspection of the TV monitors carried out at night to ensure that the cameras are all working correctly?

Security Officers

- Are the security officers contract or in-house employees?

- If contract officers, have they been vetted?

- Have they received pre-assignment training in:

  - Criminal law and powers to detain and search?

  - Security equipment and procedures?

  - Safety and fire regulations?

  - Fire-fighting procedures?

  - CPR and basic first aid?

- Are they licensed or certified as may be required by law?

- Is the number of security officers considered adequate for the site?

- Are officer replacements and reinforcements available?

- Do the work shifts have the correct number of officers?

- Are the work shifts too long or too short?

- Does the site have 24-hour coverage?

- Is the guard organization structured to facilitate a clear chain of command?

- Are security officers rotated between stationary posts?

- Do the officers know how to respond when alarms are activated?

- Are officers included in emergency plans?

- Do officers understand their duties and are they tested by mock drills?

- Are officers familiar with the use of basic fire-fighting equipment?

- If there is a single officer on duty, does the contract company call him or her regularly to check that all is well?

- Are the officers equipped with radio communication for their patrols?

- Are the officers provided with written site instructions that cover all aspects of their duties?

- Were site instructions drawn up in consultation with all interested parties?

- Once on site, is training given covering:

    - Regulations that apply to the site?

    - Specific job duties?

    - Layout of the installation or offices, to include vulnerable points such as secure and hazardous areas?

    - The use and maintenance of security equipment?

    - Safety and fire regulations?

    - Emergency devices such as backup generators, uninterrupted power supply systems, control switches, and emergency radios and telephones?

- Is an updated copy of written instructions available at all times to security employees on duty?

- Is there a log book in which the following are reflected?

    - Supervisory visits.

    - Shift change.

    - Incidents/occurrences.

    - Special instructions.

- Does the person responsible for security review the log book on a regular basis?

- Is there an adequate system of supervision and monitoring of patrols?

- Are the standards of recruitment, training, and supervision by the contract firm satisfactory?

Searches

- Are searches made of bags, packages, and similar personal containers?

- If so, are the searches carried out regularly, e.g., once each week?

- Is a register maintained of all searches carried out, giving name, date, time, and result?

- Do employees sign the register to confirm they have been searched?

- Do officers have instructions on what action should be taken if a person refuses to be searched or is found in unauthorized possession of property?

- Is a register held at entry and exit points of all employees who regularly bring in laptops or other items of concern to the management?

- Is there a system of passes for persons taking out items of concern?

- Is there an up-to-date list of authorized signatures of those who issue such passes at the entry and exit points?

Receptionist

- Does the receptionist have clear written instructions related to security?

- Do these instructions cover:

  - Receiving visitors?

  - Dealing with unusual situations, e.g., unruly visitors, bomb and extortion threats made over the telephone, and public demonstrations?

- Has a panic button been installed at the receptionist's desk?

- Is it tested regularly (at least once a month)?

- Are there instructions to members of staff as to what action they should take if the panic button is activated?

Security of Information

- Has a threat assessment been made as to which departments produce or receive sensitive documents that are likely to be of interest to third parties?

- Have the following sensitive matters been considered in information security practices?

  - Acquisitions and developments.

  - Financial figures.

  - Salary data.

  - Personnel files.

  - Manufacturing processes.

  - Patents being applied for and other development issues.

- Are those who receive sensitive papers required to sign an acknowledgement of receipt?

- Is there evidence that management is committed to a clear desk policy?

- Are after-hours checks carried out to see if employees are adhering to the policy?

- Are reports of breaches sent to management with a request for corrective action?

- Has management ensured that employees have the correct storage for classified documents?

- Are office and desk keys kept in key safes?

- Are classified diskettes locked away when unattended?

- Have approved storage containers been provided for use at the homes of "at home workers" who regularly work with classified information?

Destruction of Classified Waste

- Have employees been given instructions concerning destruction of classified waste?

- Are there suitable shredders for destruction of sensitive papers?

- Are "confidential waste boxes" supplied?

- Are the locks on the boxes adequate?

- Are the boxes monitored and collected regularly?

- Once this confidential waste has been collected from the boxes, is it stored in a secure area until either being destroyed in house or collected by a contractor?

- If collected by a contractor, has the contractor signed a confidentiality agreement?

- Is a certificate of destruction issued for each consignment of classified waste?

- Are procedures in place for the destruction of magnetic tapes and disks containing confidential waste?

Security Control Room

- Is the security control room designed so that access is controlled and TV screens easily monitored?

- Are the following standard documents, security stationery items, and lists available?

    - The assignment instruction (or standing orders for the security employees).

    - Emergency plans and instructions for fire, accident, major disaster, emergency evacuation, and bomb threats.

    - Temporary instructions.

    - Daily occurrence log.

    - Telephone message log.

    - List/directory of all employees.

    - Register of employee license plate numbers and parking space numbers.

    - List of authorized contractors.

    - Register of those who regularly bring in and out portable computers or other such valuable equipment.

- Is there a process to record:

- Key issues and returns?

- Lost and found property?

- Fire alarm tests?

- Fire drills?

- Personnel and vehicle searches?

- Hot work permits?

- Security incidents?

- Fire?

- Accidents?

Computer Security

- Has responsibility for computer security been allocated?

- Does the person responsible hold copies of all currently applicable policies and procedures related to information security?

- Is this person in contact with the IT Security Committee?

- Is access to the computer suite controlled?

- Is there an up-to-date list of persons who are allowed into the computer suite during working hours and after hours?

- Are all computers, whether on-site or remote, protected from theft and unauthorized access?

- Does the protection include:

  - Physical security?

  - Access control through an appropriate security system?

  - A lock-out mechanism that automatically engages when the machine is unattended?

  - Safeguards against unauthorized log on to the system?

- Do all computers have systems or procedures to detect viruses?

- Are procedures in place for remote location authentication?

- Have employees been made aware of standards for passwords? For example:

  - That they should, at a minimum, be changed every 60 days.

  - That they should not be recycled.

  - That they must be at least six characters in length and include both upper- and lowercase letters and one number.

  - That they should not be easily guessed.

  - That they must not be words from a dictionary.

  - That they should not be shared.

  - That, if written down, they should be protected.

- Have all computer equipment and peripherals been recorded on an asset register?

- Have all computer equipment and peripherals been etched or tagged with a company identifier and a location code?

- Have employees been made aware of the following?

  - All applications must be legally acquired and proof of ownership should be retained.

  - Games should not be introduced.

  - The company forbids the unauthorized copying and use of data and applications.

  - PCs and terminals should be logged off when unattended.

  - Computer diskettes containing classified material should be securely locked away.

- Are employees aware that abuse of the computer system could be regarded as a serious disciplinary matter?

- Does the office have a disaster recovery plan?

Board Room/Meeting Rooms/Senior Manager Offices

- Are such rooms checked for eavesdropping devices on an ad hoc basis?

- Is there a record kept of when this has been done and by whom?

- Are such rooms kept locked?

- Are such rooms cleaned under supervision?

- Are meeting rooms checked after meetings of a sensitive nature to ensure that:

    - Flip chart paper used has been taken away?

    - Waste bins and scribbling pads have been cleared?

    - No slides or information have been left behind?

Mail Service/Distribution

- Do written procedures exist for dealing with mail?

- Does the mail room have a list of pointers to look for suspect letters and packages?

- Are measures in place for dealing with a suspect package and has training been given to those whose duties involve package handling?

- Has consideration been given to the use of specialist detection equipment?

- Are incoming goods checked against delivery notes?

Key Control

- Is there a master key system?

- Is a key register maintained?

- Has somebody been nominated to be responsible for the issue and receipt of keys?

- Is a list maintained in the Security office of persons authorized to draw keys?

- Are signatures obtained each time a key changes hands

- If keys are issued on a permanent basis to individuals, is this recorded in the register?

- When keys are not in use, are they kept in a locked key cupboard?

- Are all keys tagged and numbered in accordance with the register?

- Is a complete key check carried out on a regular basis?

- When keys are lost, are locks replaced?

- Are all external doors and doors providing access to sensitive areas fitted with high-security locks?

- Are keys to office furniture kept in a key cabinet overnight?

- Are procedures in place for reporting the loss of keys and replacing them?

Cleaning of Offices

- Are offices cleaned by contract or in-house employees?

- Have the employees been vetted?

- Do cleaners carry out their function at the close of daily business?

- Is their access to the building controlled?

- Are they supervised when cleaning sensitive areas?

Bomb Threats

- Is there a written contingency plan for bomb threats?

- Have telephone operators been given written instructions on how to deal with a bomb threat call?

- Do they have a checklist immediately at hand?

- Are procedures in place for networking with local police?

- Have bomb search procedures been devised and practiced?

- Have evacuation plans been drawn up?

- Have evacuation routes been selected and marked?

- Have assembly areas outside the building been designated?

- Have the evacuation procedures been tested within the last year?

Loss Prevention

- Are computers, printers, fax machines, and the like etched or tagged with the Company's name and inventory code?

- Is access restricted to areas where desirable or high-value objects and cash are stored?

- Are inventories maintained for:

  - Office furniture (desks, chairs, filing equipment)?

  - IT equipment?

  - Art objects, paintings, and antiques?

- Are replacement costs shown on the inventory?

- Is the inventory checked on an annual basis?

Personnel Issues

- Are background screening procedures used?

- Are new employees briefed on security matters when joining the company?

- Do all new employees receive copies of currently applicable security policies and procedures?

- Is there a procedure in place for briefing employees who are scheduled to travel to high-risk areas?

- When an employee is leaving, are there measures in place to verify that all identity cards, credit cards, tools, documents, and other forms of company property have been returned?

Cash Handling

- Is there a cashier office? If yes, is the office equipped with:

  - Solid walls and doors?

  - The appropriate grades of high-security locks?

  - A high-security window at the cashier station?

- A kick rail alarm and panic button?

- Are the procedures for banking and cash handling being followed?

- Is a secure container used to convey money/checks to the bank?

- Is an escort used when conveying monies to the bank?

- Do employees leave at irregular times?

- If a security company is used to do the banking, is a receipt issued?

- Does the receipt include seal numbers?

- Are negotiable instruments (e.g., cash, drafts, and checks) adequately protected?

Photocopying

- Have all reasonable steps been taken to guard against improper use of the photocopying machines?

Stationery

- Have all reasonable steps been taken to guard against improper use of stationery materials?

Cafeteria

- Are storeroom areas, refrigerators, deep freezers, and cold rooms kept locked?

- Is access to these areas restricted and controlled?

- Is the catering contracted out?

- Are sufficient measures in place to safeguard thefts from the cafeteria and vending machines?

Disaster Recovery

- Does the office have a disaster recovery plan?

- By reference to this plan, could one establish:

    - Where the switchboard could be reconstituted?

    - How data requirements could be met by linking the mainframe to new screens in new locations?

- Contact with telephone and computer supplier to reinstate communications and order extra equipment?

- The way to cascade information down through the organization so that employees would know what is expected of them?

- Employees numbers in each business area and the amount of office space available in and around the city?

- If a replacement trading floor is needed?

- Need for press release and advertising space in the national press?

PASSWORD PROTECTION

All of the Company's computer systems use passwords to grant access. Passwords are very valuable protective tools, but they are susceptible to compromise.

Actions

- Choose a password that cannot be guessed, for example:

    - Make it at least seven characters long, ideally longer.

    - Include numbers, letters, and punctuation characters where possible.

    - Do not use your name, nickname, your company user identification, social security number, employee number, telephone number, or any variation of these.

    - Choose a string that does not constitute a word in a dictionary.

- Change your password once a month. Make it completely different from any password used previously. For example, don't just change a single digit of the current password.

- Keep your password confidential. Do not tell it to others and do not write it down where it can be seen or found.

- If it becomes necessary to disclose a password, change it immediately afterwards.

- Don't leave a computer unattended that has been logged onto using your password. Anything that occurs under your password becomes your responsibility.

- Activate your password-protected screen saver.

- When your computer system is not in use, log-off from servers and mail systems.

- If you access computers via the Internet, choose a different password from the one used for the Company's systems.

PROPERTY REMOVAL

The Company intends that Company-owned property will leave the premises in one of two ways: off the loading dock or through the front door. The Procedures that relate to loading dock operations apply to tradespeople, suppliers, vendors, et al. Loading dock procedures are not covered herein. These Procedures apply to employees who carry Company-owned property off the premises via the front door.

The Property Removal Pass System

The Security Manager is responsible for implementing a property removal pass system. The system will address three classes of property:

- Company-owned materials, equipment, and supplies that do not bear inventory tags.

- Company-owned items that bear inventory tags, such as laptop computers.

- Personal property, such as radios and wall accessories.

Non-Tagged Property

The removal of property not bearing inventory tags will be controlled with the use of a property removal pass, as follows:

- Copy 1 (the original) of the pass is filled out by the employee who plans to remove the property.

- The employee's supervisor signs the pass to indicate approval. The supervisor retains Copy 2 (the first carbon) as a record and as a reminder that the property is to be returned on or before the return date indicated on the pass.

- The employee presents the pass to the security officer at the lobby security desk when taking the property from the premises. The security officer compares the pass against the property. Copy 1 is retained by the employee. Copy 3 (the second carbon) is retained by the security officer. Copy 3 is filed in the security center as a record of property removed.

Tagged Property

Property bearing inventory tags will be controlled as follows:

- The employee presents the item at the lobby security desk. To facilitate the process, the employee presents the item with the inventory tag showing.

- The security officer uses the bar code hand wand to "read" the tag. The reading creates a "removal entry" in the computer-assisted inventory system.

- When the employee returns the item, the security officer again uses the bar code hand wand. This reading creates a "return entry" in the inventory system.

Personal Property

Personal property leaving the premises will be controlled as follows:

- The employee will describe the personal property in a memo, attest that he or she is the owner of the property, and sign the memo.

- Upon leaving the premises, the employee presents the memo to the security officer; the officer compares the memo against the property and retains the memo as a record.

Sanctions

The Company's policy is to enforce property removal procedures. An employee who is found removing property without regard to the procedures can be disciplined, including termination. An employee who removes a tagged item from the premises without having the removal recorded and who loses the tagged item is required to reimburse the company, resign, or be terminated.

RAPE AVOIDANCE

These recommendations are provided for use by female employees whose gender, both on and off the job, exposes them to the risk of rape or sexual assault.

Actions to Take on the Job

If you are a female employee with reason to believe that you are in danger of rape or sexual assault, or any other crime, you should:

- Make a report to your immediate supervisor.

- If you are not confident that your supervisor has removed the danger, you should make a report to your supervisor's manager, to the Human Resources Manager, or to the Security Manager.

Actions to Take off the Job

While on the Street

- If you think you are being trailed, cross the street and change directions. If the trailing continues, don't be afraid to scream and run to the nearest business or residence.

- When you arrive home at night, have your key ready to open the door, and get inside as quickly as you can. If you return home in a taxi or a friend's car, have the driver wait until you're safely inside. If someone suspicious is loitering near your doorway, don't approach. Get help elsewhere, such as at a neighbor's home. If you come home to find a window or door forced open, don't enter or call out. Go directly to a safe place and call the police.

- Walk near the curb and avoid passing close to shrubbery, dark doorways, vacant lots, unlit parks, or parked cars. Shun short-cuts, especially through backyards, closed buildings, parking lots, and alleyways.

- Wait for public transportation in lighted areas, near other people. Don't isolate yourself.

- Walk away from strangers who approach you in the street. Threaten to scream for help if the stranger persists in wanting to talk or follows you.

- Do not attempt to walk through a group of men. Walk around them, or cross the street.

- Know the area you walk in. Be extra aware of what's going on around you. Listen for footsteps and voices nearby. Walk in a brisk, businesslike, and confident manner. Rapists, like predatory animals, look for the weak and unprotected.

When at Home and When Driving

- List only your last name and initials in phone directories and on mailboxes if you live alone.

- Keep your doors securely locked, whether at home or not..

- Leave lights burning inside and out whenever you expect to return after dark.

- Don't open your door to an unknown caller. Check the credentials of anyone who shows up uninvited. Don't let a stranger come in to use your telephone. If an unknown caller pleads an emergency, offer to summon help while he waits outside.

- Whenever practical, drive your car on well-lighted and heavily trafficked roads. Drive with doors locked and windows rolled up.

- Look in the back seat of your car before entering to make sure an assailant isn't hiding there.

- Keep your car in gear when stopped in traffic. If threatened, blow the horn and drive away as fast as possible.

- Do not hitchhike even if your car breaks down. Instead, lock yourself in the car and put a flag on the aerial or door handle to summon the police. If extreme circumstances require you to hitchhike, follow these two primary rules: Never accept a ride with more than one man in a vehicle, and never take a ride from anyone who changes direction to pick you up.

In Buildings

- Take extreme care in elevators. It's safer to remain in the lobby for a few minutes than to ride alone with someone who frightens you. When you enter an elevator, stand near the control panel and alarm button. If you're attacked, hit the alarm button and as many floor buttons as you can.

- The same cautions apply to stairwells, garages, and common area laundry rooms. These places are preferred by rapists.

If Attacked

- Your best defense is escape. Your legs are to run with and your voice is to scream with.

- If you are forced to fight, fight dirty. Bite kick gouge eyes with keys, a pen, your thumbs, your nails. And all the while, scream to attract attention.

- If your attacker subdues you, claim to have a venereal disease or act as if you are throwing up. There are no rules when resisting rape.

Your worst defense against rape could be a weapon that is taken away and used against you. There are, however, a variety of everyday items you can use as a defensive or signaling device, e.g., a plastic squirt container filled with ammonia, a key ring clenched in the fist with keys, a police whistle, a hat pin, a pencil, a corkscrew, an umbrella, and a pocket-size alarm.

REPAIR CREW ACCESS CONTROL

The Company requires of repair crews:

- That notice be given to the Company of the dates that entry will be required to perform the agreed repairs.

- That while on the premises the repair crew be under the supervision of a responsible individual.

- That the repair crew comply with Company's rules, such as observing the access control protocols, not fraternizing with employees, not touching Company property unrelated to the repairs, and not leaving the repair site. The security officer's responsibility is to enforce the rules.

Actions

The Security Supervisor will maintain a Repairs File at the Security Center. The notices will normally be issued by the Property Management Office and will reflect the repair company identity, the times, dates, places, and nature of the work and whether or not the repair crew will require continual monitoring.

The Security Supervisor will stay apprised of the file and arrange for the availability of sufficient security on the scheduled repair dates.

If the repairs involve the use of heat-generating equipment, such as welding and soldering torches, or repairs that will produce air-borne particles, the Security Supervisor will ask the Building Maintenance Engineer to issue a "hot work permit." This permit will authorize the Security Supervisor to disarm or cover heat and smoke detecting devices in the repair area during the period of the hot work. Following the repairs, the Security Supervisor will ensure (by double-checking) that the heat and smoke detecting devices are re-armed and/or uncovered.

When a repair crew arrives at the facility, the crew supervisor will provide a list of the names of the crew members. The list will be attached to the Repairs File. If a repair crew arrives at the facility without having made the required advance notice, the Security Supervisor will contact the Property Manager for guidance.

Give to the repair crew supervisor a copy of the booklet entitled "Expectations of Repair Contractors." This booklet:

- Identifies the behavior standards expected of repair crews while on the Company's premises.

- Identifies on-site privileges, such as parking of personal vehicles, use of the cafeteria, and use of certain rest rooms.

- Provides notice that the Company reserves the right to inspect any materials entering or leaving the premises in the custody of repair crews.

- Gives instructions as to the parking of vehicles and the staging of repair equipment.

- Gives instructions as to safety rules that apply to all building occupants.

- Gives instructions as to building evacuation procedures during an emergency, such as a fire.

Issue Contractor Badges to repair crew members who DO NOT require escort. These individuals, who are typically elevator and air conditioning system technicians, are identified in the Repairs File.

Collect Contractor Badges when the repair crew leaves after the job has been completed. Make an entry in the file that shows when the job was completed.

RETAIL SECURITY

Retail operations are susceptible to crime in many forms. Surveys of retail businesses in the United States show that crime-related loss is in the range of 2 to 3 percent of total sales revenues. Crime-related loss includes:

- Employee theft

- Customer theft

- Robbery

- Burglary

- Malicious damage

- Vendor/supplier theft

- Credit card fraud

- Assault on store clerks and customers

- Counterfeit money

Security Measures

A security professional should confirm that adequate measures are in place at retail operations to identify and control losses and to ensure that retail managers have access to crime prevention advice.

Retail managers should be encouraged to maintain control measures for stocks and sales to enable them to identify vulnerable areas and places where theft may occur. Preventive measures must be carefully planned and evaluated if they are to reduce the losses in a cost-effective manner. The cooperation of staff and their training and motivation to reduce losses must be given priority.

Well-designed and secured site computer systems can play a significant part in the maintenance of controls and to support preventive measures. Features such as automated stock reconciliation procedures and transaction audit trails are examples of the types of aids that can be employed.

Resources
Retail locations should have:

- An Operations Manual that includes guidance on security policies and practices. The manual should contain procedures for ensuring that security features are incorporated into the design of new retail outlets.

- A booklet that advises employees of their security responsibilities.

- A source for obtaining professional and objective advice on the installation of CCTV, alarms, safes and related security equipment, and a contact with local law enforcement regarding proactive police measures (such as frequent patrolling) and investigations.

- A training capability to enable structured sessions on security practices.

Loss Prevention

Employee Theft

Employee theft occurs in multiple ways, e.g., cash register manipulation (open drawer), short-changing, overcharging, skimming, and double imprinting credit card vouchers. Reduction of theft by employees is largely a matter of hiring and retaining honest people, motivating them, and maintaining controls on assets. Attention to the following points is essential:

- Recruitment

  - Choosing the right candidate

  - Making a good first interview

  - Checking references

- Attitude and Training

  - Motivating employees

  - Communicating at all levels

  - Instilling pride in the work

  - Training on a regular basis

- Internal Control Procedures

  - Enforcing strict rules on cash handling and collection

- Monitoring cash register transactions

- Paying attention when receiving goods

- Controlling keys

Customer Crime

Loss attributed to customers is also varied. The common forms include shoplifting, price switching, and check and credit card fraud. Shoplifting and price switching can be reduced by intelligent siting and high visibility of stocks, use of mirrors, attention by store personnel, and covert surveillance when needed. Check and credit card fraud require other countermeasures, discussed later in these Procedures.

Robbery

Robbery can be reduced to the extent that strict banking procedures are followed, e.g., keeping on-hand receipts to a minimum and utilizing a courier service for transporting receipts to the bank. Other countermeasures include placing limits on the amount of cash kept in the cash drawer, placing receipts in a safe that cannot be accessed by the cashier, making the cashier visible from outside the store, installing bullet-resistant glass around the cashier counter, and installing a CCTV taping system and a robbery alarm system. Employees must be trained in how to react in a robbery so as to minimize personal harm and harm to customers. The use of security officers at a retail location will be predicated upon the history of robberies at the location and the current perceived risk of robbery as determined by a security professional.

Burglary

Burglary prevention requires hardening of the target, i.e., strengthening the burglar resistance of doors, windows, skylights and other entrances, installing security locks, keeping valuables off the premises during nonoperating hours, hiring a security patrol, and installing a burglar alarm system. Also important is the close adherence by employees to closing procedures.

Vandalism

An effective deterrent to vandalism is good housekeeping. Retail locations that are clean, well-maintained and free of graffiti are less likely to be vandalized.

Credit Card Losses

Computer-assisted authorization and monitoring systems and electronic data capture at the point of sale can be effective deterrents to credit card fraud but are not foolproof. Fraud control is effective to the extent that point-of-sale clerks function with complete integrity and careful attention to fraud control procedures. The motivation of clerks to follow the procedures can be enhanced when they understand:

- The magnitude of credit card fraud and its impact on profits.

- The common techniques of credit card fraud.

- Actions taken by management and law enforcement to detect, investigate, and prosecute credit card fraud.

Common Techniques

Criminals employ numerous methods to illegally obtain and use credit cards:

- Fraudulent applications. Accounts are set up and cards issued to criminals who have adopted the identity of a real person or who have conceived a bogus identity.

- Account take-over schemes. These include criminals who pose as true cardholders to fool issuers into misdirecting cards, who change personal identification numbers (PINs), who obtain additional cards, and who issue courtesy checks to themselves for fraudulent use.

- Lost, stolen, and never-received cards that are used for unauthorized purchases.

- Counterfeit and altered cards. Criminals manufacture and sell counterfeit cards to other criminals. At facilities with remote collection points, this counterfeiting need only be a reproduction of a magnetic strip.

- Collusive merchants. Merchants engage in fraudulent transactions involving stolen or counterfeit cards, mail order or telephone order fraud, or draft laundering.

- True cardholder fraud. The true cardholder attempts to defraud the issuer by claiming legitimate transactions are fraudulent or conspires with others to perpetrate fraud on the account.

- Employee fraud. Cards, account numbers, or account information are stolen and used for theft at the location or given to other parties.

- Skimming. Dishonest staff sell customer credit card numbers to criminals who manufacture duplicate cards.

SECURITY PROGRAM AUDITING

Use this document as a tool for assessing a facility's security program.

Security Policy

Is the facility Security Policy in written form and signed by the senior facility manager, and does it emphasize the importance of protecting people, property, and processes against loss or compromise?

Does the security policy include guidance for:

- Larceny?

- Burglary?

- Loss or compromise of proprietary information?

- Assault on employees and visitors?

- Bomb threats?

- Arson?

- Civil disturbances?

- Ethics and business conduct?

- Alcohol and drug abuse?

Is the security policy:

- Communicated in writing to all employees?

- Conspicuously posted throughout the facility?

- Referred to during new employee orientation?

- Referred to in group meetings?

- Contained in a manual?

- Referred to in management and employee training programs?

Does senior management support the security policy:

- By periodic written communications?

- By regular security tours?

- By participating in security program audits?

Security Standards and Procedures

Are there written standards for management performance in the security program?

Are security program standards communicated to all levels of management?

Are security instructions and procedures defined in a program manual?

Program Objectives

Are annual written security program objectives set for the organization?

What percentage of managers have developed written security program objectives?

To what degree are program objectives being achieved?

Security Organization/Administration

Has a person been designated in writing to coordinate the security program?

Does this person have direct access to senior management on security program matters?

Are security responsibilities written into appropriate manager job descriptions?

Is performance to security standards included in manager performance reviews?

Are local law enforcement, intelligence, security, and regulatory agencies contacted regularly for assistance in supporting the security program?

Are the people who are selected for sensitive or critical duties and positions screened for suitability and reliability?

Does the screening and verification process include:

- Criminal record checks?

- Credit checks?

- Education?

- Employment?

- Driver's license and driving record?

- Professional certification and/or professional licensing?

- Personal identity documents?

Management Training

What percentage of managers receive orientation and induction training to the security program?

Is this orientation and induction training completed within one month of appointment to a management position?

What percentage of managers have had a formal training course on fundamentals of security?

Are written materials used in this formal security management training course?

Is there a program that requires managers to attend formal security-update training at least every three years?

What percentage of managers have had the update training?

Employee Training

What percentage of employees receive orientation/induction training to security program standards?

Are written materials included in the orientation?

Are security awareness signs and notices posted in appropriate places to reinforce knowledge of security standards?

What percentage of employees holding specific security duties have received formal training in how to perform their duties?

What percentage of contractors who have specific security duties have received formal training in how to perform their duties?

Are training manuals used to aid and reinforce security training?

Are records kept to verify security training and identify employees needing such training?

Security Needs Established

Has a survey been made to determine the need for security measures, systems, and devices?

Did the survey determine the need for:

- Perimeter fencing or walls?

- Protection of doors, windows, and openings?

- Security alarm systems?

- Camera surveillance?

- Security lighting?

- Lock and key control?

- Security signs?

- Safes, vaults, and protected storage?

- Protection of vital utilities?

- Communications?

- Access control?

- Guard force?

- Computer protection?

- Information security?

- Emergency preparedness?

What percentage of the needs, as determined by this audit, have been met?

When were the security needs last reviewed and updated?

Access Control

Are methods taken to control entry and movement of people and vehicles as a security measure?

Do these controls include the following categories of personnel?

- Visitors

- Vendors

- Service and delivery personnel

Do these controls include the following categories of vehicles?

- Employee

- Visitor

- Vendor

- Contractor

- Service and delivery

Is the duplication of keys to buildings, vehicles, and storage areas controlled?

Information Security

Are procedures in effect to address the following:

- Marking of classified information?

- Control of classified information?

- Distribution of classified information?

- Transmission of classified information?

- Copying of classified information?

- Storage of classified information?

- Downgrading of classified information?

- Destruction of classified information?

Is a Clear Desk Policy in effect?

Are all employees who have access to sensitive information required to sign a nondisclosure agreement?

Are all contractors who have access to sensitive information required to sign a nondisclosure agreement?

Are speeches, news releases, presentations, technical papers, and other forms of open information reviewed for sensitivity and protection of trademarks before release?

Is the facility engaged in classified government work or involved in a classified contract?

Financial Assets Control

Do written delegations of financial authority exist?

Are delegations made to and signed at each level of authority?

Are delegations current?

Are delegations routinely followed?

Are adequate controls and written procedures in place to maintain individual accountability for employees with cash-handling responsibilities?

Are approval, purchasing, receiving, and payable functions separated?

Are procedures in place for the disposal of scrap waste and surplus materials?

Are "right to audit" clauses included in vendor and supplier contracts?

When was the last financial audit conducted?

Security Loss Reports and Records

How often are inventories, accountings, and records checks made to identify security losses?

Are security losses and incidents promptly investigated with the findings and actions reported?

Are loss event reports reviewed for action needed?

Does the security program require a complete investigation of criminal and malicious security losses and incidents involving:

- Cash and negotiables?

- Irregularities in financial accounts?

- Equipment and materials shortages?

- Expendable supplies and inventory shrinkage?

- Production losses from disturbances?

- Product loss or theft?

- Product extortion or contamination?

- Computer theft?

- Other security losses?

Is there a central facility file of security incident investigation reports?

Are investigative and incident reports kept in an active file for at least two years?

Are the appropriate levels of facility management receiving copies of reports and investigative summaries for corrective action?

Is the appropriate level of specialized security advisor support receiving copies of reports and investigative summaries for information and corrective action?

Security Inspections

How often are inspections of facilities and operations made by line management to verify compliance with security standards?

Are checklists used to guide the security inspections?

Are the results of security inspections communicated in writing to senior management?

Is a copy of the inspection report given to the responsible affected supervisor for follow-up actions?

Is there a written follow-up procedure to ensure that appropriate remedial actions have been taken?

Is a copy of the inspection report, together with corrective actions, provided to the appropriate level of specialized security advisor support?

Planning for Emergencies

Has an overall facility Emergency Plan Coordinator been appointed in writing?

Are security requirements included in all emergency plans?

Are emergency response plans reviewed at least annually?

Do these emergency plans include:

- Death or serious injury?

- Kidnapping or hostage situations?

- Bomb threats?

- Product extortion or contamination?

- Strikes?

- Civil disorder?

- Failure of alarm and control systems?

- Natural catastrophe?

- Catastrophic fire or explosion?

- Hazardous material discharge or spill?

Are plans coordinated with local law enforcement, fire protection, private security contractors, and emergency response agencies?

How often are drills held to train employees in emergency actions and test their performance?

Reference Library

Does the organization receive security periodicals to update program and professional knowledge?

Are security articles or other written materials distributed to managers at least quarterly to update their security management knowledge?

Enforcement

Are there written guidelines on enforcement of security standards to aid supervisors and managers?

Security Management Audits

How often is an evaluation of key security program indicators made for major units to determine effectiveness of the programs in place?

Are the results of these program audits communicated to senior management?

General Promotional Materials

Are security promotional materials in use at the facility?

Are security promotional materials conspicuously posted throughout the facility?

Does security promotion include:

- Posters on bulletin boards?

- Awards that recognize employees who demonstrate exemplary security behavior?

- Presentations at employee meetings.

- Notices on the Company's Email system?

Project Security Reviews

Does the facility have written policies or directives requiring the conduct of formal security reviews at the concept and design stages of all new developments, construction, and modification projects?

How often are compliance checks of design engineering records made by an unbiased person, with results to related management, to determine the percentage of compliance with the engineering policy or directive?

SEXUAL HARASSMENT REPORTING

Any employee who believes that he or she is being sexually harassed by a manager, supervisor, co-worker, customer, or vendor should promptly take the following steps:

- Politely but firmly confront the person doing the harassing. State how you feel about his or her actions. Politely request that the person stop the unwanted behavior because you feel offended, uncomfortable, or intimidated. If practical, bring a witness with you for this discussion.

- Keep notes. Write down what happened, indicate the date, a summary of your conversation with the person you believe is harassing you, and what the person's reaction was when you confronted him or her. Keep this statement.

- If the harassment continues, or if you believe some harm may result from speaking directly to the individual, contact your supervisor or manager. Either verbally or in writing state the problem.

- If you are unable to reach one of those individuals, if your complaint involves your supervisor or manager, or if you fail to solve your problem by talking with your supervisor, take your complaint to the next level of supervision or another manager.

- If the problem is still unresolved or if you fear retaliation, contact the Manager, Human Resources, or any member of management.

- All complaints will be handled in a confidential manner; appropriate investigations will be conducted and no information will be voluntarily released by the company to third parties or to anyone within the company who is not involved in the investigation.

- If the investigation reveals that the complaint is valid, disciplinary action designed to stop the harassment immediately and to prevent its recurrence will be taken.

- You will be promptly notified of the results of the investigation.

The Company recognizes that the question of whether a particular action or incident is sexual harassment or whether it is a purely personal, social relationship without a discriminatory employment effect requires a determination based on all facts in the matter. Given the nature of this type of discrimination, the company also recognizes that false accusations of sexual harassment can have serious effects on innocent individuals. We trust that all employees of the Company will continue to act responsibly to establish and maintain a pleasant working environment, free of discrimination, for all.

STORE SECURITY OFFICER

Overall Concept

A store security officer serves three main purposes:

- Deters crime on the premises.

- Summons the police when the law is broken.

- Protects store employees and customers from harm.

Guidelines

- Present yourself professionally and courteously at all times.

- Maintain a businesslike appearance:

- Wear a uniform that is clean, in good condition, and wrinkle free.

- Maintain a well-groomed appearance.

- Use good standing posture. Keep your hands out of your pockets.

- Do not eat or smoke while on duty.

- Always appear attentive and alert.

- Do not socialize with people, but respond to their questions politely. For example:

  - Look directly at people and address them as "Sir" or "Ma'am." Avoid calling people by their first or last name.

  - Listen attentively to all requests and offer assistance within the limits of your post orders.

- Move throughout the store, serving as a deterrent to unacceptable behavior such as rowdiness and vandalism. If your presence is not sufficient to end the unacceptable behavior, notify the store supervisor and call the police.

- Notify the store supervisor if you suspect anyone of shoplifting. Follow the directions of the supervisor. Do not, however, physically touch a shoplifting suspect. The only exception to physical contact is to protect yourself or others who are endangered.

SUBSTANCE ABUSE PROGRAM AUDIT

Instructions to Auditor

This worksheet has four sections.

- Section I is designed to capture certain administrative details.

- Section II is for auditing programs subject to both DOT and the Company requirements.

- Section III is for auditing programs subject only to the Company requirements.

- Section IV is for recording the auditor's pertinent comments.

The worksheet has a rating scheme as follows:

- S means Satisfactory. Place a circle around the S when an item is answered with a definite yes. If an item requires documentary support, the support must be received in hand in order to assign the S rating. If a yes answer is offered without the required documentary support, assign the U rating.

- U means Unsatisfactory. Place a circle around the U when an item is answered with a no and when any documentary support required for an item is not received in hand. The Unsatisfactory rating requires filling in the comments section at the end of the worksheet.

- NA means Not Applicable. Few items will merit the NA rating. The NA rating requires comment in Section IV.

Section I: Administrative Details

Company Being Audited

      1.   Provide the name of the Company being audited, contact person, address, and telephone number on the lines below.

_____

_____

_____

---

2.   This audit is an audit of a:

- Company-operated program.

- Contractor-operated program.

3.   List the persons, including phone numbers, who were interviewed or who provided information in the conduct of this audit.

_____

_____

_____

_____

_____

_____

_____

4.   The Company being audited is subject to drug testing requirements of:

- Department of Transportation (DOT) and the Company. (If true, complete Section II only.)

- The Company only. (If true, complete Section III only.)

Section II: DOT and Company Requirements

Policy Issues

S U NA   1.   Does the Company being audited have a written substance abuse policy? (Note to Auditor: (If yes, attach a copy of the policy to this worksheet.)

S U NA   2.   Has the policy been communicated to the affected employees?

3.   Identify the method(s) of communication.

_____

_____

4.   Does the policy prohibit the use, bringing onto the Company premises (including all property owned, operated, or leased by the Company or under the control of the Company), possession, concealment, transportation, promotion, or sale of the following?

S U NA   a.   Illegal drugs.

S U NA   b.   Unauthorized controlled substance.

S U NA   c.   Look-alikes.

S U NA   d.   Designer and synthetic drugs.

S U NA   e.   Any illegal or unauthorized drugs or abnormal substances that may affect an employee's senses, motor functions, or alter a person's perception while working.

S U NA   f.   Alcoholic beverages.

S U NA   g.   Drug paraphernalia.

S U NA   5.   Does the policy prohibit an employee from being on the Company premises while having in the employee's body system any detectable amount of the prohibited substances described above?

S U NA   6.   Does the policy include provisions for testing (such as the analysis of urine, blood, plasma, and other biological specimens) of employees to detect in their body systems the presence of the substances prohibited by the policy?

7.   Does the policy authorize testing in the following situations?

S U NA   a.   Pre-employment drug testing (including pre-access drug testing).

b.   Reasonable cause drug testing when, for example:

S U NA   (1)   An employee is found in possession of a prohibited substance.

S U NA   (2)   A supervisor has reasonable belief or reasonable suspicion that an employee is under the influence or in possession of a prohibited substance.

S U NA   c.   Post-accident testing.

S U NA   d.   Random testing.

S U NA   e.   Return to duty testing after rehabilitation.

S U NA   8.   Does the policy require the Company to obtain from each tested employee a written consent? (Note to Auditor: Obtain a copy of the written consent.)

Program Issues

1.   Does the Company in its policy, procedures, or implementing directives address the following?

S U NA   a.   Define "accident" sufficiently to insure that drug testing is conducted when accidents occur.

S U NA   b.   Define "employee" as a person who is subject to testing, e.g., persons in so-called covered positions or who perform safety- or security-sensitive duties.

S U NA   c.   Restrict testing to the five drugs specified in the DOT procedures, i.e., cannabinoids (marijuana), opiates, cocaine, amphetamines, and phencyclidine (PCP).

S U NA   2.   Have the appropriate Company supervisors and/or employees been informed that the program must be conducted according to DOT requirements? If so, how was this information communicated?

_____

_____

S U NA   3.   Does the Company follow and keep readily available for inspection and reference a written policy, plan, procedures, or implementing directives that conform to DOT requirements? If so, do such documents contain the following?

S U NA   a.   Methods and procedures for compliance with the DOT requirements, including the employee assistance program.

S U NA   b.   The name and address of each laboratory that analyzes the specimens collected for drug testing.

S U NA   c.   The name and address of the Company's medical review officer.

(Note to Auditor: Obtain copies of the documents containing the above referenced information.)

4.   Does the Company bar from employment in a covered position on the Company premises any person who:

S U NA   a.   Failed a drug test that has been reviewed by the medical review officer? (Note to Auditor: This provision does not apply to a person who has: (1) successfully completed a rehabilitation program and passed a drug test under DOT procedures; (2) been recommended by the medical review officer for return to duty as a result of the rehabilitation program; and (3) not failed a drug test after the successful completion of a rehabilitation program.)

S U NA   b.   Refused to take a drug test?

S U NA   5.   Does the Company bar from use in a covered position on the Company premises any job applicant who failed a drug test?

6.   Does the Company's program, plan, procedures, or implementing directives call for?

a.   Post-accident drug testing:

S U NA   (1)   As soon as possible but not later than 32 hours after the accident.

S U NA   (2)   Of each employee whose performance either contributed to an accident or cannot be completely discounted as a contributing factor to the accident.

b.   Random testing:

S U NA   (1)   Of at least 50 percent of its employees every 12 months.

S U NA   (2)   That uses a selection procedure based on a random number table or a computer-based random number generator that is matched with an employee's social security number or other appropriate identification number.

S U NA   (3)   That is spread reasonably through the first 12-month period following institution of random testing in such a manner that the last test collection during the period is conducted at an annualized rate of 50 percent, with the total number of tests conducted during the period equal to at least 25 percent of the covered population.

c.   Testing based on reasonable cause:

S U NA   (1)   When the decision to test is based on a reasonable and articulable belief that the employee is using a prohibited drug as evidenced by specific, contemporaneous physical, behavioral, or performance indicators of probable drug use.

S U NA   (2)   When at least two of the employee's supervisors, one of whom is trained in detection of the possible symptoms of drug use, substantiate and concur in the decision to test an employee. (Note to Auditor: In the case of a Company with 50 or fewer employees subject to testing, only one supervisor of the employee trained in detecting possible drug use symptoms is required to substantiate the decision to test.)

S U NA   d.   Testing after rehabilitation of any person who returns to duty as an employee while subject to a reasonable program of follow-up drug testing without prior notice for not more than 60 months after return to duty. (Note to Auditor: Obtain a copy of the policy, plan, procedures, or implementing directives that support Satisfactory ratings for items 1 through 4 directly above.)

S U NA   7.   Does the Company use for the drug testing required by DOT only a drug testing laboratory certified by the Department of Health and Human Services? (Note to Auditor: Obtain the name, address, phone number, and contact person for the drug testing laboratory. An audit of the laboratory may be required to evaluate the laboratory's compliance.)

S U NA   8.   Does the Company use a medical review officer to review drug testing results? If yes, provide name, address, and phone number of the medical review officer:

S U NA   9.   Has the Company ensured that the medical review officer is a licensed physician with a knowledge of drug abuse disorders?

10.   Has the Company ensured that the MRO performs the following functions?

S U NA   a.   Review drug testing results before they are reported to the Company.

b.   Review and interpret positive test results in the following manner to determine if there is an alternate medical explanation for an individual's confirmed positive test result.

S U NA   (1)   Conduct a medical interview.

S U NA   (2)   Review the individual's medical history and any relevant biomedical factors.

S U NA   (3)   Review all medical records made available by the individual tested to determine if a confirmed positive test resulted from legally prescribed medication.

S U NA   (4)   If necessary, re-analyze the original specimen to determine the accuracy of the test result.

S U NA   (5)   Verify that the laboratory report and assessment are correct.

11.   Has the Company ensured that the MRO uses the following rules in making determinations?

S U NA   a.   That if there is a legitimate medical reason for a confirmed positive test result, no further action is taken by the MRO.

S U NA   b.   That if there is no legitimate medical reason for a confirmed positive test result, the MRO refers the individual to an employee assistance program, a personnel officer, or an administrative officer for action in accordance with the Company's anti-drug program.

S U NA   c.   That, based on available data, including other test results, the MRO may conclude a particular drug test is scientifically insufficient for further action and in such an event renders a finding that the test is negative for that individual.

12.   Has the Company informed each employee that:

S U NA   a.   Samples that yield positive results on confirmation are retained by the laboratory in secured, long-term, frozen storage for at least 365 days?

S U NA   b.   If the MRO determines there is no legitimate medical explanation for a confirmed positive test result other than the unauthorized use of a prohibited drug, the original sample must be re-tested if the employee makes a written request for re-testing within 60 days of receipt of the final test result from the MRO?

S U NA   c.   The employee may specify re-testing by the Department of Health and Human Services?

S U NA   d.   The Company may require the employee to pay in advance the cost of shipment (if any) and re-analysis of the sample, but the employee will be reimbursed for such expense if the re-test is negative?

13.   Does the Company provide:

a.   To employees a drug abuse education program consisting of at least the display and distribution of

S U NA   (1)   Informational materials?

S U NA   (2)   A community service hot-line telephone number for obtaining assistance?

S U NA   (3)   The Company's policy regarding the use of prohibited drugs? (Note to Auditor: Obtain one set of the informational materials and community service hot-line information.)

b.   To supervisors who make reasonable cause determinations drug abuse training that

S U NA   (1)   Is at least 60 minutes long?

S U NA   (2)   Teaches the specific, contemporaneous physical, behavioral, and performance indicators of probable drug use? (Note to Auditor: Examine the training records of supervisors who are designated to substantiate and concur in the decision to test employees on the basis of reasonable cause. Obtain a listing of the trained supervisors. Also examine the curriculum or lesson plans used to conduct the training. Look for teaching points that relate to the specific, contemporaneous physical, behavioral, and performance indicators of probable drug use.)

S U NA   14.   If the Company employs subcontractors that work on the Company premises, does the Company keep or have ready access to records that substantiate the required drug testing, education, and training?

15.   Does the Company keep:

S U NA   a.   Records that demonstrate that the collection process conforms to DOT requirements?

b.　　　Records of employee drug testing results that show employees failed a drug test, the type of test failed (e.g., post-accident), and records that demonstrate rehabilitation, if any, and do the records identify:

S U NA　　　(1)　　　The functions performed by employees who failed a drug test?

S U NA　　　(2)　　　The prohibited drugs that were used by employees who failed drug tests?

S U NA　　　(3)　　　The disposition of employees who failed a drug test (e.g., termination, rehabilitation, leave without pay)?

S U NA　　　(4)　　　The age of each employee who failed a drug test?

S U NA　　　c.　　　Records of employee drug testing results that show employees passed a drug test?

S U NA　　　d.　　　A record of the number of employees tested, by type of test (e.g., post-accident)?

S U NA　　　e.　　　Records confirming that supervisors and employees have been trained as specified in the DOT requirements?

16.　　　Does the Company's record-keeping program provide the following:

S U NA　　　a.　　　Information regarding an individual's drug testing results or rehabilitation may be released only upon the written consent of the individual, except that such information must be released to certain designated persons upon request as part of an accident investigation?

S U NA　　　b.　　　Statistical data related to drug testing and rehabilitation that are not name-specific and training records be available to certain designated persons upon request?

17.　　　The Company's anti-drug program is administered by:

a.　　　The Company.

b.　　　A consortium or other agency engaged for this purpose. The name, address, and phone number of the consortium or other agency are:

_____

18.　　　The samples collected for drug testing are collected by:

a.　　　The Company.

b.　　　A consortium or other agency engaged for this purpose. The name, address, and phone number of the consortium or other agency are:

_____

---

19.   The Company's records pertaining to the anti-drug program are maintained and available for inspection as shown below.

Location: _____

Custodian: _____

20.   The Company's anti-drug program commenced on the following date:

_____

Section III: Company Requirements

Policy Issues

S U NA   1.   Does the Company being audited have a written substance abuse policy? (Note to Auditor: If yes, attach a copy of the policy to this worksheet.)

S U NA   2.   Has the policy been communicated to the affected employees?

     3.   Identify the method(s) of communication.

_____

_____

_____

     4.   Does the policy:

     a.   Prohibit the use, bringing onto the Company premises (including all property owned, operated, or leased by the Company or under the control of the Company), possession, concealment, transportation, promotion, or sale of the following?

S U NA   (1)   Illegal drugs.

S U NA   (2)   Unauthorized controlled substances.

S U NA   (3)   Look-alikes.

S U NA   (4)   Designer and synthetic drugs.

S U NA   (5)   Any illegal or unauthorized drugs or abnormal substances which may affect an employee's senses, motor functions, or alter a person's perception while working.

S U NA   (6)   Alcoholic beverages.

S U NA   (7)   Drug paraphernalia.

S U NA   b.   Prohibit an employee from being on the Company premises while having in the employee's body system any detectable amount of the prohibited substances described above?

S U NA   c.   Include provisions for testing (such as the analysis of urine, blood, plasma, and other biological specimens) of employees to detect in their body systems the presence of the substances prohibited by the policy?

               d.   Authorize testing in the following situations?

S U NA   (1)   Pre-employment drug testing (including pre-access drug testing).

               (2)   Reasonable cause drug testing when, for example:

S U NA   (a)   An employee is found in possession of a prohibited substance.

S U NA   (b)   A supervisor has reasonable belief or reasonable suspicion that an employee is under the influence or in possession of a prohibited substance.

S U NA   (3)   Post-accident testing when, for example, an employee is involved in:

               (a)   An on-the-job injury.

               (b)   A potentially serious accident or incident.

S U NA   (4)   Random testing.

S U NA   5.   Does the policy require the Company to obtain from each tested employee a written consent? (Note to Auditor: Obtain a copy of the written consent referenced above.)

Program Issues

               1.   Does the Company's procedures or implementing directives address the following issues?

S U NA   a.   Provide to the Company, upon request, a certificate or letter from the Company's testing agency that attests to the existence of the Company's drug testing program.

S U NA   b.   Submit to periodic audits by the Company of the Company's substance abuse policy and program records, including but not limited to the Company's written policy, policy-implementing directives and procedures, and chain of custody procedures, and periodic audits of services provided to the Company by the drug testing laboratory.

S U NA   c.   Furnish, on request, a report of the previous 12-month period that summarizes the number of drug tests conducted in the categories of pre-employment, reasonable cause, post-accident, and random testing.

S U NA   d.   Acknowledge the Company's right and intent to conduct unannounced searches and inspections of contractors and contractors' employees, persons, and vehicles for the purpose of enforcing the Company's substance abuse policy.

S U NA   e.   Acknowledge the Company's right, at its discretion, to require contractor employees on the Company premises to submit to urine drug tests.

S U NA   f.   Provide written communication to the Company concerning employees who violated the Company's substance abuse policy or who refused to submit to a search, inspection, urine drug test, or blood and plasma test.

S U NA   g.   Remove and not allow return to the Company premises any employee who has violated the Company's substance abuse policy or who refused to submit to a search, inspection, urine drug test, or blood and plasma test.

S U NA   h.   Accept responsibility for ensuring that subcontractors (i.e., contractors to the contractor) comply with the Company's substance abuse policy.

S U NA   i.   Provide to the Company upon request a copy of the contractor's substance abuse policy and other related implementing directives and procedures.

S U NA   j.   Acknowledge that consideration for work on the Company premises is conditioned upon the contractor's implementation of a substance abuse program that is acceptable to the Company and that administration of the program is a responsibility of the contractor.

S U NA   k.   Conduct random, unannounced testing so that during each 12-month period the number of tested employees will be equal to or exceed 100 percent of the total number of employees assigned to the Company premises and that such testing will be reasonably spaced throughout the 12-month period.

Section IV: Comments

_____

_____

_____

_____

_____

_____

_____

_____

_____

_____

_____

_____

_____

_____

_____

_____

_____

_____

_____

_____

_____

TELEPHONE ANSWERING

When you answer the telephone, keep in mind that you may be the first and only contact the caller will have with the security department. Present yourself courteously and professionally, and be attentive to the caller's needs. Record every message you take, and when you pass the message on, make a note in the Daily Log as to whom and when the message was delivered.

Answering the Telephone

- Pick up as quickly as you can. Try not to bang or drop the receiver. Begin speaking without delay.

- Speak directly into the mouthpiece with an alert professional voice tone. For example, "Good morning. Security Officer Doe speaking. May I help you?"

- Always assume that the call will be important, and convey by your voice and your words that you regard the call as important.

Taking Messages

- Listen carefully to what the caller is saying. Ask questions as needed to clarify. Do not let the caller hang up until you are certain that you have the correct message.

- Ask the caller to spell out names and street addresses.

- Verify information by repeating it back to the caller.

- Do not chat.

- Thank the caller and confirm that you will have the message delivered.

- A completed message will:

  - Identify the person for whom the message has been left.

  - Identify the caller, the caller's telephone number, and the company he or she represents.

  - Clearly state what it is that the caller wants done.

- Make sure the message is delivered.

Special Situations

- If a caller asks for unpublished company information, respond by saying, "I'm sorry, but I am not permitted to release that information."

- If a caller asks for an employee's home telephone, respond by saying, "I cannot release that information, but I'll be happy to connect you with the employee's office phone." Alternatively, you can offer to take the caller's telephone number and have the employee return the call.

- Emergency messages must be delivered without delay. If appropriate, transfer the caller to the Human Resources Department. For other emergency calls that cannot be immediately delivered, get a name and telephone number where the caller can be reached. State your intention to pass on the message as quickly as you can.

- Nonemergency after-hours calls to an employee should be handled by explaining that you have no way of making a contact until the next business day. However, if the employee's telephone number is on a contact list, tell the caller that you will try to contact the employee and pass on the message.

Record Keeping

- Record calls on the Telephone Call Log. Note in your Daily Log Book that the message was delivered. Include the following information:

  - The time the call came in.

  - The caller's name.

  - The time and method of delivery.

TWO-WAY RADIO

Radio transmissions travel over open airways, meaning that they can be monitored. Care must therefore be taken as to what is communicated via two-way radio.

Guidelines

- Make sure the radio battery is fully charged.

- Carry the radio in the holder, not in your hand or pocket.

- Keep all transmissions courteous and professional. For example:

  - Do not transmit if someone else is already talking on the radio.

  - Depress the talk button the entire time you are speaking.

  - Talk directly into the speaker.

  - Maintain a moderate transmission volume. Do not let the volume become offensive.

  - Use appropriate language. Keep your messages short and do not tie up the radio longer than necessary.

  - Use the term "out" to indicate that you are through speaking.

  - Release the button to listen for a response.

  - Ensure that the other party has received the message.

- When a battery completely loses its charge, place it into the charger. Use a battery analyzer to discharge the battery fully. In addition:

  - Make sure the charger is plugged in and turned on.

  - Do not remove the battery from the charger until it is fully charged (refer to manufacturer's instructions).

- Do not place the radio in your pocket.